The Poetry of
Wallace Stevens

ROBERT REHDER

St. Martin's Press   New York

First published in the United States of America in 1988

Printed in Hong Kong

ISBN 0-312-00860-0 (cloth)
ISBN 0-312-00861-9 (pbk)

Library of Congress Cataloging-in-Publication Data
Rehder, Robert.
The poetry of Wallace Stevens.
Bibliography: p.
Includes index.
1. Stevens, Wallace, 1879-1955—Criticism and
interpretation.   I. Title.
PS3537.T4753Z7578   1987   811'.52   87-4970
ISBN 0-312-00860-0 (cloth)
ISBN 0-312-00861-9 (pbk)

To
my mother and father
Marguerite McConkie Rehder
and
Theodore Martin Rehder

Contents

Contents

Preface

Wallace Stevens is one of the most enjoyable of poets. His pleasure in language and the deep satisfaction that his poems brought him is ours as we read. He offers us at once an immense *joie de vivre* and a keen sense of life's essential sadness.

Stevens writes to Bernard Heringman, 'I believe in pure explication de texte. This may in fact be my principal form of piety' (21 July 1953). This has been the form of my piety here. I have tried in the first chapter to give some idea of Stevens as a person and of his life; I have attempted throughout the book to place the individual texts in the context of his work as a whole and to make suggestions about his development; but my major concern has been to analyse individual poems.

I am, like everyone interested in Stevens, indebted to Holly Stevens for her editions of her father's works and her invaluable commentaries. For my discussion of his character and life, I have relied, as everyone must, on his letters and journal and on her introductions to the letters (which together form a miniature biography), on *Souvenirs and Prophecies* (1977), the book that she wrote around her publication of the journal, and on her several essays. I have also, in the first chapter, made extensive use of Peter Brazeau's excellent *Parts of a World: Wallace Stevens Remembered* (1983), which provides a wealth of new material and allows the various witnesses to speak for themselves. I am grateful, moreover, to all those who have written about Stevens. They have often helped me even where I have disagreed with them. I must mention too my students, who, as always, have contributed with great generosity to the education of their teacher.

I should particularly like to thank T. M. Farmiloe for his faith and good will, and Walton Litz for the information that he gave me about Stevens and his many helpful suggestions. Also my thanks go to T. A. Dunn and A. N. Jeffares for their support; to Elspeth O'Malley, Yvonne McClymont and especially Mamie Prentice, who carefully typed the many drafts and final copy and who continually went out of their way to help; to Frances Arnold for all her help and editorial good offices; and to Valery Rose and Graham Eyre for their many useful suggestions and scrupulous copy-editing. My greatest debt is to Caroline Rehder for her patience, generosity and painstaking reading of the manuscript. Her innumerable wise suggestions have enabled me to improve every page.

R.H.

Acknowledgements

The author and publishers wish to thank the following who have kindly given permission for the use of copyright material:

Random House Inc., for the extracts from *Parts of a World: Wallace Stevens Remembered*, by Peter Brazeau; *Souvenirs and Prophecies: The Young Wallace Stevens*, by Holly Stevens; *Letters of Wallace Stevens* and *The Palm at the End of the Mind: Selected Poems and a Play*, both edited by Holly Stevens; and *The Necessary Angel: Essays on Reality and the Imagination*, by Wallace Stevens.

Random House Inc. and Faber and Faber Ltd, for the extracts from *The Collected Poems of Wallace Stevens* and *Opus Posthumous*, edited by Samuel French Morse.

List of Abbreviations and Note on Sources

Except for the works listed below, a full reference is given in the Notes the first time that a work is cited, after which a shorter form is used. All the English books were published in New York and all the French books in Paris, except where otherwise specified. All translations are mine unless otherwise noted.

Where possible, all citations of Stevens' poems are from Holly Stevens' edition (*Palm*). Those poems that she does not reprint are cited from *The Collected Poems* and *Opus Posthumous* (*OP*). Stevens' letters, unless otherwise noted, are cited from Holly Stevens' edition (*L*). For details of the publication of Stevens' works I have relied upon Edelstein's bibliography and for information about specific words on *The Oxford English Dictionary* (*OED*). Citations from these sources have generally not been noted, as the poems can be found easily through the index of titles, the letters from the dates and any published work in Edelstein's index.

In the references to 'Notes Toward a Supreme Fiction', the three main sections of the poem – 'It Must Be Abstract', 'It Must Change' and 'It Must Give Pleasure' – have been numbered 1, 2, 3, respectively.

WORKS BY STEVENS

NA   *The Necessary Angel: Essays on Reality and the Imagination* (1951)
CP   *The Collected Poems of Wallace Stevens* (1955)
OP   *Opus Posthumous*, ed. Samuel Morse (1957)
L   *Letters of Wallace Stevens*, ed. Holly Stevens (London, 1967)
Palm   *The Palm at the End of the Mind: Selected Poems and a Play by Wallace Stevens*, ed. Holly Stevens (1972)

WORKS ABOUT STEVENS

B   Peter Brazeau, *Parts of a World: Wallace Stevens Remembered* (1983)

WSC   *Wallace Stevens: A Celebration*, ed. Frank Doggett and
           Robert Buttel (Princeton, 1980)

E   J. M. Edelstein, *Wallace Stevens: A Descriptive Bibliography*
           (Pittsburgh, 1973)

SP   Holly Stevens, *Souvenirs and Prophecies: The Young Wallace
           Stevens* (1977)

OTHER WORKS

OED   *The Oxford English Dictionary*, 13 vols (Oxford, 1933)

WBMP   Robert Rehder, *Wordsworth and the Beginnings of Modern
           Poetry* (London, 1981)

1

I Was the World in which I Walked

Wallace Stevens was born on 2 October 1879 in Reading, Pennsylvania, into a horse-and-buggy world of gas-lights, ice-boxes, and cast-iron bathtubs with roll rims and claw feet. The first telephone exchanges were established in this year, six days was the record for crossing the Atlantic by steamship, and Rutherford B. Hayes was President of the United States. The North wanted to forget the passions of the Civil War and the South to remember them, and the country as a whole was engaged in the most thoroughgoing process of industrialisation that the world has ever seen. Europe was completing a period of institutional reform. George Eliot, Gustave Flaubert, Richard Wagner, Karl Marx and Victor Hugo were near the end of their lives. The year of Stevens' birth saw the composition of *Washington Square*, and the publication of the first instalments of *The Brothers Karamazov*. Browning died and Yeats' first book, *The Wanderings of Oisin and Other Poems*, appeared in 1889 when Stevens was ten. The so-called 'Death-bed Edition' of *Leaves of Grass* that Whitman authorised as the final form of his work was published, and both Whitman and Tennyson died in 1892 when Stevens was thirteen. He was nineteen when Hardy published his first book of poetry, *Wessex Poems and Other Verses* (1898). Stevens was four years older than William Carlos Williams, six years older than Pound, nine years older than Eliot and twenty years older than Crane.

Wallace Stevens was the second child of Garrett Barcalow Stevens and Margaretha Catherine Zeller Stevens. He had an older and a younger brother, Garrett Barcalow Junior (1877–1937) and John Bergen (1880–1940), and two younger sisters, Elizabeth (1885–1943) and Mary Katherine (1889–1919). There was a child still-born in 1883 and there were possibly two other children (who may have been twins) who died at birth or in infancy before Elizabeth and Mary were born. The house, 323 North Fifth Street, in which all the children (except perhaps Garrett) were born and grew up, was a

1

three-storey brick row house facing west on a dirt thoroughfare lined with elms and horse chestnuts.[1] Wallace's room was on the third floor at the front.

Very little is known about Stevens' childhood. The three brothers, because of their closeness in age, appear to have often played together and there are a number of family stories of their exploits. They stole fruit from a neighbour's tree and, when challenged, shouted as they ran away, 'God helps those who help themselves.' During the building of the steeple on a nearby church they would climb up and hide in the scaffolding, chew tobacco and spit on passers-by, often prominent citizens, and, so the story goes, were never caught. When a neighbour who was kept awake by a street light shining in his window painted it green to reduce the glare, Wallace shinned up the post, scraped off the paint and woke up the neighbour, who then repainted the light the next day – and this happened several times before Wallace was found out.[2] The most vivid evocation of his childhood is, not surprisingly, by Stevens himself, in a letter he wrote to Elsie Moll not long after their engagement:

Secret *memoires*: go back to the bicycle period, for example – and before that to the age of the velocipede. Yes: I had a red velocipede that broke in half once going over a gutter in front of Butcher Deems (where the fruit store is now, beyond the Auditorium) – and I hurt my back and stayed away from school. – On Sundays, in those days, I used to wear patent leather pumps with silver buckles on 'em – and go to Sunday School and listen to old Mrs Keeley, who had wept with joy over every pap in the Bible. – It seems now that the First Presbyterian church was very important: oyster suppers, picnics, festivals. I used to like to sit back of the organ and watch the pump-handle go up and down. – That was before John McGowan, the hatter, became a deacon. – The bicycle period had its adventures: a ride to Ephrata was like an excursion into an unmapped country; and one trip to Womelsdorf and back was incredible. – In summer-time I was up very early and often walked through Hessian Camp before breakfast. Sometimes I rode out to Leisz' bridge and back – I remember a huge cob-web between the rails of a fence sparkling with dew. – And I had a pirate period somewhere. I used to 'hop' coal-trains and ride up the Lebanon Valley and stone farm-houses and steal pumpkins and so on – with a really tough crowd. – Then I took to swimming. For three or four summers I did nothing else. We went all morning, all afternoon and all evening and I was as black as a boy could be.... I could swim for hours without resting and, in fact, can still. Bob Bushing and I were chummy then – and Felix North and 'Gawk' Schmucker. – We used to lie on the stone-walls of the locks and bake ourselves by the hour, and roll into the water to cool. – I always walked a great deal, mostly alone, and mostly on the hill, rambling along the side of the mountain. – When I began to read, many things changed. My room was the third floor front. I used to stay up all hours, although I had never, up to that time, been up all night.... Those were the days when I read Poe and Hawthorne and all the things one ought to read (unlike 'Cousin Phillis' – the book I am reading now.) – And I studied hard–very. – You know I took *all* the prizes at school! ... At High School, I played foot-ball every fall–left end. We generally won at home and lost when we were away.... Most of the fellows called me Pat. – I never attended class-meetings and never knew any of the girls belonging to the class. Well, perhaps I did; but they do not come back to me now. – I sang in Christ Cathedral choir for about two years, soprano and later, alto. Worked at Sternberg's for two weeks, once – at the Reading Hardware Company for two months. (Father was an officer of the company – my working did not interfere with swimming.) – And I went to the World's Fair, and to school in Brooklyn for a while, and sometimes to the Zoo in Philadelphia. – When I was very young, 'mamma' used to go shopping to New-York and we would meet her at the station – and then there would be boxes of candy to open at home. We used to spend months at a time at the old hotel at Ephrata, summer after summer, and 'papa' would come on Saturday nights with baskets of fruit – peaches and pears, which would be given to us during the week. – Sometimes an uncle from Saint-Paul visited us. He could talk French and had big dollars in his pockets, some of which went into mine. – Then there was a time when I went very much with Johnny Richards and Arthur Roland. They were 'bad': poker (for matches) and cigarettes. – The truth is, I have never thought much about those early days and certainly never set them in order. I was distinctly a rowdy – and there are still gossips to tell of it.... My first year away from home, at Cambridge, made an enormous difference in everything. Since then I have been home comparatively little and, but for you, I think I should have drifted quite out of it, as the town grew strange and the few friends I had became fewer still.

(21 Jan 1909)

The two major changes that he identifies – learning to read and living away from home – indicate a growing inwardness. What he records – at thirty – is a general drift away from the setting in which he grew up and a movement into himself. As an adult, he re-created, it appears, an analogous setting for himself in Hartford, but without the innocence and spontaneity of childhood and without, perhaps, its strong emotional bonds. The presents of fruit and good things to eat that in later life he constantly made to himself may be seen as re-enactments of his father's baskets of peaches and pears. His description of himself as a solitary walker – 'I always walked a great deal, mostly alone' – is virtually a summation of his entire life outside of his office or study, where he worked mostly alone. This, together with the accounts of some of those walks in his journal, suggests an intense, full and over flowing inner life that came to be so constituted that it could only be satisfied by poetry, and there is an intimation of the poet-to-be in his thought that his early memories are in disorder until he does something to 'set them in order'.

Wallace Stevens' father was born on a farm in Bucks County, Pennsylvania, in 1848. His first job was as a schoolteacher when he was seventeen, but after three years he decided to become a lawyer. In 1870 he moved to Reading, where he worked six days a week as a law clerk, studying the law when he could (and Latin and Greek, as translation from both languages was part of the law exams), and was admitted to practice in 1872. He married Margaretha Catherine Zeller in 1876. She was the same age as he and a schoolteacher in Reading, having, like him, become one at an early age. Her father had died when she was fifteen and she had had to earn her own living as soon as she was qualified. Her mother died in the same year as Garrett Stevens was admitted to the bar. Both came from large families: he had five brothers and one sister; she, four brothers and four sisters. They had met some time before Christmas 1871 as a copy of *The Poetical Works of Alexander Pope* survives inscribed by him to her on that date with 'Compliments'.[3]

As a young man Garrett Stevens was well known and well liked in Reading, and active in politics. He came close to being nominated for a seat in the state legislature, and at the time of his marriage a local newspaper praised his 'energy and application' and described him as a 'brilliant and powerful' speaker and writer.[4] During the twenty years following his marriage, while his children were growing up, he enjoyed considerable success, principally as a corporation lawyer. He was counsel for several local banks, director of half a dozen or so corporations in and around Reading, including, for a time, a bicycle factory and a steel works, and owned farms in Bucks County. His partnership in 1900 was rated as one of the most prosperous law firms in Reading, even though he had already begun to suffer a series of setbacks that caused him in 1898 to fear bankruptcy and around 1901 contributed to what his son Wallace described as 'a nervous prostration'. After a six-month rest cure in the Adirondacks, he slowly returned to the practice of law, but was never very active again. He died in 1911 at the age of sixty-three (when Wallace was thirty-two) and his wife died a year and two days later, in 1912.[5]

Towards the end of his life Wallace Stevens described Garrett Stevens as follows:

> My father was quite a good egg; agreeable, active. He was of Holland Dutch descent, and his father and his grandfather had been farmers. We had a good deal of poetry in the library. You might say we were more bookish than the average. We were all great readers and the old man used to delight in retiring to the room called the library on a Sunday afternoon to read a five-or-six-hundred-page novel. The library was no real institution you understand; just a room with some books where you could go and be quiet. My mother just kept house and ran the family. When I was younger, I always used to think that I got my practical side from my father, and my imagination from my mother.[6]

This distribution of qualities may very well be correct but in this account it is the father who has withdrawn into his imagination. Moreover, Stevens' father wrote poetry, as well as stories and short essays. When he began is not clear, but from 1906, after his collapse and after his son's successful literary career at Harvard (so the influence may have been mutual), Garrett Stevens' poems were published anonymously in the Reading newspapers. In 1911 and 1912, after his death, 'most of his writings' were reprinted under his name in *The Reading Times*, and in 1924 a group of his poems was reprinted in *The Reading Eagle*. Michael Lafferty says that his work is of 'slight talent' and 'highly conventional' in the 'tradition of Wordsworth, Longfellow, and Tennyson'. According to Stevens, his father 'wrote some poetry of a very elementary sort in his younger days, but nothing that had any significance'.[7]

At the very start of his son's university career, Garrett Stevens recognised his son's skill with words and was prepared to envisage him as a literary success. On 27 September 1897 he writes to him that he might see in Cambridge 'some nook' seen by one of the great American writers who had lived there: 'And who knows but bringing to its description your power of painting pictures in words you make it famous – and some Yankee old maid will say – it was here that Stevens stood and saw the road to distinction.' He then goes on to consider the nature of description:

> When we try to picture what we see, the purely imaginary is transcended, like listening in the dark we seem to really hear what we are listening for – but describing real objects one can draw straight or curved lines and the thing may be mathematically demonstrated – but who does not prefer the sunlight – and the shadow reflected.
>
> Point in all this screed – Paint truth but not always in drab clothes. Catch the reflected sun-rays, set pleasurable emotions – instead of stings and tears.

The metaphor of seeing as listening in the dark might have been taken from one of Wallace Stevens' poems, and his too is the emphasis on 'pleasurable emotions'. A letter written the next year is evidence that the two men may have discussed poetry as fellow craftsmen:

> Your lines run prettily in the Stanzas sent and we may soon expect the shades of Longfellow to seem less grey – I'll talk it over prosily with you when I see you –
> I am having a devil of a lot of prose in mine just now.
>
> (16 Dec 1898)

Wallace's election to the Signet Society at Harvard provided the father with an occasion to show his playfulness and linguistic virtuosity:

> Just what the election to the *Signet* signifies I have no sign. It is significant that your letter is a signal to sign another check that you may sigh no more. I suppose you thus win the privilege to wear a seal ring or a badge with the picture of a *Cygnet* on it – to distinguish you from commoner geese, or it may be you can

con*sign* all studies de*sign*ed to cause re*sign*ation, to some as*sign*ed
port where they will trouble you no more.

You will know more about it when you have ridden the goat of
initiation, and kneaded the dough enclosed.　(21 May 1899)

Certainly Wallace Stevens was aware of the decisive effect of his
father's example. He tells Jerald Hatfield, 'I decided to be a lawyer
the same way I decided to be a Presbyterian; the same way I decided
to be a Democrat. My father was a lawyer, a Presbyterian and a
Democrat'.[8] Garrett Stevens had an analogous effect on his other
sons as well. All three decided to become lawyers, and John, who
subsequently became his father's law partner, went on to be a judge
and Democratic party boss of Berks County, Pennsylvania.[9]

The principal evidence for the relation between father and son is
the more than forty letters that Garrett Stevens wrote to Wallace in
1897–1900, his years as a student at Harvard.[10] They are affection-
ate, humorous and serious, thoughtful and shrewd. He turns a
nice phrase: 'A little romance is essential to ecstasy', and 'One
never thinks out a destiny – If a fellow takes Peach Pie – he often
wishes he had chosen the Custard', but the overriding message to
his son, repeated again and again, is to work hard and succeed:[11]

the world holds an unoccupied niche only for those who climb
up . . . . (27 Dec 1897)

Do not be contented with a smattering of all things – be strong in
something.　(14 Nov 1897)

Glad to get your encouraging reports – and shall be happy always
to get the substantial evidence of your progress, for, as you are
aware – you are not out on a pic-nic – but really preparing for a
campaign of life – where self sustenance is essential and where
everything depends upon yourself . . . . (6 Mar 1898)

Take an inventory of your capacities.　(20 May 1898)

Our young folks would of course all prefer to be born like English
noblemen with Entailed estates, income guaranteed and in
choosing a profession they would simply say – 'How shall I amuse
myself' – but young America understands that the question is –
'*Starting with nothing, how shall I sustain myself and perhaps a wife and*

family – and send my boys to College and live comfortably in my old age.' Young fellows must all come to that question for unless they inherit money, marry money, find money, steal money or somebody present it to them, they must *earn it* and earning it save up for the time of need. How best can he earn a sufficiency! What talent does he possess which carefully nurtured will produce something which people want and therefore will pay for. This is the whole problem!' and to Know Thyself!   (1 Nov 1898)[12]

It will not do to put off the thought of *subsistence* as drone matter, ignoble + unworthy . . . .   (13 Nov 1898)

Stick to it my boy . . . .   (7 Mar 1899)

Keep hammering at your real work however my boy – for a fellow never knows what's in store – and time mis-spent now counts heavily.   (21 May 1899)

This advice is, of course, the echo of Garrett Stevens' exhortations to himself to work harder, at a time when he was deeply worried about his own financial future; but it is not a simple incitement to make money. On 27 September 1897 he writes,

work and study, study and work – are worth a decade of dreams – and romantic notions – but I do not believe in being so thoroughly practical that what is beautiful, what is artistic – what is delicate or what is grand – must always be deferred to what is useful.

There is something romantic about these anti-romantic notions.

The father urges his son to embrace an idealised reality; it is inconceivable to him that life can be anything but a struggle. Work ('an effort to do our best') is more important than money.[13] Action, commitment, self-discipline and self-fulfilment are the values. Everything must be self-made. Wholeness is the result of activity. These are American values, intrinsic to the culture. Garrett Stevens' letters are contemporary with Horatio Alger's novels. That Wallace Stevens absorbed these imperatives and made them his own helps us to understand the interchangeability of and tension between doing and being in his life, as well as his desire to be well off, his steady, determined working at two jobs, insurance and poetry, and his stubborn refusal, virtual inability, to retire.

Holly Stevens, the poet's daughter, states that a cousin told her 'that my grandfather looked upon open expressions of affection or other emotions as a sign of weakness, and that he thought of himself "as a Sphinx, like he was the patriarch, but that was it" '. This view is supported by Stevens' remarks on his father's essential solitariness in a letter to his niece, Jane Stone (13 Sep 1943). This is the father of 'The Auroras of Autumn' and 'the impersonal person, the wanderer, / The father, the ancestor, the bearded peer' of 'Things of August', as remote as the thinker of the first idea:

> He wasn't a man given to pushing his way. He needed what all of us need, and what most of us don't get: that is to say, discreet affection. So much depends upon ourselves in that respect. I think that he loved to be at the house with us, but he was incapable of lifting a hand to attract any of us, so that, while we loved him as it was natural to do, we also were afraid of him, at least to the extent of holding off. The result was that he lived alone. The greater part of his life was spent at his office; he wanted quiet and, in that quiet, to create a life of his own.

On this passage Holly Stevens comments,

> If that was true of my grandfather, and I can easily imagine it was since I have heard that he would not even talk on the telephone at home, it certainly was true of my father and of our house as I grew up; we held off from each other – one might say that my father lived alone.[14]

These two comments furnish a poignant context for the statement in 'Esthétique du Mal' that

> It may be that one life is a punishment
> For another, as the son's life for the father's.

The apartness of the father became the apartness of the son. How much sadness there is in that 'discreet affection' and how far removed it is from love. It was the son's thoughtfulness, the steady, dispassionate intelligence, manifest in his letter to Jane Stone as in his work, that enabled him to live through the effects of his father's character and, in the quiet of his mind, 'to create a life of his own'. Poetry was absolutely necessary to him because it was the one place he did not hold off.

Wallace Stevens' mother is an even more shadowy figure than his father. Most of what we know about her as a person comes from an interview with her granddaughter, Mary Catherine Sesnick, who also spoke of what her mother, Sarah Stayman Stevens (the wife of Garrett Junior), thought of her mother-in-law. Garrett and Margaretha Stevens, Mary Sesnick said, 'were both strong willed':

> The household was hers; the other was his. I remember Mamma saying that Grandpa Stevens never set foot in the kitchen, that was woman's work. They had servants. She always referred to the Stevenses as Blue Book. She always stood a little bit in awe of the Stevens family: they reacted a little bit differently from a social standpoint and everything was properly done.

Margaretha Stevens appears to have shared some, at least, of her husband's reserve, although, according to Mary Sesnick, her mother had liked her 'very much':

> She said she was quite an austere type of woman and probably wasn't too friendly with a lot of people. But she did take Mamma under her wing and was very good to her. Mrs Stevens said my mother was like her daughter, but the other two wives [of Wallace and John] were daughters-in-law. And that was that. She was short, sort of pioneer-looking in a way.[15]

Wallace Stevens' mother and father appear to have been very concerned about their social standing and as a result made difficulties about their children's marriages. According to Mary Sesnick, when Garrett Junior proposed to marry Sarah Stayman, 'They sent someone to Carlisle to check my mother's parents out to see if my mother was good enough to come into the family.' The Staymans were so indignant that the engagement was nearly broken off.[16] Both his father and mother strongly objected to Wallace marrying Elsie Moll, and the bad feeling was such that, after a quarrel in 1908, Wallace and his father never spoke to each other again (which Wallace later very much regretted). He visited his mother after his father's death in 1911, but Elsie did not attend Margaretha Stevens' funeral, 'although she was vacationing only a few miles from Reading'.[17] Wallace's father wrote to him on 17 November 1907 emphasising how useful Sarah's connections were to her husband, Garrett Junior; they had recently moved to

Baltimore, where the Staymans knew 'good, strong, plain people: Doctors and Preachers and others of importance'.[18] Elizabeth Stevens wanted to marry a Catholic in Reading, but the young couple, said Mary Sesnick, 'just had a terrible time: so she gave him up. I think that, too, alienated her from her family to a certain extent'.[19]

Margaretha Stevens traced her ancestors and joined the local chapter of the Daughters of the American Revolution. She did not, however, want to remember her own background too accurately, to the exasperation sometimes of other members of her family. During the period of family disagreements over their engagement, Stevens writes to Elsie Moll,

> By the way, I don't in the least mind what your grandmother said either about her relatives or mine. It is amusing to think of that washer-woman. Mother must be worried to death when she thinks of her. You know she is a Daughter of the Revolution and traces herself through two or three generations to an officer in the American army. You can imagine her crowding out the details. Father once told her that she was a shoemaker's daughter and that he was a farmer's son. . . . They both belonged to large families and both were poor. It is very silly for people in a country town to bother about such things. Besides you can't get around a washer-woman. (31 Jan 1909)[20]

Her austerity, strong-mindedness, assumption of the house as her domain, genealogical interests and concern for her social status are characteristics of Margaretha Stevens that were shared by Elsie Moll Stevens. Both came from poor families, had had to manage on their own at an early age and married very successful men.[21] For the poet probably the most important thing about his mother was that he 'was her favorite', or so Mary Sesnick tells us:

> But I know she really doted on Wallace. He was rather sick as a young child; he was rather delicate. And that's why his mother doted so. She had lost I don't know how many babies, and she didn't want to lose any one of those three boys. He was the delicate one; I remember Mamma saying that.[22]

Wallace began his education in private schools. He attended a kindergarten near his home run by a French lady, where he may have learned some French and German (which was widely spoken in Reading at that time). He then attended the school attached to St John's Evangelical Lutheran Church and, for one year, the school of St Paul's Lutheran Church in Brooklyn, where his uncle was the minister. The month before his thirteenth birthday, he entered Reading Boys' High School, where he studied Latin (Caesar, Virgil, Cicero, and Livy or Sallust), Greek (Xenophon, the *Iliad*, Herodotus), the history of Greece and Rome, English, mathematics, physical geography, physics and, in his last year, elocution, 'Mental Philosophy' and American literature. He had to repeat his first year, because, he said, 'of too many nights out', but it may have been because of illness. As a result, for the next three years he had his brother, John, as a classmate. He became a good student (one term John was second and he was third in the class), and his first published work almost certainly appeared in the school newspaper.[23] In his third year he won *The Reading Eagle* prize for the best essay (written in the classroom in a fixed period of time on a subject announced only at the start), and in his fourth and final year he won the gold medal for oratory on Alumni night, speaking on 'The Greatest Need of the Age'. *The Reading Eagle* (23 December 1896) reports:

> The judges were unanimous. Then the boys in the audience broke loose, clapped their hands and applauded. The winner is a son of Garrett B. Stevens and a favorite in the school, as was proven by the send-off his classmates gave him. When he received his medal he bowed his thanks. Then the boys gave him the school yell and a cheer.[24]

He was subsequently invited to give the oration at graduation. This, entitled 'The Thessalians', *The Reading Eagle* of 24 June 1897 calls 'a splendid effort', saying that he 'spoke as though he were a veteran speaker accustomed to address large audiences', and both he and the valedictorian had their pictures in the paper.[25]

Only the text of the Alumni night speech survives. 'Men live their lives by hard fights', Stevens begins. Existence is a struggle. 'But I dissemble', says the young orator:

> My tears start, my voice chokes and I am filled with futile emotion at the appalling, the pitiable desperation of a man who cannot rise because he has not the opportunity. Gentlemen, write it on your

hearts, there is no greater need in this or any other age than the
need of giving the man an opportunity.

His heroes are Luther, Bismarck, Wellington, Charles Martel,
Columbus, Lincoln and Jesus. As in Horatio Alger, to have an
opportunity is equivalent to making the most of it. Every man is a
potential success.

> There is one triumph of a republic, one attainment of Catholicism,
> one grand result of Democracy, which feudalism, which caste,
> and which monarchy can never know – the self-made man. We
> cannot help but admire the man who with indomitable and
> irrepressible energy breasting the wave of conditions, grows to
> become the concentration of power and worth.[26]

This praise of men such as his father shows that the seventeen-year-
old Wallace Stevens was already imbued with his father's values.
The oration, however, is more than a simple affirmation of family
myths. These are the values of the culture as a whole. After all, they
are the sentiments that won the gold medal and caused the boys in
the audience to break loose with their applause. Perhaps this
energetic self-making with its stress on realising potential called
forth in Stevens a desire to discover a self already complete,
contingent upon nothing and totally present, instead of predicated
on future activity.

The autumn following his graduation from Reading High School,
Stevens enrolled at Harvard. He registered as a special student, as
was customary for many of those planning to go on to a professional
school, and therefore attended for three years (1897–1900) rather
than the usual four. His major subject was English. Every year he
took courses in English (in both composition and literature), French
and German. He studied the whole history and development of
English 'in outline' and then in four specialised courses: 'From the
Death of Dryden to the Death of Swift' (1700–45), 'From the Death of
Swift to the publication of the Lyrical Ballads' (1745–98), 'From the
publication of the Lyrical Ballads to the death of Scott' (1798–1832)
and 'From the death of Scott to the death of Tennyson' (1832–92). He
did French and German composition; a course that required him to
read Corneille, Racine, Molière, Beaumarchais, Hugo, Musset and
Balzac; and a 'General view of French Literature', 'Goethe and his
Time' (with lectures in German) and 'History of German Literature

to the Nineteenth Century'. In addition, he studied government, economics, European history and 'The Fine Arts of the Middle Ages and the Renaissance'. He was a good student, receiving eight *As*, eleven *Bs* and three *Cs* in three years.[27] The cosmopolitanism of Stevens' work was solidly grounded upon early study. His ambition to become a poet appears to have formed while he was at Harvard (although his first published poem appeared in the magazine of the Reading Boys' High School, *The Red and Black*, in January 1898).[28] His second poem was published in *The Harvard Advocate* on 28 November 1898, and thereafter he became a regular contributor to it and the *Harvard Monthly*, publishing eleven items in his second year and twenty-four in his third, including ten short stories and eight editorials that he wrote as President of *The Harvard Advocate*, (a post to which he was elected in his final year).[29] During the autumn of 1898 he started keeping a journal.[30] Murray Seasongood, who was one of his colleagues on *The Harvard Advocate*, describes him as follows:

> I used to see him rather frequently and sometimes we would take long walks together. He was always very modest, simple and delightful ... a large, handsome, healthy, robust, amiable person, with light curly hair and the most friendly of smiles and dispositions. To keep up with his rolling, vigorous gait and animated, frank and amusing talk, while striding alongside of him was both a feat and a privilege. He was modest, almost diffident, and very tolerant and kindly towards, alike, his colleagues and contributors of manuscripts. Even then a magnificent craftsman, he could write noble sonnets, odes and mighty lines in the traditional forms of poetry.[31]

After leaving Harvard, Stevens went to New York and tried to make a career as a newspaperman. He lived in rented rooms, experimented with special articles on 'A Happy-Go-Lucky Irishman' and 'Wharves and the Sea', and wrote up band concerts, Stephen Crane's funeral and speeches by William Jennings Byran. After working on space for several months, he was employed as a regular reporter by *The New York Tribune*.[32] The work, however, did not suit him and he was neither very successful nor very happy. Consequently, after about a year, he resigned his job, and, taking his father's advice, in the fall of 1901 he entered the New York Law School and began a clerkship in the firm of W. G. Peckham. He was invited a number of times to Peckham's home and accompanied him in the summer of 1903 on a hunting-trip to the Rocky Mountains in Canada, one of the longest journeys that Stevens ever made. He was admitted to the New York bar in June 1904 and, returning to Reading for the summer, met Elsie Moll.[33] On the brink of choosing a new career, he fell in love.

Although both his brothers and his father were practising law in Reading at the time, Stevens does not seem to have seriously considered following their example. He went back to New York in September, and with Layman Ward, whom he had known at Harvard, set up the firm of Ward and Stevens. The partnership failed in a matter of months.[34] During the next two and a half years or so Stevens worked unsuccessfully for three New York law firms: Eugene A. Philbin; Eaton and Lewis; and Eutis and Foster; and, when in the summer of 1907 he was dismissed from Eaton and Lewis (a prominent firm whose clients included Marconi and Edison), he spent over three months unemployed before he could find another job.[35]

His love, however, called for poetry, and in the spring of 1907 he began composing short, playful lyrics for Elsie Moll. His letter of 12 April 1907 consists of one such poem, and on 19 April he mentions writing and tearing up 'a disquisition on April star-light, very poetical'. If Holly Stevens is right, he kept a copy or made another version, as a manuscript of what appears to be the same poem survives in Stevens' papers, with the lightly pencilled note, ' "The Imagination Revived" ', indicating his sense of his own development.[36] This note cannot be dated, but that he had at the time an intimation of what was happening is shown by his letter of 18 March 1907:

> I am no longer a poet. Yet it may be that the sight of Spring waters will restore that faculty, with many others. You must be my poetess and sing me many songs. I shall hear them in strange places and repeat them afterwards as half my own – Good-night, dear poetess![37]

This, it can be said, is more or less what happened except that it was Stevens who sang the songs. Perhaps, in part, it was her imagined presence that he fell in love with and that made him feel more fully himself. He suggests as much to her when he distinguishes between the reality of their meetings and the imaginary communion of their letters:

How do you look in my thoughts? Oh, you would know yourself at once. . . . You are perfectly yourself and that is a little different I think, although not so very much, from the way you are sometimes when we are together. I wonder whether, in saying that, I haven't stumbled across the reason for our being easier in our letters than we are – when we are together. It must be because you are more perfectly yourself to me when I am writing to you, and that makes me more perfectly myself to you.   (10 Mar 1907)

For Christmas 1907, Stevens wrote a series of three quatrains for the flyleaf of Elsie's copy of Bliss Carman and Richard Hovey's *Songs from Vagabondia* (1894), and, the idea of a group of poems growing in him, some time in this period he refers to one of the poems he is sending her as 'for my collection of "Songs for Elsie" '.[38]

Between 1905 and 1907, as he moved from one New York law firm to another, Stevens began to specialise in surety bonds, so after being discharged by Eaton and Lewis he decided to look for a job with a surety company and was fortunate enough to find a place with the American Bonding Company in January 1908. This was a turning-point in his career. After seven years of apprenticeship and failure, at the age of twenty-eight he began the work at which he was going to succeed. The bonding-business was a relatively new one and, although only fourteen years old, the American Bonding Company had been one of the pioneers and was now one of the four largest such firms in the United States.[39]

On her twenty-second birthday, 5 June 1908, Stevens presented Elsie Moll with *A Book of Verses*, a collection of twenty numbered lyrics, his first major poetic effort since he had left Harvard.[40] By December 1908, he was satisfied enough with his prospects to buy her a Tiffany solitaire engagement ring. About this time he was made assistant manager of the New York office and resident assistant secretary.[41] For Elsie's birthday in 1909, Stevens produced another set of twenty poems, *The Little June Book*.[42] One poem from *A Book of Verses* was one of 'Two Poems' published in *Trend* in November 1914, and five poems from *The Little June Book* formed part of the series of eight that appeared in *Trend* in September 1914 as 'Carnet de Voyage', the first poems of Stevens to appear in print in fourteen years. This work represents the beginnings of *Harmonium*. Courtship and business success generated new poetic energies. He married Elsie Moll on 21 September 1909, (he was nearly thirty and she was twenty-three) and they moved into an apartment at 441 West Twenty-first Street in New York.[43] There were no more June books; with one or two exceptions, possession of his beloved brought an end to poetry composed especially for her.[44]

Stevens continued to live in New York for another seven years. When the American Bonding Company was bought by the Fidelity and Deposit Company of Maryland in 1913, he stayed on as law officer. The next year he accepted a job as vice-president and second-in-command of the New York office of the Equity Surety Company of St Louis, and when in 1915 Equity Surety merged with the New England Casualty Company of Boston to become the New England Equitable Insurance Company, Stevens retained his position. However, in February 1916, after financial difficulties, New England Equitable announced that it was going out of all but the industrial-accident insurance business, and Stevens found himself at thirty-six suddenly out of work along with most of the New York office. Fortunately, James Kearney, who was head of the bond department of the Hartford Accident and Indemnity Company and for whom he had worked when he joined the American Bonding Company, immediately offered him a job and Stevens moved to Hartford in May 1916.[45]

The American insurance business had been steadily expanding during this period, and since 1900 many new types of cover had been devised.[46] The Hartford Accident and Indemnity Company, which was three years old when Stevens joined it, had been established as a wholly-owned subsidiary of the Hartford Fire Insurance Company (one of the oldest American insurance companies), because many states would not allow fire-insurance companies to write other types of policies. The new company had concentrated on such new and profitable forms of casualty insurance as automobile insurance and it decided early in 1916 to expand its surety business.[47] One of Stevens' first tasks, however, was to incorporate in New York another Hartford subsidiary, the Hartford Live Stock Insurance Company, of which he became a vice-president and board member. The corporation was only a form maintained by three or four meetings a year as the day-to-day business was run from Hartford, but it was Stevens' responsibility for the rest of his career to see that everything was prepared for the meetings and recorded in the proper legal form.[48]

Stevens' major occupation was the settlement of bond claims, and this meant, especially at first, a considerable amount of travelling, all over the United States and occasionally to Canada. From 1916 to

1921 he was on the road about three months of every year. 'It's just like being a bag-man as they call them in England,' Stevens writes to his wife (15 Aug 1913), 'travelling with a strange line, however, for I go around to patch up trouble or else to cause it.' A separate fidelity and surety claims department with Stevens as its head was established in 1918, and, when in 1921 the company moved to its new office building at 690 Asylum Avenue, Stevens employed an assistant who did most of the travelling.[49] John Ladish, who later took over much of the travel from Stevens and his assistant, explains what was involved:

> The work was mainly a fact-finding assignment and, based on the facts, determining and recommending what should be done. For example, it would be [the bond-claims man's job] to check the financial position of the contractor, his assets, how far the job had progressed, what it would cost to complete the job by getting other bids, and whether we should finance the contract to completion. But when it came strictly to court work that was farmed out.[50]

Stevens, contrary to the practice of casualty claims, deliberately kept his department small, finding it cheaper to refer the whole responsibility for the settlement of claims to attorneys in various parts of the country than to maintain a large staff and pay travelling-expenses. Even so, his department grew from six in 1924 to around twenty (including the secretaries) at his death in 1955.[51] The department handled all the claims resulting from two major types of bonds: fidelity which guaranteed the honesty of an employee and surety which guaranteed the fulfilment of a contract. By 1924 Stevens was specialising almost exclusively in surety bonds, including judicial, court; contractor and appeal bonds, and reserved for himself most of the road-paving and construction cases.[52] Surety bonds are commonly posted by contractors to guarantee the satisfactory completion of any large building-project and in the event of non-completion or unsatisfactory completion the guarantor of surety can be called upon to perform the work.

> But not having taken on full responsibility for all the details [in] the contract initially, the surety is going to make darned certain that every inch of the way the person wanting the work done has performed his side of the bargain. If he's been sloppy, if his

specifications are bad, if he has failed to make payment in due course, if he's done anyone of a number of things that any contracting party can do and do badly, then the surety is going to assert those defenses, because he sees himself moving into the position of the contractor. This is where it becomes arcane. This is where underwriters and claims people alike have to be very sharp-eyed and understand all the details of exactly what the contract was, who said what to whom, what defences are available. All of the facts have to be dug out and disclosed. And where you're talking about the construction of a dam, a highway or a coliseum roof that collapses, an awful lot of expertise has to come into play.[53]

This', says Hale Anderson Junior, a lawyer at the Hartford who sometimes worked with Stevens, 'is where he had his expertise.' The work called for the mastery of an enormous amount of legal, financial and technical detail. Very large sums of money were at stake and in a company as big as the Hartford many claims had to be dealt with at the same time and a large number had to be kept constantly under review, often for years. Anderson comments,

> The net result is a huge accumulation of files that have to be kept track of. . . . Every day a load of these files, several feet high in total, would be placed on his desk. They would be dragged out on diary. He would go through them, peruse his last notations, and decide whether something had to be done or whether to leave it to the people in the field to carry on. If something had to be done, he would dictate his correspondence. If not, for some period, he would . . . leave it to the clerk to pick up . . . at the end of the day.[54]

Stevens did not like what he did not know. He 'was a perfectionist, and he didn't want to do anything he didn't think he was fully capable of doing', remarks Manning Heard, who became Stevens' assistant in 1933 and later President of the Hartford.[55] Stevens' mastery gave him the confidence to trust his own judgement and, therefore, to be able to follow an independent course. Heard states,

> He was a very imaginative claims man. I mean that he was never satisfied to handle cases entirely according to routine. One of the things in the old days was, if you had a contractor that defaulted,

don't try to finish the contract, you'll lose your pants. Well, Stevens very often violated that principle, and he finished contracts, and he was always pretty successful. He was at the time and for many years before his death, the dean of surety-claims men in the whole country.[56]

This 'very imaginative claims man' is the poet who is such a connoisseur of reality. Heard's judgement of Stevens' ability is confirmed by Anthony Sigmans, another associate for many years:

> He certainly was the most outstanding surety-claims man in the business; I think I'm prepared to say that, because I was in the business for a number of years and had occasion to meet a lot of the big surety men. And Stevens, whenever his name was mentioned, 'Oh, hell, he must be right.'[57]

Heard continues,

> To be a successful surety-claims attorney you have to be highly practical, realistic; you have to watch a dollar because you [can] throw away money handling surety claims like nobody's business, like taking over a contract when you shouldn't. I've always wondered how he could separate his mind between poetry ... and this mundane, realistic, surety-claims world. They're two ends of the pole: one is fantasy and the other is real as real can get.[58]

For Stevens, however, surety claims and poetry were not opposites, but complementary. They made one life. Together they enabled him to act out and to satisfy what he called his 'reality–imagination complex', and to feel whole. From another point of view, too, his insurance business and his poetry were analogous: in both he immersed himself through language in the infinite minutiae of the world, living in a sense vicariously, at second-hand. In his article 'Surety and Fidelity Claims' for *The Eastern Underwriter* (25 Mar 1938) Stevens writes,

> A man in the home office tends to conduct his business on the basis of the papers that come before him. After twenty-five years or more of that sort of thing, he finds it difficult sometimes to distinguish himself from the papers he handles and comes to

believe that he and his papers constitute a single creature, consisting principally of hands and eyes: lots of hands and lots of eyes.[59]

Both the insurance man and the poet are 'Men Made out of Words'.

His very heavy caseload caused Stevens to work methodically and steadily, and everyone who worked with him was impressed by his diligence. According to John Rodgers, who was the manservant for the executives at the Hartford in the 1920s and 1930s (and later professor of black history at the University of Hartford),

> Stevens was a very meticulous worker. He worked hard. He was the only man I'd ever seen do research the way he did it. I've seen Stevens with as many as thirty lawbooks at one time. He would get these books day after day: you'd see him with maybe twenty or thirty books, all place-marked, all around him, on a certain subject.... You'd have to bring in extra chairs to hold the books... he was a worker. Lots of others leave to play golf; not Stevens. Stevens was right there, grinding. He was the grindingest guy they had there in executive row.[60]

Richard Sunbury, the mailboy in the bond department from 1931 to 1934, declares, 'I never saw such a terrific worker as Mr Stevens'[61] 'He was always very busy', says Richard Cross, another company lawyer, and Anthony Sigmans describes him as 'a prodigious worker'.[62] This capacity for total commitment, a thoroughgoing conscientiousness both obsession and gift, he brought with him to his poetry. Stevens said to Monroe Wheeler that at the weekends 'he would retreat to [his] study and just come down for meals – and sometimes not even then, when he would be absorbed in his work. He mentioned a particular Sunday when he hadn't appeared at all'.[63] He told the poet Richard Wilbur, who always remembered the seriousness with which he said it, 'You must be like a monk. You must sacrifice yourself to your work'.[64]

Stevens arrived at his office at about 8.45 or 9 a.m., usually went for a walk at lunchtime, as he was always trying to lose weight, and went home at 4.30 p.m.[65] Sometimes he worked late, but, he did not take his insurance work home with him; evenings and weekends were reserved for poetry. He did, however, work on his poems in the office, and at the Hartford, in the midst of the intricacies of surety-bond work, surrounded by files and law books, he was visited by the muse – as his colleagues noticed. Hale Anderson states,

> there were times when he would just put everything aside and be working on some personal notes. He would quite frequently amble into the library, settle down with Webster's dictionary and amble out again, apparently having satisfied himself as to a word. . . .[66]

On occasion, he would ask his secretary to type what he had written. At other times, he 'would stop right in the middle of dictating', take a sheet of paper from the lower right-hand drawer of his desk, write something, put the paper back and continue dictating. The lower right-hand drawer was where he kept 'his poetry notes'; and Stevens usually had it partly open so that his papers were instantly accessible – another indication of how his mind constantly went back and forth between reality and imagination. That his colleagues who saw him composing refer to his manuscripts as 'notes' suggests that he may have worked from isolated words and phrases (or even prose statements) as well as from actual drafts; that they refer to many such notes suggests that he worked on a number of poems at the same time, as he did bond cases. On the contents of the lower right-hand drawer Richard Sunbury remarks;

> It seemed to me that there were sheaves and sheaves. And sometimes he would reach down, and he'd shuffle through three or four. He'd scratch out something or put something in. Or he might take the top one and just add a line or two. All of a sudden, he'd be reading a case, and I have seen him reach down in his drawer and just pick something up. His private copies of his commercial work or his business letters would go in his lower left-hand drawer. And when he finished signing the mail at night, the signed copies of his letters would be thrown on the right-hand side of his desk and the cases that were to go back to file would be thrown on the floor on the left-hand side. He called it his 'freight-yard method'.[67]

Certainly among the notes were definitions of words. Before the company had its own legal library, once or twice a week one of Stevens' assistants would be sent to the Connecticut State Library to look things up and, as Manning Heard recalls, they were invariably asked to undertake a private commission:

> Before I went, I'd go into his office. He'd say, 'Wait a minute. Will you do me a favour?' This is every time I went. 'Will you look up in the Oxford Dictionary the meaning of this word.' And I'd go and I'd just copy the definition, the whole thing, drew the Greek and all that business.[68]

Stevens was interested in the full definition, in all the nuances and connotations, and would often specify several dictionaries. 'He asked us . . . to look up certain words . . . ', says John Ladish, 'not only in the American dictionaries but the Oxford English and any others that he would tell us to check'.[69] Stevens clearly spent a considerable amount of time meditating on individual words. 'The guy I saw using the big dictionary in the law library more than anyone else was Wallace Stevens', says Charles O'Dowd.[70] His noon-hour walks very often produced poetry. Sunbury sometimes accompanied him: 'He most always had some envelopes stuffed in his pocket, and he'd just pull them out and write on the back. Just walking, he'd say, "Wait just a minute, please." He'd pull out an envelope. He always had about a half-dozen in his pocket.'[71] Stevens told Monroe Wheeler that he composed while walking to work and upon his arrival dictated the results to his secretary.[72] As these comments indicate, the presence of other people made very little difference to him. Although he was an extremely private person, he made no attempt to hide his poetic activity and composed, in a sense, in public, or perhaps it is more accurate to say that even in company Stevens always kept himself to himself. He appears as operating in a world of his own.

This essential loneliness made his relations with other people difficult. He was uncomfortable and abrupt in company and never very close to anyone. He separated himself from his family, his marriage does not seem to have been happy, and for many years he was on bad terms with his only child. Although he lived for twenty-three years in the same house, he did not know his neighbours well and after thirty-nine years in Hartford he had no good friends either in the Hartford Accident and Indemnity Company or in the town. His closest friends, Judge Arthur Powell and Henry Church, he saw only intermittently, Powell for two weeks or so on the annual business-vacation trip that Stevens made to the south every winter

(1922–40) and Church from time to time for lunch in New York (1939–47).[73] To explain why he did not know many people in other sections of the Hartford, Stevens remarked: 'Being in bond claims is like being in Oriental languages at a university'.[74] Bond work appeared to suit him because it did not require him to work closely with others, and indeed a number of his colleagues believed that he would not have succeeded in a general legal practice or as a businessman because of his difficulty in getting on with other people. He was thought to be a poor negotiator and did not cultivate the insurance agents on whom the company's business ultimately depended – or anyone else for that matter.[75] Beyond being an officer, he had no ambitions to rise in the company, although he was jealous of his authority within his own department.[76] As ready to snap at the President of Hartford Fire as at his secretary, Stevens was respected for his sharp tongue and explosive nature.[77] His deadpan, sardonic humour was not always appreciated and the aggression often showed through. His jokes were another means of keeping his distance. He showed to Anthony Sigmans the letter he had written to the Statler Hotel in Boston to reserve rooms: 'I would like a room overlooking the Common. I will have with me Sigmans who can be assigned a room overlooking almost anything.' Telling this to Peter Brazeau, Sigmans felt it necessary to explain: 'He meant no offense; he thought that was a joke, because he wouldn't hurt me for all the tea in China' – which was probably the truth.[78] Another episode is related by Wilson Taylor:

> I recall one time when I was in Hartford, we were seated in his office after lunch when a most charming young miss, probably of high school age, who was working for the summer appeared at the door of his office with a handful of checks to be signed. Stevens motioned to her to come in. She laid the checks before him, and he started the process of signing each one. Without looking up, without disturbing the rhythm of signing, and without any preliminary remarks he said: 'This is that girl I was telling you about at lunch today, Taylor.' The child was embarrassed beyond words and, of course, pictured herself as having been thoroughly discussed and critically analysed by each of us at lunch. While the incident was amusing, one could not help but feel for the young lady. To completely allay any lingering suspicions to the contrary, let me assure all readers that the young lady was not discussed by us at lunch.[79]

Asked, at a reception in his honour given by the president or trustee of a university that was awarding him an honorary degree, how he liked the house, Stevens replied, 'My wife and I have tried very hard *not* to create this effect'.[80] His host's response is not recorded, but most of his colleagues responded more or less as Leslie Tucker, a book-keeper whom Stevens encouraged to go to law school:

> To me he was wonderful. He treated me like a gentleman always. But he did have a caustic tongue. He never did or said anything I could take offense at really except on a couple of occasions he was kidding with me. For instance, when I'd go on a trip out of town for him he'd say, 'Be sure to stay at the YMCA.' But of course I never did. You didn't know sometimes whether he was kidding or whether he was serious. I think that was one of his shortcomings: he didn't let people know.[81]

Perhaps it can be said that Stevens himself did not always know, and that often he was expressing ambivalent feelings. Most recognised him for what he was: a competent, hard-working man of integrity who had difficulty in sustaining any real relation with other people. They sensed his ambivalence, and gave him credit for his virtues, respecting both his difficulty and his gift for words. He was granted a poetic licence for his character.

Contrary to what was said before Peter Brazeau interviewed Stevens' colleagues, Stevens did not try to conceal that he was a poet from the people with whom he worked. Although he said little about it (the office learned of his publications and honours from the newspapers), the people at the Hartford knew from the beginning and were proud of their poet even before they had any sense of his greatness.[82] Many people in the company bought his books and tried to understand the poems. 'Everybody' at the office, according to one of the secretaries (who wrote poetry herself), 'was trying to figure out what was meant by ["The Man with the Blue Guitar"]' and some had passages by heart.[83] *Ideas of Order* was much discussed, and, because one of the chauffeurs was named in 'Certain Phenomena of Sound' in *Transport to Summer*, there was considerable curiosity about the identity of Redwood Roamer.[84] Paul Dow collected Stevens' books, Herbert Schoen bought most of them (including at least one book of criticism about Stevens) and Anthony Sigmans started in the mid thirties clipping articles about him from the newspapers.[85] James Powers gave a copy of

Harmonium to his wife while he was courting her, and Stevens' explanation to Richard Sunbury of some Chinese poems in a book he had just bought started Sunbury writing poems.[86] One can conjecture that Stevens received a certain comfort and perhaps even incentive from this support by his fellow workers.

Stevens was appreciated for his general command of language. His fellow workers at the Hartford enjoyed as well as feared his verbal powers. On one occasion, after a field office had recovered 5 dollars of a many-thousand-dollar loss, Stevens acknowledged the payment by saying 'that he now knew how the hippopotamus felt when someone threw him a handful of raspberries', and on another occasion he referred to a lawyer whom he disliked 'as having a smile that was like the silver plate on a coffin'.[87] Moeover, he was famous for his short answers – once in reply to a long letter he wrote back simply: 'No'.[88] 'I loved his letters. He'd attach a note to the bond, and it would say yes or no, and that was it. When it came to business he didn't mince words', says Harry Williams, a president of the Hartford.[89] Stevens took great care not to have to repeat himself – A. J. Fletcher, who handled North Carolina bond claims for him 'for at least thirty years', explains his standard practice as follows:

> he analyzed everything in his first letter so he didn't have to go back if anything should come up concerning the case that had to be clarified. . . . His analysis of the case in his first letter [was peculiar to Stevens among the surety lawyers Fletcher knew]. It made it awfully easy to communicate with him or get an answer to a question. It would have been, nine times out of ten, already set forth in the letter by which he sent the claim to you. As to the character of the letter, I'd say that he never wrote one to me that didn't sound exactly like a prose poem: he was just that clear, and concise, and beautiful.[90]

Another lawyer who worked in Stevens' department, Clifford Burdge, Junior, speaks of his 'beautifully lucid legal writing' and one of the underwriters, Charles O'Dowd, sometimes used to make copies of Stevens' letters, because 'they were so beautifully written'.[91] His secretary, Marguerite Flynn, states, 'His command of English was perfect and if you took his dictation just as he gave it, you never had to hesitate in transcribing it'.[92] Sunbury in his praise reinvents Aristotle: 'His vocabulary was something you just sat down and said, "Oh, boy!" If you could sit down and listen to that man talk, you'd be entranced. It was almost like music to listen to the man talk. He was a master of metaphor.'[93]

About 6 feet 2 inches tall and weighing around 250 pounds (18 stone), Stevens was physically imposing. He towers above the other officers of the Hartford in a photograph taken on the front steps of 690 Asylum Avenue in 1938.[94] Those who knew him were impressed by his presence:

> You immediately had respect for him. He was such a big man physically that he impressed you, and you sort of stepped aside a little bit when he would come.

> . . . tall, austere, very dignified, an unusual-looking man . . . .

> . . . everybody was in awe of him. That was my impression seeing him walk around the company. He was a big man and he carried himself very well.

> He was a huge man and moved with a great deal of solemnity. It was very pleasant, but he was rather awe-inspiring.   (B, p. 146)

> . . . a great tall giant . . . .

> He was very austere; in fact, frightening. He was a very large man, with a great belly and a head like a melon. And a difficult fellow.[95]

These are representative reactions. He always wore dark grey suits, a red tie usually, high shoes and had his hair cut very short.[96] He was very particular about his clothes, as he was about most things, and dressed with the formality of his period. He wore a suit and tie when he went for a walk by himself in the park on Sundays.[97] He was not, however, totally conventional. He wore coloured shirts, pink and blue, in the 1930s, when few others did.[98] He bought his clothes in New York rather than in Hartford. His suits were made to measure by a Norwegian tailor in East Orange, New Jersey; his shirts, underwear and socks came from Newell's on Park Avenue and he also went to New York to obtain 'the right handkerchiefs'.[99]

Elder Olson, in talking to Stevens, was struck that he did not argue but meditated: 'He would hear something, and you could see him think about it; you could almost hear him think about it'.[100]

Stevens absorbed things, and slowly and deliberately made up his mind about them. His attention was meticulous and painstaking, and very small things could engage him. His Cuban friend José Rodriguez Feo recalls that, the first time Stevens took him to Chambord, one of the best and most expensive restaurants in New York, he said,

> 'José, we will have one of your tropical fruits because I see on the menu that they have avocados, alligator pears.' They brought us half of the avocado, which was very expensive; in the center they had cheese. To him that was a beautiful thing; it became almost a poetic object, to be eaten, but to be enjoyed, to be looked at. . . . from the very beginning, I noted this love of life in his enjoyment.[101]

Stevens took voluptuous pleasure in his perceptions. Every object was potentially a poetic object – a surety bond, an avocado or the right handkerchief – to be savoured because it offered a 'Holiday in Reality'. 'He spoke in sentences, not in paragraphs. There was no such thing as a connected argument', says Olson. 'What you had instead was a series of intuitive and highly perceptive remarks. When he got on a subject, he would talk with flashes of intuition. That was not a man who thought consecutively.' This was perhaps because connections meant a rearrangement of his self. What he savoured in an object was its newness, its differences from other objects – that is, its unconnectedness. Moreover, the regular routine of his life can be seen as a way of creating a set of connections between unrelated, unrelatable, objects and as a way of creating enough order to allow him to remain in doubt about the world and to continue making ever-new arrangements of its objects. 'I don't have ideas that are permanently fixed', he writes to Ronald Latimer (31 Oct 1935), and in his next letter (5 Nov 1935) he states, 'The only possible order of life is one in which all order is incessantly changing.'

Stevens loved to eat. Gourmet and gourmand, he enjoyed his food immensely, although from 1926 onward he was usually trying to keep to a diet because of high blood pressure and a tendency to diabetes. He commonly went without lunch and ate very little on Sundays, but he could not resist anything that looked particularly appetising in a baker's window or on the table.[102] Robert De Vore recalls that, on the way to a business meeting in Philadelphia,

Stevens stopped at Lahr's, as he explained he always did when he came to Philadelphia, to buy cinnamon buns. He had a dozen sent to Hartford, took another dozen with him and started the meeting with 'Let's have a cinnamon bun.'[103] He walked miles in New York to buy raisin buns at a particular bakery, always turned up at the Powers' summer house in Cornwall, Connecticut, with 'great batches' of croissants and brioches, and, when the wife of one of his colleagues made pecan buns like those he bought in Philadelphia, he ate six as well as his lunch.[104] His attitude to wine, says Rodriguez Feo, was that of a Frenchman or Italian, not of an American.[105] He had a big wine-cellar and ordered wine by the case, although his wife did not drink and they very rarely entertained.[106] Stevens dined whenever he could in the best New York restaurants and complained that Hartford was a hard place to live in because there were neither any great restaurants nor grocers where he could buy 'the really fine fruit'.[107]

Buying fruit for Stevens was virtually a passion. 'He was always going to fruit stores to buy things', says Rodriguez Feo.[108] Stevens' walk instead of lunch to keep his weight down very often included a stop to buy fruit. Dow, who frequently walked with him, states, 'He would go to a fruit store where they had great big grapes; he just loved them.'[109] He ordered dried fruit from California, and fresh fruit, whenever he was in New York, from a shop on Madison Avenue – enough for them to send it by train, and he would arrange for someone to pick it up and take it to his house.[110] The quality of his interest is indicated by the following *excerpts* from his letters to Wilson Taylor (15 Aug 1944 and 25 Sept 1945):

I imagine that Mrs Batchelder sold her business with the orchard, and that what she used to sell her successor will sell. I hope so because her prunes were the only real equals of old Dr Barker's. Be careful to get this year's crop. As a matter of fact, all of these things, except possibly the pears, ought to be available already. The drying process in that climate takes only a few days. Dried cherries are very difficult to get. You will probably have to get them in the country yourself.... I suppose by now you have discovered Goldberg-Bowen, the big grocery shop in San Francisco. They used to put up a mountain grove prune which was distinct.... I don't want these unless it is completely impossible to get something like Mrs Batchelder's prunes....

It is really a little early to be ordering prunes for the winter, but I am sending you $50.00 for which I should like to have four 5-pound boxes and twenty-five pounds of apricots. this is about as much as I am likely to use during the course of the winter and in fact, now that you have introduced me to Bee Ritchie and I have had stoned prunes, it may even be too much. . . . Moreover, I made a deposit with these people. It seems that they dip their prunes in chocolate and sometime next month I expect to receive a load of those.

The reason I am sending you $50.00 is that you may see some other things that you think I ought to have, especially fine pears, peaches, or cherries. One gets fed up on too much of the same thing.[111]

Virtually everything received this meticulous attention, and somehow his passion for the fine print of any subject with which he was concerned appears to have contributed to the good-humoured gusto and spontaneity so evident in everything he wrote. Both characteristics demonstrate his capacity to live fully in the present. Friends in Florida regularly sent him wild lemons from there because he had enjoyed them so much on a visit.[112]

Stevens' life appears as a continuous effort of private, home-made, mundane connoisseurship, not in order to associate himself with any tradition, but to get through the day, a habit of mind rather than an end in itself – a way of accommodating the luxuriant sensuousness of his perceptions. He wrote poems because these feelings were not self-sufficient. Poetry was a way of giving them form, of making them significant, of raising them to another power of seriousness. There is no doubt of the very real pleasure that he took in objects of all kinds, but the structure of arrangements, that everything had to be chosen and that only those things that had been carefully considered would do, suggests that abandonment was only possible within a form and that contact with the world was felt as self-surrender. This connoisseurship is a response to chaos. The buying of special things from special places incorporates pleasure into a routine and makes the appearance of the object appear as an act of the will, creation *ex nihilo* – and the pleasure of discriminating between sensations is one of mastery. Perhaps such habits are part of the management of greed and the introduction of an element of self-restraint into self-indulgence; certainly they show us Stevens constantly offering himself little treats, something extra.

Each transaction is the appropriation or consumption of an object, the re-creation, it might be said, of a feeding-situation in which the object, to some degree personified by the ceremonies of enjoyment, provides company in addition to other nourishment. This equivalence, such as it is, between possession and communication may help us to understand why Stevens so often involved others, including those he did not know, in his efforts to obtain things.

As he asked his colleagues to look up words in the dictionary for him or to fetch or send him things, so he sometimes asked them to take him places. According to his fellow director of the Hartford Live Stock Insurance Company, Arthur Polley, any of his subordinates who offered Stevens a ride to work took a risk:

> Now, if he had been my boss, I never would have picked him up in God's world, because every once in a while he'd just get the idea that he wanted to go some place, and by gosh you drove him there. One of the men that worked for him [once] picked him up, and it was the time of the World's Fair in New York. Wallace was very much of a gourmet, and he says, 'Well, now, it's a nice day. I guess we won't go to the office. Just keep driving.' And, my God, he made him take him down to the World's Fair to have lunch. But then he didn't have lunch with him. He says, 'You get what you want, and you meet me here an hour later.' . . . And it wasn't only once but twice he made him take him down.[113]

Stevens arranged through Harriet Monroe for her sister, who was in Peking, to send him a selection of Chinese objects of her choice and some tea. He was delighted with the things she sent. Although his letter to Harriet Monroe describing them shows how carefully he studied each one and how they fed his imagination, nevertheless, he was not totally content: the carved figure of an old man 'is so humane that the study of him is as good as a jovial psalm. *I must have more*, provided he is not solitary. But *I intend to let that rest for the moment* for Mrs Calhoun has clearly gone to a lot of trouble' (28 Oct 1922, emphasis added). Years later, when Harriet Monroe went to Peking, he writes to Morton Zaubel, the assistant editor of *Poetry*, to ask 'if [he] thought that she would be interested in doing a little shopping' (22 Oct 1934), and upon her return he asks her, 'Do you suppose your sister would care to do a little more shopping?' (13 Mar 1935). For Stevens each of these ventures was an excursion in fantasy. Obtaining the address of a Chinese student from James Powers, he reports:

I sent Mr Qwock some money last spring, with a request for some erudite teas. It appears that, when this letter reached Canton, he had left on a holiday in Central China, or in the moon, or wherever it is that learned Chinese go in the summer time. But on his return to his studies in the autumn he wrote to me and said that he had written to one of his uncles, who lives in Wang-Pang-Woo-Poo-Woof-Woof-Woof, and has been in the tea business for hundreds of generations. I have no doubt that in due course I shall receive from Mr Qwock enough tea to wreck my last kidney, and with it some very peculiar other things, because I asked him to send me the sort of things that the learned Chinese drink [*sic*] with that sort of tea.   (17 Dec 1935)

Ten days later Stevens tells Powers that Kwok is in Macao, 'where, I assume, he is gathering pickled apricots, candied gold fish and sugared canaries' knees for me' (27 Dec 1935). Similarly, Stevens writes to Leonard van Geyzel to ask him if he would mind 'getting together a few things from Ceylon' (14 Sep 1937). This letter was the start of a epistolary friendship that lasted the rest of Stevens' life and entered into the substance of his poetry.[114] Again Stevens was delighted with what van Geyzel had chosen, but his thank-you letter reveals that his appetite was undiminished:

When summer comes round I shall be wanting to do something of this sort again, but in some other place, say, Java or Hong Kong or Siam. Do you know of anyone in any of those places to whom I could write as I wrote to you, and who would be likely to take my letter in the same spirit in which you took it? I am not trying to work my way round the world on the basis of other people's courtesy; I should be quite willing to pay for the trouble. . . . The great difficulty is to find people of taste: people who are really interested in doing this sort of thing as part of the interest of living.

These various orders can be seen as the acting-out of a fantasy of omnipotence. The world is domesticated when objects are sent in a package from Peking to be arranged in a house in Hartford; the far-away is brought near at hand, the unknown becomes knowable and the object consumed and ingested by the senses is transferred from the outer to the inner world. Thirteen years before he wrote to Harriet Monroe's sister, Stevens writes to Elsie Moll, 'I do not know if you feel as I do about a place so remote and unknowable as China – the irreality of it. So much so, that the little realities of it seem wonderful and beyond belief.' (18 Mar 1909). The 'little realities' verify the imagination, merging, in fact, the imagination and the world and bringing them both *within* belief. Stevens' poetry suggests that for him the whole world was like China. Each object, each poem, creates a new perspective, new vision, new knowledge: Hartford is altered; he is renewed.

He sought the vividness and originality of his first impressions and to this end his correspondents were invited to make the final choice as to what they would despatch. Wilson Taylor was sent extra money because 'you may see some other things that you think I ought to have'. Stevens wanted his presents to himself to come as a surprise. Thus, they have a value analogous to that of Duchamp's *objects trouvés* or 'readymades'. Stevens confides to Elsie Moll,

> You wonder why I didn't go into the country to see apple-blossoms and the like. The truth is, or seems to be, that it is chiefly the surprise of the blossoms that I like. After I have seen them for a week (this is great scandal) I am ready for the leaves that come after them – for the tree unfolded, full of sound and shade.
>
> (9 May 1909)

Change means growth – and the chance of fulfilment. There is, in addition, a sense in which the poem is the counterpart of the carved Chinese figure or lunch at the World's Fair, an object moved from the inner world to the outer; and every transfer, in either direction, is a taking-possession, so that 'the little realities' are as wonderful as poems and the poems as nourishing as fruit. This interchangeability is suggested by Stevens' comments to his wife on 17 June 1910:

> Somehow, I do not feel like reading. It isn't in the air in June. But I *do* like to sit with a big cigar and think of pleasant things – chiefly of things I'd like to have and do. I was about to say 'Oh! For a world of Free Will!' But I really meant free will in this world – the granting of that one wish of your own: that every wish were granted. – Yet so long as one keeps out of difficulty it isn't so bad as it is. For all I know, thinking of a roasted duck, or a Chinese jar, or a Flemish painting may be quite equal to having one. Possibly it depends on the cigar. And anyhow it doesn't matter.

The objects that came to him through the post were like wishes coming true. They enabled him to think through the transition between the dream world and the world. They were metaphors for things as they are.

At 118 Westerly Terrace, according to his daughter, Stevens did most of his writing in the study adjoining his bedroom on the second floor.[115] The objects that Harriet Monroe's sister had sent him from Peking were on his desk. There he kept a number of his books, a first edition of *Ulysses*, some limited editions published by the Cuala Press, his collection of Alain and books of reproductions of Klee, there hung the portrait of Anatole Vidal by Jean Labasque.[116] These two rooms were Stevens' sanctum, where he often retired after meals to work or read or think. 'There is no passion like the passion for thinking which grows stronger as one grows older', Stevens writes to Rodriguez Feo (17 Oct 1955). 'Spend an hour or two a day [thinking]', he recommends, 'even if in the beginning you are staggered by the confusion and aimlessness of your thoughts.' His vocabulary indicates the power of the forces at play in his meditations. Mental 'aimlessness' and 'confusion' are 'staggering', almost overwhelming, and thinking is an ever-increasing passion, gaining in strength as it establishes order, however tentative or temporary. Stevens is recommending what he had always done. He arranged his life so as to attempt to satisfy this 'passion for thinking'. (How could he had done otherwise if we take the word 'passion' seriously?) 118 Westerly Terrace was a large house, eleven rooms on three floors, and one reason Stevens bought it was to give himself space in which to think. When his daughter asked why three people needed such a big house, Stevens replied, 'To be together when we wish'; then added, 'and to get away when we wish'.[117]

Stevens rose at six o'clock and thereby had two hours to meditate and breakfast before starting his two-mile walk to the office.[118] For Stevens, walking was an integral part of the process of composition. He regularly walked to and from the Hartford, took a walk during his lunch hour and on Sundays walked in the 100 acres of Elizabeth Park. Another reason for buying 118 Westerly Terrace was that it was only a block and a half from Elizabeth Park, the destination of innumerable walks. Holly Stevens states that the park was *home* for her father and that he 'spent some time there almost every day'.[119] His visits to New York were also the occasions for long walks (as well as opulent lunches) as Rodriguez Feo testifies:

He would walk a lot when we were in New York. He would say, 'Oh José. You Spaniards, you get tired of walking.' I'd say, 'Oh, Mr Stevens, but you've already walked fifteen blocks.' He'd say, 'Yes, but it's so nice to walk and look at the stores, walk down Fifth Avenue and down the streets in the Italian sections, look at the fruits, look at the shops, look at the flowers.' And he would never get tired.

When they talked, says Rodriguez Feo, Stevens always emphasised 'that I had to think more' and told him, 'You should be more in contact with the real things of life, not be so absorbed in literature.' He sends Rodriguez Feo (10 June 1945) what he calls 'a precious sentence in Henry James' as a summation of his view:

To live *in* the world of creation – to get into it and stay in it – to frequent it and haunt it – to *think* intensely and fruitfully – to woo combinations and inspirations into being by a depth and continuity of attention and meditation – this is the only thing.[120]

For Stevens the great division was not between the country and the city, but rather between reality and imagination. Walking was a way of taking possession of the world and plunging, simultaneously, into 'the world of creation'. Walking generated the objects, the metaphors, of thought. Although he had a bias in favour of the country, Fifth Avenue or the Lower East Side would do, and he had a decided preference for what was immediately at hand. To Rodriguez Feo he writes: 'I almost always dislike anything that I do that doesn't fly in the window' (20 June 1945).

Stevens was a person who needed a considerable amount of time to himself and he created a life that fulfilled that need. Any thought that it was in some ways a lonely life and of a loneliness not wholly of his own choosing has to be set side by side with his comment on Santayana: 'I doubt', he writes to Rodriguez Feo, 'if Santayana was any more isolated at Cambridge than he wished to be' (4 Jan 1945). Stevens' self-isolation seems, to some degree, a result of the discomfort he felt in being with other people and an unhappy marriage – and these two things are clearly related. There is perhaps nothing more difficult to know than the nature of someone else's marriage, and Elsie Stevens was an even more private person than her husband. She destroyed those sections of his journal and correspondence with her that she thought were too personal,

objected to the writing of a biography and was offended by Stevens'
fame.[121] She declares to Samuel Morse (20 Dec 1960), who was
working on a biography,

> Mr Stevens' poetry was a distraction that he found delight in, and
> which *he kept entirely separate from his home life*, and his business life
> – neither of them suitable or relevant to an understanding of his
> poetry. Particularly his home life, which I would regard as an
> intrusion and an intervention. The publicity that Mr Stevens'
> renown offers, is offensive to me . . . .[122]

Such evidence as there is indicates that Stevens and his wife were
frequently not on good terms. No one in his family understood why
he had married Elsie Moll. His father and mother had opposed the
marriage, and, while his brothers and sisters did not dislike her,
their views appear to have been those of his sister Elizabeth. Elsie,
she said, years later, was 'a pretty doll-like creature who never said
anything. We couldn't understand Wallace having an interest in
somebody like this'.[123] Stevens' daughter also did not understand
why her father had married her mother, and, when she once asked
him, he replied that it was because she was the prettiest girl in
town.[124] This estimate of her beauty is confirmed by early
photographs of her, and the delightful letters that Stevens wrote to
her during their courtship and the early years of their marriage show
a man very much in love.

An entry in his journal during his first summer in New York after
Harvard reveals some of his fantasies about marriage as well as his
feeling of the emptiness of being alone. On 26 July 1900 he writes.

> Tonight I received no assignment & so I am in my room. I almost
> said at home – God forbid! The proverbial apron-strings have a
> devil of a firm hold on me and as a result I am unhappy at such a
> distance from the apron. I wish a thousand times a day that I had a
> wife – which I never shall have, and more's the pity for I am
> certainly a domestic creature, par excellence. It is brutal to myself
> to live alone. . . . I don't know – sometime I may marry after all. Of
> course I am too young now etc. as people go – but I begin to feel
> the vacuum that wives fill. This will probably make poor reading
> to a future bachelor. Wife's an old word – which does not express
> what I mean – rather a delightful companion who would make a
> fuss over me.[125]

Some three and a half years later and some four months before he met Elsie Moll, on 14 February 1904, there is one of the strongest statements of his need for company:

> I'm in the Black Hole again, without knowing any of my neighbors. The very animal in me cries out for a lair. I want to see somebody, hear somebody speak to me, look at somebody, speak to somebody in turn. I want companions. I want more than my work, than the nods of my acquaintances, than this little room. I do *not* want my dreams – my castles, my haunts, my *nuits blanches*, my companies of good friends. Yet I dare not say what I do want. It is such a simple thing. I'm like that fool poet in *Candida*. Horrors!

The 'fool poet' is Shaw's Marchbanks, who says in Act II of *Candida*, 'That is what all poets do: they talk to themselves out loud; and sometimes the world overhears them. But it's horribly lonely not to hear someone else talk sometimes', and the reference suggests that, even in this period when he was writing no poetry, Stevens had some idea of himself as a poet.[126]

What Elsie Moll meant to Stevens is shown by the way in which she suddenly becomes the major subject of the journal, and the letters to her gradually take the place of the journal. This substitution might have occurred sooner if she had written to him more often. He confides to his journal on 13 September 1904, some three months after their meeting, 'I could write to her every night – but she will answer only once a week, and then four pages are all I get'.[127] The remark is an indication of how much he had to say that he could not say to himself. The fading of the journal after 1907, moreover, also coincides with his beginning again to write poetry: the poems on the flyleaf of *Songs from Vagabondia* are dated Christmas 1907; *A Book of Verses* is dated 5 June 1908; *The Little June Book*, 5 June 1909 – all specifically composed for Elsie Moll.[128] She was his muse; knowing her brought the poet to life, although when reading some of his poems to friends in 1914 he began by saying, 'She doesn't like them. Perhaps you will', and she is reported as saying, 'I like Mr Stevens' things when they are not affected; but he writes so much that is affected.'[129] Her dislike, from what her daughter says, was, among other things, founded on a recognition of the part she had played in her husband's beginning again. She felt that his poems belonged to her:

While I was growing up my mother did not read my father's poems, and seemed to dislike the fact that his books were published. Questioning her about this after my father's death, she told me that he had published 'her poems'; that he had made public what was, in her mind, very private. At the time I did not understand what she meant but, with the discovery that when he first began publishing in 1914, he had used some of the poems in the books he made for her birthdays, her logic becomes clear, her resentment comprehensible.[130]

His poetry after *The Little June Book* aroused her jealousy as a turning-away from full and exclusive communication with her. She appears, however, to have taken at least an intermittent interest in his work toward the end of his life. Discussing with Louis Martz 'An Ordinary Evening in New Haven', composed for the sesquicentennial of the Connecticut Academy of Arts and Sciences in 1949, Stevens explained that he had written more sections than it was possible for him to read at the ceremony:

Now I read every section as is my custom to my wife as I wrote it. She put her hands over her eyes and said, 'They're not going to understand this.' I was very careful to pick out the sections I thought would go over with an audience. But even so, my wife was terribly concerned about it.

Martz definitely had the impression that 'it was his habit to read – at least at that time of his life – the poems he was writing to his wife and get her responses'.[131]

There is also another way in which she can be said to have figured as or like a muse. The Stevens' landlord at 441 West 21st Street in New York, where they rented an apartment from 1909 to 1916, was the sculptor Adolf Weinman, who lived in the apartment below them. Struck by Mrs Stevens' beauty, he asked her to pose for the designs he was doing for new American coins. The designs were accepted and Elsie Stevens' head appeared on the Mercury dime and Liberty half-dollar. This meant that, for the rest of his life, whenever he paid cash or received change, the transaction probably involved handing over or being handed an effigy of his wife, and that she, who rarely saw or conversed with anyone except her husband, could think that her portrait was the common currency of nearly 200 million people. The effects are incalculable. Stevens almost never spoke of it, although Weinman's statue had a place of honour on their living-room mantlepiece.[132]

The course of Stevens' marriage is obscure. Weinman's children remembered that, when Elsie Stevens was angry, she would pace through the apartment slamming all the doors, including the doors to the closets.[133] Carl Van Vechtan, who saw a certain amount of Stevens in 1914 (and met his wife on only one occasion) describes her as painfully uncomfortable in company. He presents the poet as hen-pecked and states that Stevens said to him, 'I always say that I don't talk about my fear of my wife, but I'm always doing it!'[134] According to their sons, Mr and Mrs Gray, who rented the downstairs of their house at 735 Farmington Avenue in Hartford to Stevens from 1924 to 1932 and lived in the upstairs, thought:

> he was very lonely and they always felt sorry for him, always felt his wife was crazy. He used any kind of excuse in paying the rent to come up and hand them the check. That would be during Prohibition; I have an idea they'd have a drink together. They thought it was awfully sad: he always seemed to be alone. . . . He would have to kind of steal the time to talk, and he would have to be very careful not to cause any disturbance in his own domestic scene. It was kind of surreptitious.[135]

The rumour among Stevens' colleagues at the Hartford was 'that he and his wife used to fight like cats and dogs', and Stevens once remarked to Charles O'Dowd, 'Mrs Stevens and I went out for a walk yesterday afternoon. We walked to the end of Westerley Terrace and she turned left and I turned right'.[136]

By all accounts Elsie Stevens was a very neurotic person. Most people who met her found her strange or odd. Her daughter comments, 'All her life, at least during the time I knew her, she suffered from a persecution complex which undoubtedly originated during her childhood . . .' Her mother, she learned, was 'different' from her friends' mothers, and tells the following story as an example:

> the first time I called her 'Mommy', as I had heard my playmates address their mothers, I was told never to use that word to her again: it sounded like 'Mummy', which indicated to her that I thought of her as an Egyptian mummy, a dead body wrapped in rags.[137]

Elsie's niece, who stayed with the Stevenses in 1941 states, 'She was remote, just remote. She said very little. . . . You didn't know the next moment what Elsie was going to say to you or whether she was going to disappear in thin air, because half the time she wasn't there.'[138] She dressed sombrely and austerely in the style of her youth, wearing long-sleeved blouses, her skirts down to her ankles and her hair in a severe bun.[139] A meticulous housekeeper, she objected to Stevens drinking (a colleague remembers helping him smuggle French wine into the house at night so that she would not know) and did not allow Stevens or anyone else to smoke in the house.[140] 'She was a very hard person', says the mother's help who worked for her for two years; 'Very strict. She had her own way. You just had to follow it. She made you nervous if you didn't'.[141] Elsie Stevens appears to have had no friends. When they moved to Hartford she belonged to two study groups for a time and a music club, but, as she grew older, she seems to have become more and more of a recluse and the neighbourhood children called her 'the witch'.[142] She was an excellent cook, but they entertained only very rarely. Only a small number of people ever set foot in the house, and many were puzzled or hurt at Stevens' abrupt and evasive excuses as to why he could not invite them to his home.[143] After their first years in Hartford, his wife never accompanied Stevens to other people's houses. They had separate rooms in 118 Westerly Terrace and a neighbour says, 'I don't remember ever seeing them together; they never walked together as a couple.' None the less, something, whether loyalty to their youthful passion or their shared need to live apart from others or some other psychological interdependence, kept them together, as the marriage endured forty-six years and ended only with Stevens' death.[144] They had a common interest in genealogy, and his wife's researches and their success (she became a member of the Daughters of the American Revolution in the late 1930s) may have stimulated Stevens' interest in tracing his family.[145] Also they were both keen gardeners, and, although Stevens said that he had to give up gardening because they clashed over what they wanted, a letter to Wilson Taylor (30 Oct 1944) describes them gardening together, so perhaps a more satisfactory *modus vivendi* was achieved at the end of their lives. Only the most tentative speculation is possible on this subject, about which we are unlikely ever to know the truth.[146] Perhaps it can be said that the nature of Stevens' marriage altered the significance for him of life at the office.

Wallace Stevens was a man of very considerable energy. He

worked a full day as an insurance lawyer and at the same time steadily produced poems of the highest quality (between 1930 and 1955 he published an average of over eight poems a year in periodicals). From 1936 to 1951 he gave a number of lectures on the theory of poetry and from 1941 to 1952 he did extensive research into the history of his family.[147] 'What we shall have when I am through with it', he writes to Orville Stevens, 'is not a scrapbook of an amateur but a really scholarly study of the family' (20 Dec 1943).[148] Over 2500 genealogical items in the Wallace Stevens Collection at the Huntington Library ('including carbon copies of his own genealogical letters, letters from professional genealogists and interested relatives; books, pamphlets and periodicals; copies of wills, church records, gravestone inscriptions and Bible flyleaves; notebooks filled with notes on his reading; printed and hand-drawn maps; memoranda and photographs') testify to the effort that Stevens put into the project.[149] The routine of his life would appear to have worked to maximise the amount of effective energy, as if the outer quiet was a condition of the rich and intense inner activity.

Only occasionally in some of the stories told about him do we catch a glimpse of the exuberance, extravagance and freedom that is so obvious in the poetry. John O'Loughlin, who worked in the bond department, recalls a party that he attended with Stevens where Stevens had had a number of drinks: 'The waiter came along with a tray of hors d'oeuvres, and he kicked it right out of her hand, and it went right up to the ceiling'.[150] There is a story of Frost and Stevens walking home arm-in-arm along the beach after a night's drinking at Key West, falling down and rolling into the surf together before being able to right themselves. Stevens in company usually had several drinks (commonly dry martinis) in order to relax, and by all accounts held his liquor very well. According to O'Loughlin, 'Mr Stevens was not a drinking man, and when he got a little bit more, he'd become very joyous and not mean or cantankerous.' Stevens' winter visits to the South appear to have been occasions when he let himself go and drank a great deal. He describes his first visit in a letter to Ferdinand Reyher:

> Now that trip to Florida would have unstrung a brass monkey. . . .
> I was the only damned Yankee in the bunch. I was christened a
> charter member of the Long Key Fishing Club of Atlanta. The
> christening occupied about three days, and required just two
> cases of Scotch. When I traveled home, I was not able to tell

whether I was traveling on a sound or a smell. As I remember it, it was very much like a cloud full of Cuban senoritas, cocoanut palms, and waiters carrying ice-water. Since my return I have not cared much for literature. The southerners are a great people.

(2 Feb 1922)[151]

Florida was the setting for perhaps the most violent episode of Stevens' career and one of the most spectacular and unlikely literary encounters: the fight between Stevens and Hemingway at Key West in February 1926. As Hemingway describes it, his sister had left a party in tears because of what Stevens had said about him. He had then gone looking for Stevens, who, it is alleged, had gone away saying 'that if Hemingway had been there he would have flattened him with a single blow'. When Hemingway confronted Stevens he swung on Hemingway and missed, whereupon Hemingway knocked him down several times. Stevens hit Hemingway on the jaw and broke his hand. Stevens was fifty-six, Hemingway thirty-eight. The two men made it up soon afterwards and Stevens laughed when he told the story a day or two later and said that he had been a fool to drink so much. According to Hemingway, Stevens did not want his colleagues to know of the fight and they agreed, he says, to say that Stevens had fallen downstairs. Stevens, however, did talk about it and the story did reach Hartford, although, when he returned to the office with a puffy eye and broken hand, neither he nor his assistant mentioned it.[152] The episode perhaps even increased Stevens' esteem for Hemingway, because six years later he recommended him to Church (2 July 1942) as 'the best man that I can think of' for the chair of poetry that Church was thinking of establishing. Hemingway is, says Stevens, 'the most significant of living poets, so far as the subject of EXTRAORDINARY ACTUALITY is concerned'.

In 1949 Paul Dow went with another colleague to Stevens' house to discuss a business matter because Stevens had been ill and not at the office. Wearing a bathrobe, Stevens received them in his study on the second floor and talked about the Tal Coat painting in the room and the sesquicentennial celebration of the Connecticut Academy of Arts and Sciences, where he was going to read part of 'An Ordinary Evening in New Haven', which he had composed for the occasion: 'He read part of it to Ladish and myself, just a few sections, and commented on it. And he jumped around to show us how healthy he was. Picked up the tails of his bathrobe and jumped around. I was amazed.'[153] A year or two later this vitality was undiminished. When the New York office gave an anniversary party at the Biltmore Hotel and invited the chief executives of the company (the president, comptroller, Stevens and Wilson Jainsen, another vice-president), Coy Johnston was present:

> An accordion player played as we ate. Everybody seemed to get pretty liquored up as the evening wore on, and then the dancing began. All men. You never saw such a sight: Jainsen dancing with Stevens, swinging him around the room to a Polish polka. Wallace Stevens would throw up a foot as he would twirl. That's a side of Stevens nobody knew existed. The party started about four in the afternoon. Stevens disappeared at eleven o'clock; so did the whole Hartford crowd.[154]

These episodes that suggest pent-up forces need to be set against Manning Heard's statement that he never saw Stevens excited.[155] The contradiction emphasises the deep and comprehensive satisfaction that Stevens received from his work, both surety bonds and poetry, and reveals how easily these forces found expression in his poetry.

Wallace Stevens was seventy when he 'picked up the tails of his bathrobe and jumped around'. As the Hartford required an annual report on employees over seventy before deciding whether they could continue working, he was probably concerned, especially after a period of illness at home, that there should be no doubt about his condition.[156] Stevens did everything he could in order to go on working, even, unlike other department heads, to the extent of not preparing anyone to succeed him.[157] He was furious when fidelity claims were transferred to E. A. Cowie, as Cowie reports:

> I can remember going down to talk to him one day [that winter of 1955], and he was seething. At first he refused to talk to me. Then he got to arguing how they had insulted him by taking his authority away. All of a sudden he got over it. He mellowed, and talked about what I wanted to talk about, but he was pretty blue about that. He had been practically shaking; he was almost having a tantrum. I was prepared to leave his presence, but finally he softened and he said, 'I'm not blaming you.'[158]

About a year before his final illness, Stevens requested a colleague to

ask the president to give one of his assistants a rise, because he was
afraid that if the president saw him he would ask him to retire.[159] He
suffered great pain rather than stop work. Hale Anderson Junior
comments,

> I want to make the point that of all the individuals I've seen go
> through this, he was the most capable in knowing how to die.
> During his last illness, he would come and sit [in the company's
> reception room at lunchtime], and put his thumb and forefinger
> under his chin and rest, with his eyes closed, and never indicate
> by word or manner that he didn't feel well. And about the time
> people began to hustle back to work, he would get up and go back
> to his office and tackle that pile of files again. He was a true
> stoic.[160]

Stevens' poetic career can be divided into three periods: 1898–1900,
1907–24 and 1928–55. His major work begins in the second period,
with the poems that he published in 1915. Stevens resembles Yeats,
Valéry and Rilke in that they all composed most of their best poems
after the age of forty, and, in the case of Stevens and Yeats, the bulk
of their best work was done when they were over fifty. Theirs is the
poetry of maturity.

The earliest evidence that we have of Stevens' extraordinary
verbal gifts are some of the letters that he wrote to his mother as a
boy. At fifteen, away from home on a summer holiday, he describes
his brother Garrett, who was nicknamed 'Buck':

> At present he is on the top of the house, with his Rosalie, author of
> 'Listigzaneticus or Who Stabbed the Cook', and while they
> together bask Buck's kaleidescopic [sic] feelings have inspired the
> keen, splattering, tink-a-tink-tink-tink-tink-a-a-a that are gambol-
> ing off the hackneyed strings of his quivering mandolin[.]
>
> (4 Aug 1895)

The next summer, age sixteen, he writes from the same resort,

> The piping of flamboyant flutes, the wriggling of shrieking fifes
> with rasping dagger-voices, the sighings of bass-viols, drums that
> beat and rattle, the crescendo of cracked trombones – harmo-
> nized, that is Innes band. Red geraniums, sweet-lyssoms, low,

heavy quince trees, the mayor's lamps, Garrett playing on the organ, water-lilies and poultry – that is Ivyland.   (31 July 1896)

This joyous and free-wheeling exuberance does not show itself in his published work until the poems of *Harmonium*. Stevens had to live another twenty years before he could command these powers.

Stevens discovered his vocation as a student at Harvard, and most of his early work was published in *The Harvard Advocate* (1898–1900). He wrote both poems and short stories. The poems are uninterestingly conventional, with regular metres, regular rhyme schemes and echoes of Shelley, Keats, Tennyson and Robinson, as well as many of the minor poets of the period, such as Dante Rossetti and Austin Dobson. Stevens shows a preference for quatrains and Petrarchian sonnets. He submitted a series of fifteen sonnets for English 22, his second-year composition course.[161] This early work is smooth, competent and unremarkable. The poet's skill is obvious, but the melodies are somewhat banal, the thoughts are very general, the logic is often vague or uncertain and many of the poems are touched by a jejeune sentimentality. Although there are a number of ideas that presage the later poems, only occasionally is there a phrase that suggests the mature poetry.[162] The poems, in and of themselves, are of no lasting value and one can understand the response of Charles Copeland (Copey), Harvard's famous teacher of composition (which may have been partly humorous as he was a friend of Stevens at Harvard). Witter Bynner recounts, 'I remember Copey's asking him just before he left Cambridge what he was going to be and when the undergraduate answered, "A poet", Copey's exclaiming, "Jesus Christ!"' [163]

During the next fourteen years Stevens wrote little and published nothing – beyond those items that he contributed as a reporter to *The New York Tribune* (1900-1). Toward the end of his life he said, 'When I got to New York I was not yet serious about poetry'.[164] He did, however, want to become a writer and continued to keep his journal. Between 22 and 26 June 1900 he copied in the revised version of a poem, 'A Window in the Slums' and on 20 February 1901, two days after being 'charmed' by Ethel Barrymore in *Captain Jinks of the Horse Marines*, he declares, 'Hang me if I don't write a play myself' and writes a plot summary of *Olivia: A Romantic Comedy in Four Acts*.[165] He was still working on *Olivia* when in March he returned to Reading and talked to his father about his future: 'We talked about the law which he has been urging me to take up. I hesitated – because this literary life, as it is called, is the one I always had as an ideal & I am not quite ready to give it up because it has not been all that I wanted it to be.'[166] Not long after this he decided that he would like to take his chances as a writer. On 12 March 1901 he writes in his journal,

> I recently wrote to father suggesting that I should resign from the Tribune & spend my time in writing. This morning I heard from him and, of course, found my suggestion torn to pieces. If I only had enough money to support myself I am afraid some of his tearing would be in vain. But he seems always to have reason on his side, confound him.[167]

The tone is not one of great disappointment, and the father's reasons find a sympathetic ally in the son.

He made a new start in 1907, when he began composing poems for Elsie Moll, but it was only in 1913, after his marriage (1909) and the death of his father (1911) and mother (1912), that he began seriously 'trying to get together a little collection of verses again'. Although the poems 'are simple to read, when they're done, it's a deuce of a job (for me) to do them', he writes to his wife (7 Aug 1913), who was spending the summer in the mountains of Pennsylvania. His lingering doubts emerge with his growing pleasure as he cautions her, 'Keep all this a great secret. There is something absurd about all this writing of verses; but the truth is, it elates and satisfies me to do it. It is an all-round exercise quite superior to ordinary reading.' That there is no hint of these poems being for her and that her birthday is just past indicates that this 'collection' is for himself. Which poems he was working on is uncertain, but it is likely that they were the series of eight short lyrics that he published as 'Carnet de Voyage' in *Trend* (Sep 1914), his first poems to appear in print since he had left Harvard. Stevens published thirteen poems in 1914, although none that he chose to include in *The Collected Poems*. He had abandoned the older conventions of Shelley and Robinson for the new conventions then being established. These poems are adaptations, attempts at learning a language, rather than true experiments, and show the effects of *Songs from Vagabondia*, Flint, Hulme and Pound as well as of Stevens' study of French poetry (especially Mallarmé) and Chinese and Japanese art – interests that he shared with many of his contemporaries.

The poems are, except for 'Phases', descriptions of moods in which an effort has been made to exclude any explicit statement of ideas. They are deliberately brief, but no attempt has been made to reduce the images to the minimum. Pale and somewhat clumsy foreshadowings of the poems of *Harmonium*, they are brighter and fresher than his Harvard work, possessing a charm and an energy that it lacks. The great change, however, is from these poems to 'Peter Quince at the Clavier' and 'Sunday Morning', published respectively in August and November 1915. Stevens in the two years from 1913 to 1915 made himself into a great poet. Not surprisingly, he referred to this period as his 'awakening', and, having obtained a sense of his inner powers, he continued to the end of his life the work of discovery.[168] When Herbert Schoen asked him why he had started to write poetry again, Stevens affirmed, 'Herb, I just had to begin again' – according to Schoen 'as if it was some kind of upwelling pressure within himself'.[169]

Stevens, however, was not as yet exclusively committed to poetry. He submitted *Three Travelers Watch a Sunrise* to a contest sponsored by the Players' Producing Company for the best one-act play in verse and won the prize. The play was published in *Poetry* in July 1916 and the director of the Wisconsin Players liked it enough to ask Stevens if he would write a play for her. He sent her *Carlos among the Candles* and *Bowl, Cat and Broomstick*, which the company performed in October 1917 at the Neighbourhood Playhouse in New York. The performances were such failures that the management of the theatre would not allow them to be performed a second time. According to Stevens, the sets for *Carlos among the Candles* were the opposite of what he had asked for (and painted by a schoolboy) and the single actor forgot something like a third or quarter of his lines.[170] Stevens, none the less, did not simply blame the performance: 'the possibility remains', he writes to Harriet Monroe on 31 October, 'that there was little or nothing to perform'. The purpose of *Three Travelers Watch a Sunrise* is 'to demonstrate that just as objects in nature offset us, . . . so, on the other hand, we affect objects in nature, by projecting our moods, emotions, etc.'[171] *Carlos among the Candles* 'is intended to illustrate the theory that people are affected by what is around them'.[172] Thus, the great reciprocal relation of Stevens' poetry was first conceived in dramatic terms and only slowly worked its way into the poems. The failure of his plays, Stevens writes to Latimer on 5 November 1935, 'taught me what poetry is, and is not, proper for the theatre', and, when *Three*

Travelers Watch a Sunrise was finally produced at Provincetown in 1920, he did not go to see it. To Harriet Monroe, he explains, 'So much water has gone under the bridge since the thing was written that I have not the curiosity even to read it to see how it looks at this late day. That's truth, not pose' (4 Mar 1920). He retained the whole experience as a metaphor. Again and again in his poems, individuals are actors, poetry is a script and we are in the world 'As at a Theatre'.

Between 1914 and 1919 Stevens published thirty-nine poems that he chose to include neither in *Harmonium* (1923) nor *The Collected Poems* (1955). Of the work that appeared in *The Harvard Advocate*, he comments to Donald Hall, 'Some of one's early things give one the creeps' (16 Feb 1950), and, having made his selection for *Harmonium*, he writes to Harriet Monroe, 'I have omitted many things, exercising the most fastidious choice, so far as that was possible among my witherlings. To pick a crisp salad from the garbage of the past is no snap.' (21 Dec 1922). He was aware of the distance he had travelled and how much he had changed. The poems of *Harmonium* are the first in which his free, colourful and vivacious style makes its appearance. In his Harvard work there is almost no sign of the savouring of objects and enjoyment of language for its own sake that is so characteristic of *Harmonium*. The earliest poems chosen for *Harmonium* were composed when he was thirty-six; he was forty-three when the collection itself was published. His six other books were issued when he was between fifty-five and seventy-five.

The freshness of Stevens' vision in *Harmonium* is such that everything is exotic. He uses an extraordinary vocabulary of strange and rare words, such as 'princox', 'scurry', 'chirr', 'lacustrine', 'unburgherly', 'gubbinal', 'funest', 'alguazil', 'nincompated', 'dibbled', 'diaphanes', 'shebang', 'dits', 'verd', 'planterdom', 'muzzy', 'ructive', 'rapey', 'palankeens', 'embossomer', 'tunk-a-tunk-tunk' and 'feme'. There are more of these words in *Harmonium* than in his other books, and more in 'The Comedian as the Letter C', the longest and most ambitious poem of *Harmonium*, than in any other poem. Stevens employs his words in unexpected combinations ('Pulse pizzicati of Hosanna', 'Trinket pasticcio', 'Exchequering from piebald fiscs unkeyed' and 'fubbed the girandoles'), so that at first glance their syntactical function is very often unclear. We are required to look again for their meanings and their grammar. There is perhaps no great English poet who writes such an extremely distinctive and idiosyncratic style. As Richard Blackmur comments,

Good poets gain their excellence by writing an existing language as if it were their own invention; and as a rule success in the effect of originality is best secured by fidelity, in an extreme sense, to the individual words as they appear in the dictionary. If a poet knows precisely what his words represent, what he writes is much more likely to seem new and strange – and even difficult to understand – than if he uses his words ignorantly and at random. . . , there is a perception of something previously unknown, something new which is a result of the combination of the words, something which is literally an access of knowledge.[173]

Naming is for Stevens both creation and initiation – 'an access of knowledge'. This prodigality of rare and precious (in all senses) words is a manifestation of the extravagant generosity that informs the whole process of composition. To William Benét, Stevens writes: 'I dislike niggling, and like letting myself go' (24 Jan 1933). This is not a matter of vocabulary alone. His best poems, he thought, were instances of letting himself go: 'Poems of this sort are the pleasantest on which to look back, because they seem to remain fresher than others.'

Although most of the poems in *Harmonium* are elaborations of single moments of perception or states of mind, many of them appear to be as much moments of fantasy as of a specific place and time. Stevens, however, is very clear about their relation to the world. He states to Latimer,

I wonder whether if you were to suggest any particular poem, I could not find an actual background for you. I have been going to Florida for twenty years, and all of the Florida poems have actual backgrounds. The real world as seen by an imaginative man may well seem like an imaginative construction. (31 Oct 1935).

Not only do his poems have 'an actual background', but he believes he could locate each one of them at a specific point in space and time. His comment suggests the value of his poetry to the poet in keeping his past vividly present to him. The words 'background' and 'imaginative construction' are indicative of what happens to actuality in Stevens' poetry, and show that actuality is not the same as so-called realism. 'Realism', Stevens says in *Adagia*, 'is a corruption of reality'.[174] For him the poem is a working-through of experience involving a deliberate discarding or suppressing of the details of personal history in the interests of greater inwardness. He talks about his inner life in such a way as to protect it from the disclosures that he feels compelled to make. Stevens is as impersonal as Hafiz, and as intimate – except that he wrote very few love poems. If love is the most intense relation between two persons and possible only to the fully-organised self, then Stevens is concerned with the period anterior to love, that of the formation of the self (as is most of the great poetry from Wordsworth to the present). Crispin, the protagonist of 'The Comedian as the Letter C', has no real relations with others, not even his wife and daughters. They merge with his surroundings, and, as Stevens points out to Latimer, Crispin was not ready for other persons: 'It is hard for me to say what would have happened to Crispin in contact with men and women, not to speak of the present-day unemployed. I think it would have been a catastrophe for him' (21 Nov 1935). Stevens' poetry is about the first relations with the first object. He has an unrequited passion for reality.

Stevens is interested in the image not for its own sake, but as a revelation of the nature of perception and thereby of self and of the world. He observes in *Adagia*,

> The bare image and the image as symbol are the contrast: the image without meaning and the image as meaning. When the image is used to suggest something else, it is secondary. Poetry as an imaginative thing consists of more than lies on the surface.[175]

Stevens is always looking beyond the sense data – and for meaning. He seeks to analyse and interpret rather than to simplify. Unlike Pound and Williams, he does not believe that to minimise the image maximises its suggestive power. There is a tendency for images in his work to form series. He believes that objects have different values: 'Not all objects are equal. The vice of imagism was that it did not recognise this.'[176] This comment in *Adagia*, like the previous one, was part of his effort to separate himself from imagism, perhaps the most powerful poetic force of the period in which he was composing the poems of *Harmonium*, and to work out a view of poetic form that would empower his own development.

George Santayana, whom Stevens knew and admired, said that everything in life is comic in immediacy, tragic in perspective and lyric in essence, and the three come together in the poetry of Stevens such that one rarely appears without at least a suggestion of the other two.[177] Stevens is remarkable for the joyousness with which he writes about solitude. Humour in poetry is usually the sign of a refusal to go deeper. The comedy of Stevens, however, can be said to derive from the richness – the immediacy in Santayana's terms – of his perceptions and from the profound pleasure that he takes in perceiving. *Harmonium* is the most humorous, in all senses, of his collections and the most sensuous. As a poet, Stevens is intensely playful and utterly serious, as serious as Mozart.

Between August 1924 and June 1928 Stevens composed no poetry. He 'jotted down' one very brief poem in New York on 19 June 1928 and sent it to Harriet Monroe to 'add to your *private* library' (20 June 1928, emphasis added), and the next year he sent another short lyric to Louis Untermeyer (11 June 1929) for an anthology that he was editing. Only in March 1930 did he start composing regularly again. Even so, he writes to Lincoln Kirstein on 10 April 1931, 'Nothing short of a coup d'état could make it possible for me to write poetry now', and as late as 5 August 1932 he tells Harriet Monroe, 'Whatever else I do, I do not write poetry nowadays.' This interregnum in a poet of his quality, especially considering the profound need that drove his poetry, that his work had always met with recognition and the apparent decisiveness of his late start, is very difficult to interpret. He explains events to Latimer,

> many years ago, when I really was a poet in the sense that I was all imagination, and so on, I deliberately gave up writing poetry because, much as I loved it, there were too many other things I wanted not to make an effort to have them. I wanted to do everything that one wants to do at that age: live in a village in France, in a hut in Morocco, or in a piano box at Key West. But I didn't like the idea of being bedeviled all the time about money and I didn't for a moment like the idea of poverty, so I went to work like anybody else and kept at it for a good many years.
>
> (6 May 1937)

There is no evidence that he was bedevilled about money in 1924 or that his financial situation changed radically in the period 1924–30.[178] Holly Stevens suggests that her father was discouraged by the reception of *Harmonium*.[179] The reviews, except for Marianne Moore's, were unsympathetic and uninterested, and the book did not sell well. 'My royalties for the first half of 1924 amounted to

$6.70. I shall have to charter a boat and take my friends around the world', Stevens comments wryly to Harriet Monroe (July 1924?). Stevens' comments at the very end of his life to Stephen Langdon are more plausible and imply the importance of his marriage to him. Langdon remembers his saying that

> he experienced what he called 'lapses of grace' . . . when he put aside writing poetry entirely. He said nevertheless the desire to write was gnawing at him all the time. He tried to do without it to make life a little more livable personally, with his wife, I think.[180]

The plural 'lapses' suggests the inner similarity of the two periods of silence.

Harmonium was published on 7 September 1923. On 18 October, Stevens and his wife sailed from New York in the *Kroonland* on a cruise to California, by way of Havana and the Panama Canal. They returned overland through New Mexico, arriving back in Hartford about 10 December. This was the first long vacation they had taken together since their marriage in 1909, and Holly, their only child, born on 10 August 1924, was conceived on this trip.[181] The arrival of a baby was, according to Stevens, a major reason why he stopped writing, and in some sense, as for Crispin in 'The Comedian as the Letter C', perhaps a daughter was a substitute for poetry. Many of Stevens' surviving letters of this period are letters excusing himself from sending any work. He writes:

> Holly . . . babbles and plays with her hands and smiles like an angel. Such experiences are a terrible blow to poor literature. But then there's the radio to blame, too.
>
> (To Harriet Monroe, 12 Jan 1925)

> The baby has kept us both incredibly busy. . . . I have been moved to the attic, so as to be out of the way, where it ought to be possible for me to smoke and loaf and read and write and sometimes I feel like doing all of these things but, so far, I have always elected to go to bed instead. . . . There's a poet from Paris visiting in Hartford. . . . But Oh la-la: my job is not now with poets from Paris. It is to keep the fire-place burning and the music-box churning and the wheels of the baby's chariot turning and that sort of thing.   (To William Carlos Williams, 14 Oct 1925)

... there is a baby at home. All lights are out at nine. At present there are no poems, no reviews. I am sorry. (To Marianne Moore, 19 Nov 1925)

Stevens' daughter's account of this period, despite its reference to the noise of the traffic and the landlord's young children, presents a picture of a relatively quiet existence:

Stevens spent a good deal of his time listening to the radio and, later, the phonograph as he accumulated an impressive library of classical records, many of them imported. He also read a good deal at this time, as well as becoming an avid gardener, installing flower beds ... and a large asparagus patch at the bottom of the yard. ... His energy, in this period between the ages of forty-four and fifty-two, went largely into his work at the insurance company.[182]

Stevens started again slowly. He wrote one poem in 1928, one in 1929, three in 1930 and one in 1931. The two earliest poems both use the metaphor of the sun emerging at the end of winter. This is Stevens' comment on his own condition. 'The Sun This March' (1930) begins,

> The exceeding brightness of this early sun
> Makes me conceive how dark I have become ....

What moved him to become a poet again? His daughter was no longer a baby and by 1929 she was ready to start school. Knopf wrote to him in the spring of 1930 suggesting a second edition of *Harmonium* and asking about new material (the book was reissued in July 1931), and in 1932 Stevens purchased 118 Westerly Terrace, moving in in the autumn of that year.[183] He was pleased to feel less 'the creature of circumstance' and more 'the master of the situation'. 'I think that buying a house is the best thing that I have ever done', he declares to James Powers (12 May 1933), and when Powers bought a house he thoroughly approves: 'For my part, I never really lived until I had a home, my own room, say, with a package of books from Paris or London' (17 Dec 1935). Stevens' sense of security was further increased when in February 1934 he was made a vice-president of the Hartford Accident and Indemnity Company, one of four in the home office. This was a major promotion (the chief executive officer at that time was also only a vice-president) and meant a substantial rise in salary, and it is likely that business success contributed to poetic success.[184] Most powerful of all, probably, was the need to satisfy the 'desire to write' that 'was gnawing at him all the time'. This was as 'The Sun This March' makes clear, a drive to explore the inner darkness, a desire for self-knowledge:

> Oh! Rabbi, rabbi, fend my soul for me
> And true savant of this dark nature be.

Stevens' final period (1928–55) yielded five collections and *The Collected Poems* (1954). The five collections are *Ideas of Order* (1936), *The Man with the Blue Guitar* (1937), *Parts of a World* (1942), *Transport to Summer* (1947) and *The Auroras of Autumn* (1950). This is the work that establishes him as a great poet. 'One of the most difficult things in writing poetry is to know what one's subject is', Stevens writes to Latimer (26 Nov 1935). Perhaps the major difference between Stevens' earlier and later poetry is that it is only after 1929 that he discovers that his subject is poetry, or, in other terms, what he calls his 'reality – imagination complex'. This discovery is certainly foreshadowed in *Harmonium*, but it is only in the later poems that it is clearly understood and stated, and perhaps Stevens' inability to find his subject is a reason for both his stopping to write poetry and his beginning again. As part of this search, he devises his own notation in which to work out his problems. In the later poetry, blue and red, moon and sun, north and south, and winter and summer are metaphors for imagination and reality that recur as constants, as a language within a language, as do transparence and being at the centre as metaphors of perfect communication and perfect know-ledge. The poems are more and more about the nature of perception rather than the perceptions themselves, about the order and ordering-process instead of the data; they are thus more abstract than the earlier poems. This greater theoretic interest can also be observed in Stevens' correspondence – the discussion of poetry with Latimer (1934–8), the explication of his own poems to Simons (1938–45), and the letters on the establishment of a chair of poetics that he exchanged with Church (1939–45); it can be seen too in his decision (beginning in 1936) to lecture on the nature of poetry and in the publication of those lectures as *The Necessary Angel* (1951).

The poems of the final period speak with ever greater certainty about the uncertainties of being. They are at once freer and more rigorous forms, and there is more repetition. Stevens repeats so that he can mark more nuances in an effort to get as close as possible to his experience, as if language were a kind of touching or holding, and proximity were understanding. The later poems tend to be longer and to consist of more than a single image. To discover 'a value that really suffices' in a world that is 'permanently enigmatical' 'involves something more than mere imagism', Stevens writes to Simons (29 Dec 1939). His use of *value* in the singular is indicative of the type of unity that he is seeking. Also he wants more than a series of images. This demand for unity, connection and development not only changes the shorter poems, but also results in long poems. Of his twenty-two longer poems, nineteen were composed after 1933.

The glamorous sensuousness of *Harmonium* disappears. When Theodore Weiss asked Stevens about this in 1945, Stevens said simply, 'One grows older.'[185] For him, however, aging was growth. 'One grows tired of being oneself and feels the need to renew all one's thoughts and ways of thinking', he says to Thomas McGreevy; 'Poetry is like the imagination itself. It is not likely to be satisfied with the same thing twice' (1 June 1950). As new perception, new imagining renovates the self, self-renewal restores the freshness of the world. Thus Stevens needed change and was ready for it. He maintained to the end his belief in what he calls in a letter to William Benét 'the essential gaudiness of poetry' (6 Jan 1933).

2
The Grand Poem: Preliminary Minutiae

'The Grand Poem: Preliminary Minutiae' is the title that, after second thoughts, Stevens suggested to Alfred Knopf on 12 March 1923 should be substituted for *Harmonium*. Six days later he had changed his mind again. He telegraphed Knopf, 'USE HARMONIUM' (18 May 1923). The alternative title reveals Stevens' belief that all his poetry constitutes a single work. It shows us that he saw his poems as interrelated, as if bearing on some unstated problem, and himself as searching for some all-encompassing form, as yet, and perhaps always, in the future. The problem is the relation between reality and imagination, and the form, which Stevens came to call the supreme fiction, is a solution to the problem. The most complete statement of this view is 'Notes Toward a Supreme Fiction', whose title resembles that of the alternative title to *Harmonium* in that the individual poems are said to be only small indications, tentative sketches, of something greater, *preliminary* and *notes toward* – a conviction reaffirmed in the title of Stevens' fourth collection: *Parts of a World*.

This sense of working in small can be seen in the metaphor that Stevens chooses at this time to express his dissatisfaction with his work. He writes to Harriet Monroe, 'All my earlier things seem like horrid cocoons from which later abortive insects have sprung' (28 Oct 1922). The capacity of the small to contain or represent the large depends upon the small being understood as endlessly complex so that it is commensurate with the large for the purposes of metaphor. Then a short poem can be as serious as a long poem and we can 'see a World in a Grain of Sand'.[1] The invention of the microscope, telescope, calculus and still-life would appear to mark stages in the development of this feeling, although it is only with Wordsworth that a new type of lyric emerges, when each poem is conceived of as part of a life history. The minutiae that poets after Wordsworth, including Stevens, seek to order are the infinitely small and infinitely significant data of perception, the innumerable transient mental states that make us what we are.[2] The title that Stevens decided on for his first collection of poems asserts the harmony of these many discrete events – *Harmonium* – and he wanted to call his collected poems *The Whole of Harmonium* to make clear his sense of all of them as the music of a single instrument.

Something of Stevens' method of composition – and of his way of apprehending the world – can be observed in the letter he wrote to Harriet Monroe on 25 April 1920 after travelling that day to Indianapolis:

I

The cows are down in the meadows, now, for the first time.
The sheep are grazing under the thin trees.
My fortune is high.
All this makes me happy.

II
Fickle Concept

Another season of illusion and belief and ease.

III
First Poem For The Meditation Of Infants

Gather together the stones around the tree and
let the tree gather its leaves and fruit.

IV

Earth-creatures, two-legged years, suns, winters . . .

V
Poupée de Poupées

She was not the child of religion or science
Created by a god as by earth.
She was the creature of her own minds.

VI
Certainties cutting the centuries

Je vous assure, madame, q'une promenade à travers the soot-
deposit qu'est Indianapolis est une chose véritablement
étrange. Je viens de finir une belle promenade. Le jour aprés
[*sic*] demain je serai à Pittsburg d'ou je partirai pour
Hartford. Au revoir.

These jottings, 'preliminary minutiae' in every sense, show how
poems formed in his mind and how any perception could form the
basis of a poem. He starts from an image – the cows and sheep
grazing in the fields; then, as he tries to sum up ('fortune',
'happiness', 'illusion and belief and ease'), he produces new images
(the tree, the doll, Indianapolis), and particulars and abstractions
appear almost alternately, as if they represented distinct processes
instead of a single way of working. In Stevens' poetry, as in
Wordsworth's, there is a tendency for interpretation to separate
from description, even though in this case we do not know whether
these six sections should be considered as notes for one poem or
several. Moreover, it seems that this decision has not yet been taken
by Stevens, which is part of the interest of the letter and offers
confirmation of the idea that Stevens' longer poems are of
essentially the same structure as his shorter poems, and can be
thought of, in a sense, as composed of short poems. The letter also
reveals how Stevens generates ideas by playing with words, and
rhetorical figures (in this case, paradox) as forms. Here he keeps
opposing the particular and the abstract, certainty and uncertainty:
illusion and belief, stone and fruit, earth-creatures and time ('years,
suns, winters'), the mind (the multiplicity of which is emphasised
by 'her own *minds*') and systems of belief ('religion or science'), and
certainties and centuries (time again). The assonances and conso-
nances of the two titles that organise these antitheses make *fickle* and
concept, and *certainties* and *centuries* seem like oxymorons, and it is as
if the titles have originated in an almost random play with sounds.
The French creates the strangeness of Indianapolis (and there is an
added contrast in that the ordinary news of the letter is
communicated in a foreign language). The passage shows Stevens'
need to double things; even his language must have its counterpart.
Everything must have the structure of metaphor.

Many of the poems in *Harmonium* start from images as simple as
that of the cows in the meadows – for example, the well-known
'Thirteen Ways of Looking at a Blackbird', which is composed of
numbered sections like those in the letter to Harriet Monroe:

I
Among twenty snowy mountains,
The only moving thing
Was the eye of the blackbird.

II
I was of three minds,
Like a tree
In which there are three blackbirds.

. . .

XII
The river is moving.
The blackbird must be flying.

XIII
It was evening all afternoon.
It was snowing
And it was going to snow.
The blackbird sat
In the cedar-limbs.

This is a poem about perception which demonstrates that each act of vision re-creates reality and that every perception is a metaphor. Where the meaning of the cows in the meadows is happiness, the significance of the blackbird changes with its context, as if it were a word; and yet, owing to the form of the poem, it is both a variable and a constant. Interpretation is kept to a minimum so that the image interprets itself. Our attention, in being so completely focused on the thing seen, is thereby concentrated upon itself, and we are compelled to an imaginative re-enactment, made self-conscious of our seeing.

The images in Stevens' poems are not simple representations of the world. They are metaphors right from the go. What is seen is the mind in operation. Consider 'Bantams in Pine-woods', that remarkable poem that even after long familiarity retains its capacity to surprise:

Chieftain Iffucan of Azcan in caftan
Of tan with henna hackles, halt!

Damned universal cock, as if the sun
Was blackamoor to bear your blazing tail.

Fat! Fat! Fat! Fat! I am the personal.
Your world is you. I am my world.

You ten-foot poet among inchlings. Fat!
Begone! An inchling bristles in these pines,

Bristles, and points their Appalachian tangs,
And fears not portly Azcan nor his hoos.

The poem's organisation is unusual: the sound-play that dazzles us
and holds our attention like a magician's gestures occurs only at the
beginning and the end – as if to suggest that all statements gradually
take shape in, and return to, the murmur of thought, while the
whole poem is summarised in the middle stanza, in three very
short, point-blank sentences, conjugating the verb *to be*. The playing
with sound tests the nature of language and creates new means of
signifying. Chieftan Iffucan of Azcan is how the poet addresses the
bantam. The name, with its vague Mayan or Aztec associations,
adds to the bantam's exoticism and (along with *caftan*, *sun* and
blackamoor) makes his rich red-browns and blazing reds tropical, as
well as intimating that he is the indigenous inhabitant of this space
(although *Appalachian* makes this somewhat problematic). Who is
the intruder in the pine-woods is an important question in the
poem. The rooster is not only his world, but all of reality: he is
'universal', the sun is his slave and all but eclipsed by him. He is so
very large – 'Fat! Fat! Fat! Fat! – that for a moment he seems larger
than life, 'a ten-foot poet' dwarfing the speaker, who remains an
'inchling' beside him. As the representative of reality, he is
associated with possibility (if-you-can and as-can) and questions the
poet about his own identity. His challenge is who (hoo)? Thus, as
Stevens tells us in 'Notes Toward a Supreme Fiction', when 'the
grossest iridescence of ocean / Howls hoo and ... hoo', 'Life's
nonsense pierces us with strange relation' (1. III. 19–21)

The poet insists on the difference between himself and the
bantam. They are worlds apart: 'Your world is you. I am my world.'
He is 'the personal', the individual, the particular – anything that
can, metaphorically, be measured in inches – in opposition to the
bantam's portly universality. The cock is so all-encompassing that

the brightness of his 'blazing tail' subordinates and darkens the sun – to an oxymoronic black. There is also an antithesis of size between the bantam and the sun, and between both bantam and poet and the pines, and another contrast of light and dark in the bright bantam against the evergreen background. The bantam, whose very name denotes smallness, is big in every way and emphatically fat, fat with the world's plenty, just as at the close of 'Notes Toward a Supreme Fiction' Stevens addresses the world as 'my green, my fluent mundo' and 'Fat girl, terrestrial...' (3. x. 20, 1). The poem is a confrontation between the poet and reality in which the poet is intent on maintaining their separateness. He orders Chieftain Iffucan to halt and begone. Among the dark fluent greens of the pines, he 'Bristles and points their Appalachian tangs'. *Bristles* suggests the threatening feather-ruffling and hackle-raising of the bantam, the way pine needles grow from the branch and the alertness of the poet to the moment's distinctive qualities. *To point* is to indicate, to direct and to give point to, as well as to mark for chanting. *Tang* is the part of the arrow-head by which it is secured to the shaft (or of the knife blade to its handle), a pungent odour or after-taste and the ringing note produced by plucking a tense string or suddenly striking a large bell: the word amalgamates here the bristling, the smell of the pine-woods and the echoing hoos.

'Bantams in Pine-woods' dramatises the poet's feelings about being in the world. The metaphor is acted out, generating a special poetic realm. The poem creates a place in which to happen. The poem's apparent point of departure is the brightly coloured bantam rooster, but Stevens toys with his image rather than reports it, and it is this playing with the data that reveals him as interested in something other than mere verisimilitude, especially as much of his play is with the words that the scene suggests rather than with any of the so-called real items of which it is composed. Stevens is a poet who rejoices in the babble of sensation, but like Wordsworth he is concerned with what the eye and ear 'half create, / And what perceive' and seeks in his sound-play to describe how the world merges with language as well as the quirkiness, the nonsense, of reality.[3] The poet's wish is to see his ideas, as if perhaps he can thereby understand his mind's mysteries, and this produces landscapes that are very unlike those produced by the attempt to imitate or represent nature. The poet in these special landscapes is a witness to his own imaginative processes. Stevens writes in *Adagia*: 'Reality is a cliché from which we escape by metaphor. It is only *au pays de la métaphore qu'on est poète'* (*OP*, p. 179). The pines and the bantams are *au pays de la métaphore*. Stevens wants neither to escape from reality nor to create an alternative reality, he desires to escape from hackneyed perception. This is a reason for quirkiness, why his poems are full of surprises. The world is strange, uncanny in its own way, because it is seen as if for the first time. Metaphor, he believes, cannot be a substitute for reality, nor does it possess any independent value: 'There is no such thing as a metaphor of a metaphor. One does not progress through metaphors. Thus reality is the indispensable element of each metaphor' (*OP*, p. 179). Stevens, however, wants to progress. Poetry for him is knowledge of reality, a statement of things as they are. 'Poetry seeks out the relation of man to facts.' The apparent unreality of some of his poetry is from its simultaneous representation of the inner and the outer world, including what he calls 'the symbols of one's self': 'It is the explanation of things that we make to ourselves that disclose our character: The subjects of one's poems are the symbols of one's self or of one of one's selves' (*OP*, p. 164). The progress for which Stevens works is towards greater self-knowledge, self-explanation, but, in a world that changes such that *selves* are perceived instead of a *self*, this is an everlasting process of affirmation, always demanding one more poem.

Stevens is acutely conscious that every perception transforms us and that we alter in response both to our own inner processes and to the world's mutations. The artist lives through the world, as his poet, Crispin, in 'The Comedian as the Letter C', crosses the Atlantic:

> What word split up in clickering syllables
> And storming under multitudinous tones
> Was name for this short-shanks in all that brunt?
> Crispin was washed away by magnitude.
> The whole of life that still remained in him
> Dwindled to one sound strumming in his ear,
> Ubiquitous concussion, slap and sigh,
> Polyphony beyond his baton's thrust.
>
> Could Crispin stem verboseness in the sea,
> The old age of a watery realist,
> Triton, dissolved in shifting diaphanes
> Of blue and green? A wordy, watery age

That whispered to the sun's compassion, made
A convocation, nightly, of the sea-stars,
And on the clopping foot-ways of the moon
Lay grovelling. Triton incomplicate with that
Which make him Triton, nothing left of him,
Except in faint, memorial gesturings,
That were like arms and shoulders in the waves,
Here, something in the rise and fall of wind
That seemed hallucinating horn, and here,
A sunken voice, both of remembering
And of forgetfulness, in alternate strain.
Just so an ancient Crispin was dissolved.

                                        (i. 29–52)

The world's mutability makes it infinitely rich, infinitely elusive, and this accounts for the many restatements, the series of metaphors, in Stevens' description of the sea. Crispin as he absorbs the wave-gestures, submerged music and diaphonous blue-greens undergoes a sea-change:

What counted was mythology of self,
Blotched out beyond unblotching. . . .
The dead brine melted in him like a dew
Of winter, until nothing of himself
Remained, except some starker, barer self
In a starker, barer world. . . .

                                        (i. 20–1, 59–62)

The sea's vividness is the intensity of his own perceptions; and its indescribable richness forces him back upon himself: 'Crispin / Became an introspective voyager' (i. 67–8). To apprehend means to take in, to understand and to fear. The sea-sounds verge on speech, adumbrations of meaning that come and go. Crispin's perceptions are haunted by inscrutable possibilities of significance. Because perceiving and language-making are one process or analogous processes, he expects the world to be a text and is baffled when he cannot read it.

Reality in Stevens' poetry is watery because it is always in motion and the poet's response to it is usually introspection. However, he welcomes change:

> Let the place of the solitaries
> Be a place of perpetual undulation.

This poem, 'The Place of the Solitaires' (which intimates that we live at the centre of a diamond and that each perception is a facet of a fixed, light-filled structure), demands that:

> There must be no cessation
> Of motion, or of the noise of motion,
> The renewal of noise
> And manifold continuation ....

It is as if the poet is afraid that the world might stop and half-believes that his thoughts keep it going. There must be no cessation 'of the motion of thought/ And its restless iteration', because the poet is sustained in his solitude by the world's motion, and the continuity and integrity of his being depends on its continuation. He emphasises 'the noise of motion' almost as if change had a voice that could be apprehended in the willed stillness of meditation. That *solitaires* is plural suggests that every thinker is solitary; thus 'The Place of the Solitaires' is the world of each of us.

There are moments when the poet's sense of his own apartness is total, as in 'Tea at the Palaz of Hoon':

> I was the world in which I walked, and what I saw
> Or heard or felt came not but from myself;
> And there I found myself more truly and more strange.

Then everything contributes to his self-discovery. His identity is simple: he is his perceptions and there is no need to make any distinctions and no room for doubt, yet the otherness of the world's objects, their inexplicable, disconnected variety, makes him feel strange – unlike himself. Tensions such as this are the basis of Stevens' poetry. Paradox is a way of living with ambivalence. The same idea is restated in the short poem entitled 'Theory':

> I am what is around me.
>
> Women understand this.
> One is not duchess
> A hundred yards from a carriage.

These then are portraits:
A black vestibule;
A high bed sheltered by curtains.

These are merely instances.

The poetry of Stevens is a search for meaning in a world of unending change where every interpretation is tentative, a theory, only one way among many of seeing things. He believes in the irreducible polysignificance of the world and makes poetry out of the possibility of rearranging every perception. Like Whitman, he feels himself to contain multitudes and each item is simultaneously himself, itself and virtually every other thing. Meaning resides in the relations between things and can easily become tenuous, as when the duchess is out of sight of her carriage. Every object is interesting as soon as it occurs to Stevens, because it is immediately incorporated into the network of relations that we call the self. Vestibule and high, curtained bed, blackbird and pineapple, the parts of the world are known – and can only be known – as statements about the identity of the perceiver, and, as our identity is continuously changing, they are merely instances, preliminary minutiae.

'SUNDAY MORNING'

There is one poem in *Harmonium* that by its seriousness stands out in the same way as 'Lines Written a Few Miles above Tintern Abbey' stands out in *Lyrical Ballads*. This is 'Sunday Morning', the first great poem that Stevens wrote and probably his best-known work, offering a definition of genius in that it seems to come almost from nowhere. None of his previous poems have exactly this tone or are anything like as good. 'Sunday Morning' can be said to inaugurate Stevens' first period of major work (1915–24). Here, all at once, the poet is in full possession of his powers. The poem consists of eight 15-line stanzas in blank verse of a power unmatched by any English poet since Wordsworth, except Browning.

The poem represents the thoughts attributed by the poet to a woman who sits comfortably over a late breakfast on a Sunday morning musing upon the Crucifixion. Although her emotions upon this occasion become clear to us, she remains a shadowy figure without either a personality or a history – Stevens' way of keeping

the thoughts at a remove from himself without handing them over
to anyone else, and a sign that he sees them as somehow feminine.
The woman appears to have just got up, and in her 'sunny chair'
'She dreams a little'. The poem is a daydream, a meditation on the
near edge of sleep that emerges from a darkening calm:

I

Complacencies of the peignoir, and late
Coffee and oranges in a sunny chair,
And the green freedom of a cockatoo
Upon a rung mingle to dissipate
The holy hush of ancient sacrifice.
She dreams a little, and she feels the dark
Encroachment of that old catastrophe,
As a calm darkens among water-lights.
The pungent oranges and bright, green wings
Seem things in some procession of the dead,
Winding across wide water, without sound.
The day is like wide water, without sound,
Stilled for the passing of her dreaming feet
Over the seas, to silent Palestine,
Dominion of the blood and sepulchre.

Where the woman is is not specified, only that she is far away in
space and time from the scenes of the New Testament story. The
death of Jesus, in Stevens' carefully muted references, is an 'ancient
sacrifice', 'that old catastrophe', almost suggesting that there might
be some temporal limit to belief, although the woman is so pervaded
by the story that she thinks of walking on the water to Palestine.
Removed from the scene of the action, she feels that in order to
understand it she has to go and see for herself. The repetition of
'wide water without sound' in successive lines lulls us into her
daydream. Reality is watery here, too. Her thoughts feel like
twilight on water, and the day is like a soundless expanse of still
water. The major antithesis in the poem is stated in the first
sentence: the world when vividly apprehended dissipates any
unwordly belief. This is a contrast of moods: comfort *versus* sacrifice,
living in the world set against living for another world. Peignoir,
coffee, oranges, sun, chair and rug negate metaphysics, or, rather,
produce their own ontology. Because the woman lives in considerable comfort, her longings bespeak the limits of the body's

pleasures. Her surroundings are described with a deliberate sensuality, a luxury of feeling – hinting vaguely of the jungle with the tropical oranges and cockatoo. The force of the oranges and cockatoo is increased by repetition; in the second half of the stanza they reappear with emphasis, *pungent* and *bright*, in order to characterise the procession of the dead, which as a result seems to belong more to Yucatan than to Palestine. Thus, they are absorbed into the daydream, 'green freedom' subdued, for the moment, to the 'Dominion of the blood and sepulchre'.

The second stanza opens with three questions that sum up its arguments, and in six of the poem's stanzas the main ideas are similarly set forth in clear, simple sentences. That these sentences are usually questions shows the poet's uncertainty about his answers and that tentativeness is an answer. He is satisfied by the play of possibilities; the willing suspension of belief is for him an act of affirming the nature of the world. The difficulty of 'Sunday Morning' derives from the richness of its nuances and the intrinsic difficulty of its subject, that of making meaning of our lives. The poem exemplifies Stevens' knack for plain statement and his habit of combining summary statement and metaphor. This alternation between preliminary minutiae and supreme fictions is one of the many ways in which he resembles Wordsworth. His capacity to keep the poem going frequently appears to depend on repeatedly collecting his thoughts in an abstract form, and this process appears to generate metaphors and often series of similar or connected metaphors. Abstractions are to Stevens almost like a language within language, the theme from which he derives his variations, Diabelli's waltz to Beethoven. He enjoys the sound of finality, but it is a delight to be savoured as a relish to his scepticism. It tempts him with the possibility of another world. Every absolute, however, is putative, no more than one of many possibilities, and Stevens frequently rehearses them all as if he needs to prove that no form is final. He seeks to come to true conclusions with unfixed forms. This, in itself, is an act of interpretation and one that perhaps can be said to be modelled on the rhetorical figure of paradox (the form of so many of Stevens' summary statements): the attempt to create a form that signifies a range of meanings, the substitution of an activity or process for a finite set of denotations and connotations – an effort to interpret change itself.

II

Why should she give her bounty to the dead?
What is divinity if it can come
Only in silent shadows and in dreams?
Shall she not find in comforts of the sun,
In pungent fruit and bright, green wings, or else
In any balm or beauty of the earth,
Things to be cherished like the thought of heaven?
Divinity must live within herself:
Passions of rain, or moods in falling snow;
Grievings in loneliness, or unsubdued
Elations when the forest blooms; gusty
Emotions on wet roads on autumn nights;
All pleasures and all pains, remembering
The bough of summer and the winter branch.
These are the measures destined for her soul.

The three questions subsume the argument of the entire poem. The final stanza, like the last eight lines of this one, is an answer to the third question, and the poem, in a sense, does not progress beyond this point: the remaining six stanzas are a development of the first two. The poem is, as Stevens says of another poem 'A Thought Revolved' – and thoughts are revolved in his poetry so that they can be seen from all sides. His poems usually develop not as a series of steps towards a destination, but as variations on a theme. They go round and round and over and over their subjects, which is how we respond to the thoughts that deeply trouble us. Stevens knows 'The Pleasures of Merely Circulating', but in the nature of his compulsion to repeat there is something that, despite the playfulness and comedy, convinces us of his profound seriousness. The stanza is commonly the unit of repetition, and in many of the longer poems successive stanzas often perform the same activity. The poems do not merely represent the mind's mulling and churning; they are doing what they are describing – like all art, they *are* thinking.

The woman wonders why she should give what she possesses to the dead, implying that religion is a tax on her substance and centred on death. To ask 'What is divinity . . . ?' calls all religion, not Christianity alone, into question and makes it a depersonalised abstraction like 'the thought of heaven'. The woman's questions answer themselves. They reveal her slowly forming conclusion that religion is a fantasy, an act of the mind, and show us her thoughts turning back to her surroundings. Tacitly she acknowledges the need for thoughts that can be cherished. Although religion is rejected, she searches her experience of the world for something to take its place. Divinity is not rejected, but confined to the inner world. *Passions* refers what is experienced in the rain to the suffering of Jesus, and *soul* at the close is another indication that this anti-religion is modelled on Christianity. She wants a secular religion based in transitory things, 'comforts of the sun' and moods. She desires the emotion of religion without the theology, and in the poem the negation of religion produces a freeing and proliferation of feeling of all kinds: passions, moods, grievings, elations, emotions. There is a need to feel deeply and variously, and for feeling to be measured. Certainly the soul in its new mode of belief is to have 'measures'. This appears to mean that every pleasure and pain is to be recognised as corresponding to an event in the world, as each enumerated set of feelings (except 'Grievings in loneliness') is presented as a response to the world and its changing weather. There is a difficulty because the beginning of the sentence is separated from the end by so many juxtaposed elements. The basic sentence is

> Divinity must live within herself: . . .
> All pleasures and all pains, remembering
> The bough of summer and the winter branch.

What is suggested is that the divine is no more than a sum of human feelings; what is stated is the woman's resolution. The *must* appears to represent her decision to contain her longings for a supernatural realm. Pleasure and pain are to be referred to the changing seasons, bounded by the extremes of summer and winter. Our irreversible lives are to be interpreted in terms of a cycle. 'Remembering' takes place 'within herself'; meaning is to be looked for within nature. The lack of subordination in the sentence makes pleasure a green branch and pain a black branch, as well as allowing that each may have its summer and winter.

III

> Jove in the clouds had his inhuman birth.
> No mother suckled him, no sweet land gave
> Large-mannered motions to his mythy mind.

He moved among us, as a muttering king,
Magnificent, would move among his hinds,
Until our blood, commingling, virginal,
With heaven, brought such requital to desire
The very hinds discerned it, in a star.
Shall our blood fail? Or shall it come to be
The blood of paradise? And shall the earth
Seem all of paradise that we shall know?
The sky will be much friendlier then than now,
A part of labour and a part of pain,
And next in glory to enduring love,
Not this dividing and indifferent blue.

The account of Jove is a new beginning, deliberately abrupt. The god appears as if from nowhere. There is no reference to the woman at her late breakfast. The subject remains religion, but the argument of the previous stanzas is abandoned and only resumed with the second set of three questions. However, before this happens Stevens introduces the strange image of Jove moving 'as a muttering king ... would move among his hinds'. 'Hind' is an old word meaning household servant or farm labourer. The king is continually speaking, but what he says is barely heard and unintelligible. He is the master, admired but not understood. Jove, moreover, is separate from his believers in that he is the personification of the antithesis of everything human. He has no birth (in any human sense), no mother, no suckling and no intimate relation with any landscape. He is magnificently present, but his origins are not explained. He is mythy, not of the world of 'pungent oranges' and 'wet roads on autumn nights', and he instigated a desire that he did not satisfy. He moved among us until our blood interacted with heaven. This commingling in which the body and an idea are married and the blood remains virginal (more subtle than the earlier mingling to dissipate), and in which a star represents fulfilment, is paradoxical and strange. There is a small difficulty with the pronoun *it*: the blood commingling with heaven 'brought such requital to desire' that even the 'hinds discerned it [our blood? requital? heaven?], in a star'. Our blood is, I think, what is discerned in the star, although each of the choices comes to much the same thing. That star is apparently the star of Bethlehem, and thus connects Jove and Jesus. The commingling suggests the virgin birth. The thought of Jesus' death causes the woman to consider the birth of gods, as if knowing their origins would explain our destiny – as if birth and death were the same mystery.

Religion becomes in these metaphors of blood, where immortality depends upon the blood's failure or success, physical and instinctive, the form of the body's longing to live for ever. The idea of the blood's failure is entertained before that of its success, and the similar start to the next two questions – 'Or shall', 'And shall' – masks their demand for opposite answers. That the earth shall *Seem* all of paradise that we shall know indicates that, whatever the answers, we are confined to a world of appearances. The poem then returns to the sky, the cloudy site of Jove's inhuman birth, and this stanza, like the preceding one, closes with an affirmation of the comforts of the earth, our 'sweet land'. The values are those of the harmonious relations between people – friendship and love; and their introduction at this point without any preparation is characteristic of Stevens. He is a poet of surprises, unexpected comparisions, imaginative jumps. Our impression frequently may be of discontinuity, but this in fact is the sign that a new relation between things, a new order, is being established. This is a poetic principle in *Adagia*: 'Poetry constantly requires a new relation' (*OP*, p. 178).

The surprises here are that the world will be friendlier if it is all that we can know, that this friendliness includes labour and pain, and that the sky resembles enduring love. The sky as the way to heaven is dividing, an opaque gateway that separates us from paradise, and, because it does not recognise our existence, indifferent. The sky as the sky of earth is friendlier because it shares our labour and our pain, and is not a place of inhuman births. To compare the sky with its infinity of colours and the ever-new splendour of its shifting light to the glory of enduring love (as that is what Stevens does in putting them next to each other) is to suggest the many-mindedness of love, its infinity of shades. This is to interpret any sustained emotion or any enduring feeling (including that of self) as a succession of states of mind and 'a permanence composed of impermanence' ('An Ordinary Evening in New Haven', x. 11). The changing, ever-enduring sky is set against not love, but enduring love, a lasting finiteness, as love ends in death. Metaphors, however, are statements of reciprocity. The sky is 'next in glory' because in the poem human values are paramount. To assert this is the poem's purpose. Thus, the finite is more glorious, more valuable, than the infinite, and the sky – as the sky of earth – has only a putative permanence. The metaphor introduces the possibility of the earth's death, that as love ends so may the sky. The poem moves between belief and disbelief, which is, of course, only another form of belief – in this case, in mortality rather than immortality, and until the poem's conclusion this new belief is in the process of becoming. '*This* dividing and indifferent blue' marks the return of the woman's thoughts from the future, when the sky '*will be* much friendlier', to the *now* of the poem and the condition of vestigial faith that was the starting-point of her reverie.

IV

> She says, 'I am content when wakened birds,
> Before they fly, test the reality
> Of misty fields, by their sweet questionings;
> But when the birds are gone, and their warm fields
> Return no more, where, then, is paradise?'
> There is not any haunt of prophecy,
> Nor any old chimera of the grave,
> Neither the golden underground, nor isle
> Melodious, where spirits gat them home,
> Nor visionary south, nor cloudy palm
> Remote on heaven's hill, that has endured
> As April's green endures; or will endure
> Like her remembrance of awakened birds,
> Or her desire for June and evening, tipped
> By the consummation of the swallow's wings.

As the woman upon waking has tested the reality of the encroaching dark of Jesus's death and the cloudy sky of Jove's birth, so the birds challenge the misty fields, and perhaps she is content because she feels that their 'sweet questionings' are a confirmation of hers. That reality is tested by song is a statement about the nature of poetry. Songs, however, exist in time: 'A poem is a meteor' (*Adagia*, *OP*, p. 158). The woman imagines the birds disappearing and the fields vanishing in the mist. If the earth vanishes, she asks, 'where then is paradise?' Her answer is a repertory of the stuff of old religions, complex because it is composed of many images. To negate she finds it necessary to enumerate. She lists six locations of paradise. The first two are very comprehensive: *any* shadowy future place envisaged in presumably any prophecy and any fantasies about graves. *Old chimera* suggests ancient Greek notions (older even than Jove), as *prophecy* suggests the prophets of Israel, but the references are unspecific, unlike the next pair, which appear to refer to the Roman and Greek conceptions of the underworld and the isles of the blest. The archaic construction, *gat them home*, subtly emphasises that these are the outmoded beliefs of long ago. *Haunt*, *chimera*, *spirits*, *visionary* and *cloudy* stress their ghostly, insubstantial dream-like nature. *Golden* and *Melodious* are Stevens' embellishments indicating his craving for a sensuous paradise, a sensuousness that in his poetry is embodied by the tropical south, and the final two paradises are his personal and eclectic additions to a group of otherwise traditional notions. The 'visionary south' seems 'the warm South' of Keats' 'Ode to a Nightingale' and 'cloudy palm' 'The palm at the end of the mind' in 'Of Mere Being' that marks the limits of thought and existence. With this list the poem has completed its move from the disappearance of god to the negation of paradise, from the absence of a person to that of a place. These imaginary places, other 'misty fields', test, like the birds' tentative songs, the earth's reality; each is a culmination of a desire to go home to an earlier happiness, to escape the world and yet possess it.

The woman states that none of these ideas has lasted as long as 'April's green'. This is a reversal of the order where religious truths are eternal in contrast to the ephemeral events of the world. The result is a comparison of two forms of transience – one linear, the other, cyclic. 'April's green', by definition, cannot survive the first of May; nevertheless, its reassuringly regular recurrence makes its intermittence an image of the world's continuity, unlike religion, whose beliefs die never to be reborn. The poet affirms, moreover, that the woman's personal memories and desires will retain their potency longer than any vision of paradise. Her vivid apprehension of the world even in retrospect or prospect is more powerful than any imaginary creation. Permanence – only Stevens employs the word *endure* to emphasise that existence is a struggle – is the permanence of moments: the apprehension of the new green of April (the month of Easter Sunday), the memory (a metaphor of intermittence and temporality) of bird-song, and the desire for a future moment noted at the instant of its consummation. Set equal to each other, their interchangeableness in itself communicates the feeling of change as does the presence of the swallow. Swallows return to the north with the spring and are most in evidence at evening, when they swoop and turn, doubling back and crisscrossing, in an image of rapid and continuous movement. The phrasing, with the verb *tipped*, makes it seem that the woman's desire is fulfilled by the fleeting and delicate touch of a single swallow's wing-tip and that consummation is extra, as if desire itself were all but self-sufficient.

V

She says, 'But in contentment I still feel
The need of some imperishable bliss.'
Death is the mother of beauty; hence from her,
Alone, shall come fulfilment to our dreams
And our desires. Although she strews the leaves
Of sure obliteration on our paths,
The path sick sorrow took, the many paths
Where triumph rang its brassy phrase, or love
Whispered a little out of tenderness,
She makes the willow shiver in the sun
For maidens who were wont to sit and gaze
Upon the grass, relinquished to their feet.
She causes boys to pile new plums and pears
On disregarded plate. The maidens taste
And stray impassioned in the littering leaves.

The woman observes that her contentment contains a residual restlessness. As in the opening stanza, the sheer pleasure of being in the world, of coffee and oranges in a sunny chair or watching a swallow on a June evening, gives rise to a yearning for something more, or other, for another world; and in both cases this sensuousness produces the thought of death. The perceiver's death is implied in perception of the world as continuously changing. Object, verb and subject become transitive – in that order. The poem is an exploration of the nature of happiness. Stevens' poetry is remarkable for the full range of its feelings, especially the innumerable intermediate emotions of the meditative mind and the many shadings of happy moods. 'Sunday Morning' includes the complacency of comfort, 'unsubdued elations', 'gusty / Emotions on wet roads on autumn nights', the contentment of hearing birds sing in the morning when the mist is on the fields, and the consummated desire for a June evening. Sick sorrow has only one path; triumph and love, many paths.

The question-and-answer or statement-and-response structure of the poem enables Stevens to engage in a dialogue with different parts of himself and to attempt to go beneath the surface of thought. The virtuality of this structure – that it is neither exactly question-and-answer nor statement-and-response, nor any regular dialectic structure – helps unify the poem. Opposing views do not split it. They develop as a process of self-questioning. The whole needs to be spoken by a single voice. Stevens' notion of form depends upon incomplete patterns. He is a poet of irregular regularities, of almost and more or less. The number of lines in the stanza is the only unvarying element in 'Sunday Morning', and this is typical: stanza-length is most often his only constant, although the length of his lines varies only between narrow limits, usually nine and twelve syllables. These two characteristics set him apart from Whitman, who uses less form than any other great English poet; even so he is closer to Whitman than he is to Hardy or Yeats. As there is for Stevens neither any final form nor any form commensurate with the world as a whole, every poem is an approximation and it is a matter of accuracy that the poem be partially or asymmetrically regular. Total irregularity would be as imprecise as total regularity. Every order, in Stevens' view, seems to be arbitrary, personal and, to an extent, an act of violence; none the less, he cannot commit himself whole-heartedly to chaos. The best orders are those that generate other orders, self-transforming, such as poetry itself, and are extrapolations of that order that is the maker's self.

The woman's terse statement that in contentment she feels the need of an imperishable bliss is a summary of all her longings so far. Suddenly she is able to interpret the feelings that sent her dreaming feet over the seas to Palestine. This is hunger born of fullness – of satisfied desire and sensuous delight. Her need is for some lasting happiness in a world of temporary pleasures, the ecstasy of stillness in a world of unending motion; and her flat, succinct, abstract declaration calls forth a rich, slowly building hymn of death, motherhood and beauty that fills the rest of this stanza and the next. The idea of death as a mother is as unexpected as that of the sky being friendlier for overseeing labour and pain; Stevens in both cases makes a virtue of ambivalence. Death creates beauty and thereby offers us the only fulfilment possible. Our lives are wanderings in a wood, and our achievements and our mistakes shall be buried with our bodies. The paths that we have taken, whether in sorrow, triumph or love, are certain to be destroyed without a trace remaining by dead leaves in autumn. There is no stronger word than *obliteration* in this context. The falling leaf is an image of our passion. Death is the finality of all change, and involves the finest nuances. The willow leaves trembling at the least breath of wind that cause the maidens to look up from the grass – these are movements as subtle as the flash of the swallow's wings and are the death of, a change from, their previous states. The plums and pears are *new*, just gathered from the grass and picked from the trees. Their harvest and its effect shows how every moment comes to fruition and passes to oblivion.

The introduction of death as a mother suggests that the need of 'some imperishable bliss' is a primary hunger. Stevens elucidates this not with glimpses of reality such as the 'wet roads on autumn nights' or the wheeling swallow, but with a symbolic picture of children, of the maidens and boys, that is like a *tableau vivant*. The unreality, such as it is, of this picture is appropriate to the subject of dreams and desires. Fulfilment comes only from death as the mother of beauty; it is not found in death. The scene is a re-enactment of the events of Eden, as if performance of the myth is the rite of passage from childhood to adulthood, the way to passion and enduring love. The maidens awake to new emotion as if from sleep. As in the story of Eden, eating is associated with sexuality, but here the sexuality is only implied: the maidens wander off impassioned; the poet does not say that they go with the boys or that anything happens. To define his notion of fulfilment, Stevens isolates the moment of desire. Death the mother hovers about her children and is the prime mover of all the action. She makes and causes. Her activity is governed, and interpreted, by the *Although*, so that the shivering of the willow, the piling of the plums and pears, and the tasting and straying are presented as the compensation for 'sure obliteration', what we receive in exchange. Beyond this the meaning of the episode is left open. The words *strews*, *stray*, and *littering*, as well as the possibility of many paths, suggest the randomness of life, and that so much is implied and unexplained, merely enacted, emphasises its incomprehensible mysteriousness, a mysteriousness present in the smallest details: the archaic *wont*, why the grass is *relinquished* and the plate present yet *disregarded*.

The next stanza imagines the scene of the plum- and pear-trees as paradise. One myth becomes another. The sequence of cause and effect is suspended. The fruit remains on the branch ripe and untasted, and the poet is overcome by sorrow at the thought of this static perfection.

VI

> Is there no change of death in paradise?
> Does ripe fruit never fall? Or do the boughs
> Hang always heavy in that perfect sky,
> Unchanging, yet so like our perishing earth,
> With rivers like our own that seek for seas
> They never find, the same receding shores
> That never touch with inarticulate pang?
> Why set the pear upon those river-banks
> Or spice the shores with odors of the plum?
> Alas, that they should wear our colors there,
> The silken weavings of our afternoons,
> And pick the strings of our insipid lutes!
> Death is the mother of beauty, mystical,
> Within whose burning bosom we devise
> Our earthly mothers waiting, sleeplessly.

Beauty is change. Paradise in the image of our world is a contradiction in terms, and, as soon as the poet tries to imagine rivers in paradise like those of earth, movement enters the description. The continuous flow of our rivers appears as a never-ending searching, and confrontation of opposite shores appears as a going-away, an intensification of their failure to touch. The 'inarticulate pang' is a wish for completion, the emotion of change, like the 'need of some imperisable bliss'. The poet's *Alas* is his inarticulate cry of regret that colours created in the play of earth's changing light are worn in paradise. The gerundive *weavings* indicates that they are the result of a process and *silken*, that they shimmer as the willow shivers. The *Alas* also affirms the reality of the image that the poet now contemplates. His view of paradise is withheld from the poem as a way of making the imagination itself present *there* where those others wear our colours.

The poet regrets even the transfer of 'our insipid lutes' to where there can be no melancholy and dullness; moreover, *insipid*, which means *without taste*, both indicates the poet's lacklustre mood at this place where ripe fruit never falls and suggests how our music, that art that most embodies change, must sound in paradise. This unemphatic exclamation of sadness is followed by a reprise and an affirmation so powerful that it is almost as if another voice were speaking and the rhetorical questions belonged to another mode of thought. Certainly the way in which the poem works at this point reveals how little belief has to do with any formal dialectics. The logic of the poem is the logic of the unconscious, and what is affirmed here is the imagination's self-sufficiency. By implication, the only imperishable bliss is art. The woman's need can be answered only by the world's temporal beauty and by the recognition that paradise is another version of our earthly mothers ready to care for us eternally. *Mystical* appears to place the beauty-creating finality of death beyond any logic. The awesomeness of death's incomprehensible motherhood is indicated by its burning bosom. The burning is the bonfire of earth's perishing, the craving and satiety of the Heraclitean fire, with overtones of Elijah's chariot and horses of fire or the effulgence of the celestial rose in the *Paradiso*. The home truth that we want our mothers always is touched by the apocalyptic. *Sleeplessly* echoes *imperishable*, showing by its impossibility that this is a dream within a dream – and that hope is possible only in a changing world.

VII

Supple and turbulent, a ring of men
Shall chant in orgy on a summer morn
Their boisterous devotion to the sun,
Not as a god, but as a god might be,
Naked among them, like a savage source.
Their chant shall be a chant of paradise,
Out of their blood, returning to the sky;
And in their chant shall enter, voice by voice,
The windy lake wherein their lord delights,
The trees, like serafin, and echoing hills,
That choir among themselves long afterward.
They shall know well the heavenly fellowship
Of men that perish and of summer morn.
And whence they came and whither they shall go
The dew upon their feet shall manifest.

This stanza abounds in exuberant and positive vitality: *turbulent, orgy, boisterous, savage, delights* and in this context, *chant*, as if the interpretation that closes the previous stanza had freed a great quantity of new energy. Unlike the wakened birds who question the misty fields, their doubts exemplified in the invisibility of the landscape, the men who assert their allegiance to the sun that makes all things visible do so with a vigor that all but creates the world. Every important event in 'Sunday Morning' is an interaction between a person (or persons) and a landscape – even the Crucifixion is thought of as a vestigial landscape. Despite the value attributed to enduring love, the poem, like most of Stevens' poems, is not about the relations between persons but about the relations of the individual with himself – although for Stevens the individual is never alone with his self, never self-contained: there is always a context, a setting, a landscape, a world that becomes a language. The poem has moved almost imperceptibly from spring to autumn to summer, the season for Stevens of the richest physicality. 'Sunday Morning' is a poem about change that pays no attention to time. The seasons are Stevens' clock, a clock of growth and emotion rather than a *memento mori*, as they are in Spenser and Shakespeare. His poetry seems constantly to refer to the period of human development before the sense of time is established and to the timeless processes of the unconscious where, in Freud's words, 'nothing can be brought to an end, nothing is past or forgotten'.[4] This is why in his poetry there is so much reiteration. The poem, in expressing the relation between the individual (conceived of as an inner world) and this always unstable context, creates a momentary stability. Steven finds all the comedy and tragedy of human life in each act of perception. The men's chant – formal musical speech between poetry and song – incorporates the world. Their formation, a ring, affirms the unity of their experience. The windy lake, trees and hill are voices that participate in the psalm or paean and 'choir among themselves long afterward', as if the world is the continuation of poetry by other means. The chant is also physical in the god-like nakedness of its style and in that it arises out of the blood. *Supple* describes either the muscles of the men or the muscular movement of the ring as they move, or perhaps dance, in a circle. Both *ring* and *orgy* imply the contact of bodies, and the metaphor with which the stanza closes tells us that the men are barefoot and in bodily contact with the world, again emphasising that their chant is a celebration of the nakedness of sensation. This touching of bodies makes the body's evanescence more bearable, as if communication were meaning, as if the immediacy of being deeply touched, any fully realised emotion, were a virtually imperishable bliss, a memory so potent as to make one sceptical of annihilation, as the mother's presence at the beginning of life enables us to endure her absence at its end.

If the previous stanza is concerned with the child's relation to the mother, this stanza is about the son's relation to the father. The sexuality of this relation is made overt by *orgy*, *naked* and the physicality of the men's devotion (*ring*, for example, suggesting that they are holding hands). The men want to be close to their god, to be at one with him: they want him to be among them. They wish, it appears, to play with their god and to admire his naked power. *Savage* indicates that he might be dangerous, and *devotion* that they will keep their distance. The relation is to be one of *fellowship*. To them the sun is not a god; rather it incarnates the possibility of divinity, becoming the alpha and omega of the world, the first cause and the sign of its finality. Their chant is a chant of paradise composed out of their bodies and the whispering and murmurous sounds of the earth, and the immortality that it offers is that of the dew of a summer morning that vanishes with the appearance of the sun. This rejection of Christianity is presented in Christian terms: *chant, devotion, god, paradise* and *serafin*. As this stanza, and the entire poem, shows, Stevens cannot conceive of the absence of religion without an anti-religion. This is not a simple substitution of one absolute for another. To destroy, he must rebuild – and this is a single process that cannot work unless the new structure in some way refers to the old. Even when he appears to free himself from this form, stating that paradise is our desire to be greeted in death by our earthly mothers, he inserts the word *mystical*. For Stevens, although absolutes are fictitious, the idea of an absolute is a prerequisite to seeing the word *as it is*, and grasping the ambiguity of its existence. Without alpha and omega, the alphabet ceases to exist and there is no language. Truth is a function of fiction. Angels (and serafin) are necessary. The angel in the late poem 'Angel Surrounded by Paysans' declares,

> I am the angel of reality,
> Seen for a moment standing in the door.
>
> I have neither ashen wing nor wear of ore
> And live without a tepid aureole,

Or stars that follow me, not to attend,
But, of my being and its knowing, part.

I am one of you and being one of you
Is being and knowing what I am and know.

Yet I am the necessary angel of earth,
Since, in my sight, you see the earth again,

Cleared of its stiff and stubborn, man-locked set,
And, in my hearing, you hear its tragic drone

Rise liquidly in liquid lingerings,
Like watery words awash; like meanings said

By repetitions of half-meanings.

He is, he says, one of them, their creation through which they
escape from themselves, even if too briefly, to a vision of the sea-
changes of the world. Half-meanings are half-truths – literature, the
fictions that complete reality.

The orgiastic chanting of the ring of men is a collective experience
in a poem that emphasises private emotion. That is why it is a
liberation. Freedom is a new form of communication with the world.
Freud suggests that it is the capacity to accept what we repress, to
assume responsibility for our guilt; Stevens, that it is the capacity to
accept change. The image of the ring of men is an idea of primitive
religion projected into the future, as if to say that the ancient past is
what shall be. This, combined with the statements that we seek our
earthly mothers in death and that the sun is as a god among us,
would make our primitive origins, our savage source, present,
and, along with the opening attempt to go back to the 'ancient
sacrifice' in Palestine, indicates that paradise, inner divinity and
imperishable bliss depend upon the restoration of some primordial
state. Stevens, like Wordsworth and Heidegger, is concerned with
the recovery of the first conditions of being. This for him is poetry's
major task. As he says in 'Notes Toward a Supreme Fiction',

The poem refreshes life so that we share,
For a moment, the first idea ... It satisfies
Belief in an immaculate beginning

> And sends us, winged by an unconscious will,
> To an immaculate end.
>
> (1. III. 1–5)

We *share* the first idea; we only *believe* in an immaculate beginning and end, belief that follows from the momentary possession of poetic knowledge. Again, whither we shall go is related to whence we came, and perhaps Stevens' archaicisms, of which there are several in this stanza – *morn, whence, whither* – are a sign of this backward looking to what we are. Certainly, in his view, life is refreshed by the enumeration of nature's features. The many inventory-like passages (in II, IV, VI, VII and VIII) that are the answers to the poem's questions are a return to the fostering matrix. They stand for what we first perceived. They are the poetic apprehension of the first idea and in them we are as if washed by the pristine dew of the summer morn. That which vanishes makes everything clear: men come from nothing and go to nothing. They evaporate like the dew, knowing during their brief existence the fellowship of other men who perish like themselves and the evanescent beauty of summer mornings. *Heavenly* in this case means *heaven-like* – that the wonder of 'our perishing earth' is all of paradise that we shall know – and is yet another demonstration of Stevens' need to declare his deeply felt conviction as to the temporality of the world in religious terms, as if all assertions about the meaning of life were imaginary.

VIII

> She hears, upon that water without sound,
> A voice that cries, 'The tomb in Palestine
> Is not the porch of spirits lingering.
> It is the grave of Jesus, where he lay.'
> We live in an old chaos of the sun,
> Or old dependency of day and night,
> Or island solitude, unsponsored, free,
> Of that wide water, inescapable.
> Deer walk upon our mountains, and the quail
> Whistle about us their spontaneous cries;
> Sweet berries ripen in the wilderness;
> And, in the isolation of the sky,
> At evening, casual flocks of pigeons make

Ambiguous undulations as they sink,
Downward to darkness, on extended wings.

With the final stanza the poem comes full circle; demonstrating how much order can be created by a single reprise, its end is its beginning. The conclusion consists of three sentences, three statements. The woman hears a voice that cries that the death of Jesus was like any other death, that his tomb is merely a grave, not the threshold of another world, and that he was merely Jesus, a man who perished, not the resurrected Christ. This speech marks the end of her daydream. Then, in a movement of gradually increasing power, one of the greatest passages of blank verse in English, the poet describes things as they are. Dream gives way to reality. There is only one enjambment before the close (lines 12–15), so that from 5 to 11 each line except 9 offers the possibility of a full stop. This series of plain statements is followed by the elaborately qualified description of the flight of the pigeons, where the simple sentence is interrupted three times in four lines by modifying clauses. The suffixed elements that prolong lines 7, 8 and 9 (*unsponsored, free; inescapable; and the quail*) can be said to be matched or balanced by the prefixed elements of 12, 13 and 15 (*And; At evening; Downward to darkness*) as the initial iambs of lines 5 to 8 are balanced by the initial trochees and spondees of lines 9–12 and 15. Moreover, the contrast between the second sentence of the stanza (5–8) and the last (9–15) is the difference between theory and practice, deduction and induction. The poem's form is the whole of these irregular, overlapping patterns and loosely related repetitions.

The poet affirms (5–8) three ways of seeing the world without religion. The repeated *Or* makes them tentative – despite the positive *We live* – and interchangeable: three versions of the same view. This view is scientific. According to Jeans, the solar system was produced by the collision of the sun with another star. That we live *in an* old chaos tells us that the earth is unorderable and that it is one fragment among many. The ancientness of this chaos is reassuring in that it suggests that such a chance explosion is unlikely to happen again, a guarantee of the earth's stability. This domesticates it by offering the opportunity of familiarity, of coming to know, if not to understand, its unique incoherence. The earth is from the sun and depends only on the sun's appearance and disappearance. This is a soberer version of the boisterous secular hymn of the ring of men. By implication, earth's morality is the black and white of night and day, whose recurrence is an image of regularity, like the endurance of April's green and, therefore, another reassurance. There is, however, no superhuman or supernatural presence, no sponsor. Stevens employs opposites to make the same point: the *dependency* is *unsponsored*, *free* is *inescapable*. Our world is a solitude rather than a loneliness, a feeling rather than a place, and its total isolation is an enrichment rather than a deprivation. 'The greatest poverty' says Stevens in 'Esthétique du Mal', 'is not to live / In a physical world'. The earth is an island in *that* wide water upon which the voice cries that there is no spirit that survives the body's death, and soundless, dream seas separate the woman from Palestine and us from paradise. This is the freedom from which we cannot escape.

These three theoretic statements that attempt to comprehend that human condition as a whole are followed by the description of the deer, quail, berries and pigeons (9–15). Each clause is a complete thought and possible sentence that advances a single item of experience. Because one series is succeeded by another, and because of the form of the account of the pigeons' flight, the second series functions both as an illustration of the first and as another theory. At the poem's close, the world is as if explained by the objects that it contains. The description is active: deer *walk*, quail *whistle*, berries *ripen*, pigeons make *undulations* and *sink*, and this movement appears as an activity of interpretation. The poem as a whole assumes that life is a question to which there is an answer, and an answer in language, as language is the model for all our systems of meaning. Stevens' pleasure in sheer perception, the unthinking surrender of the body to the world, is disturbed, subtly altered, by the idea of the sign that is at the basis of language: that each thing refers to or signifies something other than itself. Thereby every perception becomes a statement of meaning and the world's objects become language.

This is related to Stevens' elemental trust of the world. To be so open to, and to feel so free in, the world, it is necessary to believe in its thereness and capacity to hold us as a mother holds a baby; only then is the surrender that is perception possible. This is the primitive faith that Stevens substitutes for religion in 'Sunday Morning', his optimism. This is why nature is never fierce of awful in Stevens' poetry. The poet Crispin, in 'The Comedian as the Letter C', is able to assimilate without difficulty, without tragedy, the multitudinous magnitude of the Atlantic and the thunderstorms of

Yucatan. He is a 'connoisseur of elemental fate' and in the midst of these tempests 'Aware of exquisite thought'. The world is so important that the poem concludes that 'his soil is man's intelligence'. Man is commensurate with his surroundings. 'The bough of summer and the winter branch' can be the measures of our soul. A *wilderness* is a *chaos*, but this wilderness belongs to us. They are *'our* mountains'. The walking, whistling and ripening are cheerful activities that demonstrate the friendliness of our environment.

The pigeons are observed at evening when the distinction between day and night is blurred. The sky holds the light longer than the earth. Their casual groupings counter the isolation of a sky from which divinity is absent. Charged with the force of the whole poem and its insistent questioning, the word *Ambiguous* makes the flight of the pigeons questionable and causes us to try to interpret it as a metaphor. As we search for its second term, we discover our lives as metaphor and that their second term is equivocal. The pigeons sink into the shadows – as if every descent was into the night of the unconscious or of death. They fly 'on extended wings', approaching the unknowable dark at full stretch, as if reaching out for the unattainable – an image of courage in the face of adversity. The swallow's wings bring consummation to desire; the pigeons' wings, an uncertain hope of some all-important message. Their flight appears as writing that vanishes almost before it can be read, but not quite: it is of the essence of the poem that it closes with the pigeons in mid-flight. We are left on the threshold of an unsayable and perhaps imperishable communication, as if every communication were a threshold. The final metaphor is an assertion of the completeness of this incompleteness, that the unfinished can be whole, a statement in the language of change that combines the shadows and the light.

A poem by Heidegger from *Aus der Erfahrung des Denkens* (1954, composed 1947) sums up Stevens' achievement – this passage especially:

> The world's darkening never reaches
> to the light of Being.

> We are too late for the gods and too
> early for Being. Being's poem,
> just begun is man.[5]

The gods have departed. Each person in the twilight of uncertainty must make what he can of his own perceptions. Stevens' poetry is his effort to understand what it means to live in the world, to exist, to be conscious (and unconscious), to be what he is – and to assume responsibility for being. That this is done as if each of us is homesteading in reality, a pioneer of metaphor, pulling himself up by his own fictional bootstraps, and as if this were an opportunity rather than a tragedy, is a very American response to the problem.

3

Americans are not British in Sensibility

'One Must Sit Still to Discover the World' (*OP*, p. xxxi) – so reads the final entry in one of Stevens' notebooks, and it is exactly what he did: he sat in his room in the evening or at weekends and tried to take in as much as he could of the changing world around him (and the routine of his life as well can be seen as an effort to impose a kind of stillness). He had a discursive mind. An inveterate browser and note-taker, he was a connoisseur of small details, potentially interested in anything and ready to pick up a word or phrase for a poem from anywhere. When he lived in New York, he often spent his evenings in the New York Public Library. His description of his notes to Elsie Moll gives some idea of the range and variety of his interests and of how he thought:

> Scraps of paper covered with scribbling – Chinese antiquities, names of colors, in lists like rainbows, jottings of things to think about, like the difference, for example, between the *expression* on men's faces and on women's, extracts, like this glorious one from Shakespeare: 'What a piece of work is man! how noble in reason! how infinite in faculty!' and so on; epigrams, like, 'The greatest pleasure is to do a good action by stealth, and have it found out by accident' – (could any true thing be more amusing?) – lists of Japanese eras in history, the names of Saints: Ambrose, Gregory, Augustine, Jerome; the three words, 'monkeys, deer, peacocks', in the corner of a page; and this (from the French): 'The torment of the man of thought is to aspire toward Beauty, without ever having any fixed and definite standard of Beauty'; the names of books I should like to read, and the names of writers about whom I should like to know something. (9 May 1909)

On 29 June 1912 he writes to her, 'Then I drifted to the library to read a little about a painter – Delacroix', and a week or so later,

Then I plodded down to the L-br-ry, because I wanted to find out who the devil Saint Anthony really was (I only found out that I *could* find out in the unreadable works of Saint Athanasius!) and who Saul was (confound my ignorance) and the story of Jacob and Esau – and I fell sound asleep over the Jewish Encyclopedia.

(11 Aug 1912)

Things encountered casually fully engage him. Their randomness is their virtue, inciting him to the construction of new orders.

To Henry Church he recounts how, in a copy of *Gazette des beaux arts* picked up in a New York gallery, he happened upon an article by Lionello Venturi on 'The Idea of the Renaissance' that he finds irresistibly interesting; nevertheless, he apologises to Church for recommending it, aware that his interest in it is personal, not in what it says, but in what it suggests to him: 'But everything is interesting and, at the moment, Venturi is to me what a very smelly fox is to a young dog: I don't need any horn to follow him' (8 Dec 1942). He is like a person searching for something without knowing what he is looking for. Reading a volume of letters by Romain Rolland, he is fascinated by the 'glimpses of Parisian life sixty years ago' that it offers and he is glad that Rolland is 'not a man of strong ideas'. As he tries to explain to Barbara Church,

He was a man of feeling. His reactions to the artistic Goethe, the laborious Schiller, elaboration of the mass on special occasions, aspects of Rome, aspects of the Mediterranean, Mounet, etc., seem to me to be just the sort of thing that I have been greatly in need of. The letters have extricated me from contemporary life and placed me in close contact with a man who was not in any sense a big man but who was one of the most interesting men of the last generation or two.   (28 Nov 1949)

To Rodriguez Feo he remarks, 'I am finding these letters interesting beyond belief and for no particular reason. Last night one of his letters was full of complaints about a noisy neighbor. Somehow it interested me immensely to know that one has noisy neighbors in Paris' (5 Dec 1949). He is removed by Rolland from contemporary life, refreshed by the change and the new perspective on his own existence that it produces. What he appears to enjoy most in the letters is their vivid ordinariness, as if Rolland's noisy neighbors were suddenly next door, as if without Rolland he cannot believe in the validity or applicability of his own experience and needs Rolland to confirm what he is. He has no particular interest in the historicity of either the Renaissance or Rolland. As a poet, he does not have the historical feeling of Hardy, Yeats, Pound or Eliot, or even Williams. His poetry is not concerned to differentiate between different periods of time. It is imbued with the feeling of things changing rather than of time passing. The past resembles an unordered set of present moments and every landscape in this virtual or mythic present is a text to be read. Each of the miscellaneous items of his reading offers a new vista upon the self. Stevens writes to Elsie Moll, 'The love of books for the thoughts in them is like the love of the earth for its seas and distances' (9 Apr 1907, *SP*, p. 176).

Valéry, writing in 1919, observes that Europe is going through a spiritual crisis. He sees the kind of heterogeneity that we find in Stevens' reading as the essential and distinguishing characteristic of all work done at this time:

> In any given book of this epoch – and not only in the most mediocre – one finds, without any effort: the influence of the Russian ballet, a little of the sombre style of Pascal, – many impressions of the Goncourt type, – something of Nietzsche, – something of Rimbaud, – certain effects due to the frequentation of painters, and sometimes the tone of scientific publications, – the whole perfumed by something inexpressibly British to which it is difficult to assign a proportion! . . . Observe, in passing that in each of the components of that mixture one will find many other *bodies*.

This state of extreme disorder is produced, according to Valéry, by 'the free co-existence in all cultivated minds of the most disimilar ideas, of the most opposed principles of life and knowledge. This is what characterises a *modern* epoch.'[1] Such variety, it might be added, can exist in a culture only in the absence of a widespread religious belief: heterodoxy is the absence of orthodoxy. 'We are too late for the gods.' This variety means individuality, every man for himself. Each person must possess a belief in the uniqueness of his own experience and its significance in order to maintain views very different from his neighbours'. Self-consciousness demands and produces self-confidence. From the multiform and fragmentary nature of so many works of the period it appears that the lack of any shared unified system made it necessary to examine the pieces of the world one at a time to have any hope of establishing the fundamental units and reassembling them. Moreover, perhaps it was less a case of a loss of religious faith than one of a transfer of faith from an outer system to an inner structure, so that faith was not lost but transformed and each person made in effect a religion of the self – as in 'Sunday Morning', divinity now had to live within the self.

Many artists turned inward to reorder the world. The heterogeneity of their work was the consequence of each artist's trying to mark the uniqueness of his own experience. Stevens' idiosyncratic style was his effort to discover his own individuality. Discussing why he had chosen the Depression as the subject of his poem 'Owl's Clover', Stevens states in 'The Irrational Element in Poetry', 'I chose that as a bit of reality, actuality, the contemporaneous. . . . I wanted to apply my own sensibility to something perfectly matter-of-fact. The result would be a disclosure of my own sensibility or individuality . . . to myself' (*OP*, p. 219). The result, as Stevens envisaged, was the opposite of 'matter-of-fact'. Many decided that they must create their own languages if they were to have any chance of finding or knowing themselves. They became hermetic in the hope of uncovering rather than keeping their secrets. Private languages were devised so that the artist could commune with himself. Idiosyncrasy was felt to be a guarantee of authenticity. Poetry became *difficult* as the result of attempting to translate what was *sui generis*. Indeed, the variety of styles that characterises European poetry after Wordsworth is the sign of a shared concern, of finding similar solutions to a common problem:

> Every subsequent major European poet repeats Wordsworth's search for his deepest feelings, for the feeling of his own individuality and the diversity of styles is a consequence of each one attempting to devise a language appropriate to his own being. (*WBMP*, p. 214)[2]

The great changes of this time appear to have had the effect of impressing poets (and all artists) with their own singularity, as if their growing sense of the fluidity of the outside world called for a consolidation or re-formation of the self, the creation of a more dynamic identiy that changed so as to provide greater continuity. Although what happens in the inner world is in a constant, if fluctuating, relation to what happens in the outer world, the primary changes over this period are, of course, psychological. The principles of the natural world do not change; what changes is the cultural world: the man-made objects – and the relations of men with those objects, the objects of the natural world, and with themselves. Here the relations between the inner and outer worlds are symbiotic. Change (except for the weather, one of Stevens' favourite metaphors) is ordinarily not imposed upon people from without (although some persons impose it upon others): it is what they consciously and unconsciously do to themselves and to their environment.

This readiness of people to submit themselves to change meant a more vivid and energetic curiosity and a high value on the new. Stevens states in Adagia: 'Newness (not novelty) may be the highest individual value in poetry. Even in the meretricious sense of newness a new poetry has value' (*OP*, p. 177). Stevens would agree with Crane in 'General Aims and Theories' (1937) when he says,

> I put no particular value on the simple objective of 'modernity'. The element of temporal location of an artist's creation is of very secondary importance; it can be left to the impressionist or historian just as well. It seems to me that a poet will accidentally define his time well enough simply be reacting honestly and to the full extent of his sensibilities to the states of passion, experience and rumination that fate forces on him, first hand. . . . But to fool one's self that definitions are being reached by merely referring frequently to skyscrapers, radio antennae, steam whistles, or other surface phenomena of our time is merely to paint a photograph.[3]

The poet engages with his world because he has no choice. He is the world in which he walks. Contemporaneity is his birthright. The new is valuable in so far as it frees us from the old and offers us the chance of discovering something new about ourselves. The distinction that Stevens makes between invention and discovery in his analysis of surrealism (again in *Adagia*) reveals his assumption that poetry involves the exploration of the mind:

> The essential fault of surrealism is that it invents without discovering. To make a clam play an accordion is to invent not to discover. The observation of the unconscious, so far as it can be observed, should reveal things of which we have previously been unconscious, not the familiar things of which we have been conscious plus imagination. (*OP*, p. 177)

'To make a clam play an accordian' is 'to paint a photograph'. The poet is committed to self-examination; his task is the creation of new consciousness. What matters is the honesty, intelligence and resourcefulness of his response to his own states of mind – 'of passion, experience and rumination'. This is how Stevens can say in *Adagia* that 'All poetry is experimental poetry' (*OP*, p. 161). He sees every form as an inevitable limitation, like language or perception, and no form as any better or more radical or more 'modern' than any other. This is the lesson he learned from the experiments of his contemporaries, as he makes clear in the statement that he sent to Norman Holmes Pearson for *The Oxford Anthology of American Literature*:

> There is such complete freedom now-a-days in respect to technique that I am rather inclined to disregard form so long as I am free and can express myself freely. I don't know of anything, respecting form, that makes much difference. The essential thing in form is to be free in whatever form is used. A free form does not assure freedom. As a form, it is just one more form. So that it comes to this, I suppose, that I believe in freedom regardless of form.   (24 June 1973)

Freedom is the capacity to face the unconscious and to act knowing what one is doing. Form is not technique, but accuracy of statement. What matters is the poet's discoveries.

Freedom was Stevens' heritage as an American poet, established by the Declaration of Independence (1776), the Bill of Rights (1791) and *Leaves of Grass* (1855). Whitman's work was a poetic declaration of independence and offered to every subsequent poet the opportunity to disregard tradition. Stevens used this freedom to wander where he pleased among the printed words of the world. Besides reading widely and carefully in the corpora of British and French poetry, he was an insatiable reader of periodicals. There can have been very few current ideas that he did not encounter in some form or other in their pages. 'I read all the little magazines', he told Frank Jones (*B*, pp. 126–7). He enjoyed them as he enjoyed the weather, and it is, I think, difficult to overestimate their sustaining effect upon him. Stevens' reading was a private matter, a method of serendipity. Unlike Pound and Eliot, who in numerous essays re-evaluated the entire European tradition in order to make their position clear, Stevens wrote comparatively few essays and none about other authors.

After Tennyson and Whitman the new bearings in English poetry were taken on the compass of French literature – and primarily by American poets. 'There are just two things in the world,' Pound states in 1913, 'two great and interesting phenomena: the intellectual life of Paris and the curious teething promise of my own vast occidental nation.' To talk to French writers in the cafés of Paris is, he says, to be at the centre of Western literature:[4]

> For the best part of a thousand years English poets have gone to school to the French, or one might say that there never were any English poets until they began to study French. . . . The history of English poetic glory is a history of successful steals from the French. . . . The great periods of English have been the periods when the poets showed greatest powers of assimilation.[5]

Yeats in 1914, speaking at a dinner in his honour in Chicago (in itself indicative of the shift in the centre of poetic power), warns his audience that they are 'too far from Paris':

> It is from Paris that nearly all the great influences in art and literature have come, from the time of Chaucer until now. Today the metrical experiments of the French poets are overwhelming in their variety and delicacy. The best English writing is dominated by French criticism; in France is the great critical mind.[6]

Eliot, remembering his own time in Paris, remarks in 1934, 'Younger generations can hardly realize the intellectual desert of England and America during the first decade and more of this century. . . . The predominance of Paris was incontestable.'[7] Reviewing Peter Quennell's *Baudelaire and the Symbolists* in 1930, he observed,

> I look back to the dead year 1908; and I observe with satisfaction that it is now taken for granted that the current of French poetry which sprang from Baudelaire is one which has, in these twenty-one years, affected all English poetry that matters. . . . The poets of whom Mr Quennell treats are now as much in our bones as Shakespeare or Donne.[8]

Stevens not only shared the interest of Pound and Eliot in French poetry, but the French language and things French had for him from an early age a personal symbolic value.

The period after Whitman was a time of re-examination in American poetry. The poets in seeking to know themselves had to re-examine their entire relation to the world. Their acceptance of French was only part of their redefinition of their relation to European culture. It may be seen as part of a process of establishing their independence from their own immediate Anglo-American context. Freedom was imagined as a fulfilment. American poets desired to be free in order to be themselves. Their need for freedom was in a state of continuous tension with their loneliness and their need to belong somewhere. They wished for continuity with a longer past than the United States could offer *and* to affirm their self-sufficiency. Thus, they were ambivalent both about their own country (and Whitman) and about their British literary ancestry.

Pound had to go abroad in order to appreciate Whitman and see the United States as a subject for poetry. In 1909 he writes,

> From this side of the Atlantic I am for the first time able to read Whitman, and from the vantage of my education and – if it be permitted a man of my scant years – my world citizenship: I see him America's poet. The only Poet before the artists of the Carmen–Hovey period, or better, the only one of the conventionally recognised 'American Poets' who is worth reading.
>
> He *is* America. His crudity is an exceeding great stench, but it *is* America.... He is disgusting. He is an exceedingly nauseating pill, but he accomplishes his mission.
>
> ... I read him (in many parts) with acute pain, but when I write of certain things I find myself using his rhythms.... The vital part of my message, taken from the sap and fibre of America, is the same as his.
>
> ... Personally I might be very glad to conceal my relationship to my spiritual father and brag about my more congenial ancestry – Dante, Shakespeare, Theocritus, Villon, but the descent is a bit difficult to establish. And to be frank, Whitman is to my fatherland ... what Dante is to Italy.... The first great man to write in the language of his people.[9]

For Pound, Whitman is a success because he embodies his reality: 'He *is* America.' If self-definition means dis-covering, realising – creating – a self, becoming what one is, Whitman has achieved this purpose. His achievement is the *identity*: 'He *is* America.' Pound's comments show that he feels himself to be the centre of a struggle between an old world and a new.

Williams in his autobiography records the same struggle:

> Keats, during the years at medical school, was my God. *Endymion* really woke me up. I copied Keats' style religiously, starting my magnum opus of those days on the pattern of *Endymion*.
>
> For my notebooks, however . . . , I reserved my Whitmanesque 'thoughts', a sort of purgation and confessional, to clear my head and my heart from turgid obsessions.[10]

His first book of poems, published in 1909, was, he writes, 'bad Keats, nothing else – oh well, bad Whitman, too',[11]

Over thirty years later the struggle was still going on:

> At City College, New York, at a luncheon speaking engagement, I was defining our right as Americans to our own language, saying that English, its development from Shakespeare's day to this, does not primarily concern us.
>
> 'But this language of yours', said one of the instructors, himself an obvious Britisher, 'where does it come from?'
>
> 'From the mouths of Polish mothers', I replied.[12]

Stevens sums up the position with equal force in *Adagia*: 'Nothing could be more inappropriate to American literature than its English source since the Americans are not British in sensibility' (*OP*, p. 176).

This awareness of belonging to the Old World as well as the New is the subject of Stevens' first very long poem, 'The Comedian as the Letter C', and its length is an indication of the complexity for him of the subject. The protagonist, Crispin is (as Robert Buttel has shown) a descendant of Voltaire's Candide, Beaumarchais's Figaro and Laforgue's Pierrot, who embarks from Bordeaux for Yucatan. He is French – yet Stevens has not forgotten his 'English source'. His hero is also a reincarnation of Crispinus, the would-be poet of Jonson's *The Poetaster*, and the poem's extravagant language echoes the language of Jonson's comedies.[13] This thorough European, after journeying about the Caribbean, becomes the founder of a colony, a pioneer, in the Carolinas. The plot of the poem is of immigration and settlement. Thus, a basic pattern of American history is used as a metaphor for the growth of the poet's mind. Crispin's itinerary

marks the stages in the development of his imagination, expressed
as the changing relation between a man and his environment. The
movement is toward greater integration. The poem begins with the
statement, 'man is the intelligence of his soil, / The sovereign ghost'.
Half-way through this changes to 'his soil is man's intelligence', a
restatement made possible only by the reformulation of Crispin's
self brought about by his experiences in the Americas. The very
crossing of the Atlantic is presented as a self-transforming act:

> The sea
> Severs not only lands but also selves.
> Here was no help before reality.
> Crispin beheld and Crispin was made new.
>   (I. 77–80)

Crispin is newly created by his new perceptions. The newness of his
environment is a liberation:

> His mind was free
> And more than free, elate, intent, profound
> And studious of a self possessing him,
> That was not in him in the crusty town
> From which he sailed.
>   (II. 88–92)

After his sojourn in Mexico, Crispin is not European in sensibility.

Throughout his poetic career, Stevens maintained this view of the
intimate and decisive relation between who we are and where we
live. In his last prose piece, 'Connecticut' (1955), after commenting
on the number of people in the state who were foreign-born or
'children of parents who were themselves foreign born, or of
parents whose parents, generation back of generation, were foreign
born', he states,

> There are no foreigners in Connecticut. Once you are here, you
> are – or you are on your way to become – a Yankee. I was not
> myself born in the state. It is not that I am a native, but that I feel
> like one.
> There is nothing that gives the feel of Connecticut like coming
> home to it. . . . It is a question of coming home to the American self
> in the sort of place in which it was formed. (*OP*, pp.295–6)

The same view emerged whenever he spoke of the relation of American and British poetry. Asked in 1950 whether it was 'nonsense to talk of a typical American poem' and what qualities 'tend to distinguish a poem as "American"', he replied, 'At bottom this question is whether there is such a thing as an American. If there is, the poems that he writes are American poems.' Being an American poet was not something that you worked at any more than you worked at being modern, it was the inevitable consequence of living in America: 'Even if a difference was not to be found in anything else, it would be found in what we write about. We live in two different physical worlds and it is not nonsense to think that that matters.'[14]

'Academic Discourse at Havana' and 'Sea Surface Full of Clouds' are the last two major poems that Stevens published before he stopped writing poetry in the summer of 1924. The former was originally published as 'Discourse in a Cantina at Havana' in *Broom* (Nov 1923); the latter was among the new poems included in the second edition of *Harmonium* (1931). The two poems represent the culmination of Stevens' first period of major work (1915–24) and mark the transition to the next (1930–55). They also show how he needed Europe in order to define America. 'Academic Discourse at Havana' shows Stevens' relation to British literature, 'Sea Surface Full of Clouds' his relation to French literature.

'ACADEMIC DISCOURSE AT HAVANA'

'Academic Discourse at Havana' and 'The Idea of Order at Key West' are perhaps the two best poems in *Ideas of Order*, and the first can be said to be a rehearsal for the second. Both are set in the warm South of the imagination and both are concerned with speech as a way of giving form to sensation.

I

Canaries in the morning, orchestras
In the afternoon, balloons at night. That is
A difference, at least, from nightingales,
Jehovah and the great sea-worm. The air
Is not so elemental nor the earth
So near.
      But the sustenance of the wilderness
Does not sustain us in the metropoles.

Havana is at a remove from the old – and exotic – neither so elemental nor so near the earth as where we started from, a metropole of the imagination in which we hunger for the manna of an earlier existence. Genesis is followed by exodus. Upon being expelled from the Garden of Eden, Cain 'dwelt in the land of Nod [which means "wandering"], on the east of Eden' and then 'builded a city' (Genesis 4: 16–17). This poem is composed somewhere east of Eden, looking westward.

II

Life is an old casino in a park.
The bills of the swans are flat upon the ground.
A most desolate wind has chilled Rouge-Fatima
And a grand decadence settles down like cold.

The casino in a park is a condensation of metropole and wilderness and a combination of two very old topoi: the wheel of fortune and the *locus amoenus*.[15] 'Life is an old casino in a park' is perhaps the most comprehensive statement in the text, and the whole poem takes place within its aura. A casino is where we gamble our lives away, and that it is old suggests that things have always been this way, that there is nothing older than our fate. The wheel that spins and stops at random, representing all our uncertainties and the unpredictable movement of life (Stevens refers in 'The Place of the Solitaires' to 'the dark, green water-wheel' of the sea) is within the double set of containers of casino and park, and kept under control by not being named. A park is a pleasance, the wilderness domesticated, another Eden. The 'minimum ingredients' of the *locus amoenus*, as defined by Curtius, are all present: 'a tree (or several trees), a meadow, and a spring or brook'.[16] Here an impoverishing wind is blowing through the park. The bills of the swans, who stand for purity, beauty, serenity and virility, are depressed to the ground in a gesture of collapse, death or sleep. They have bitten the dust, at least temporarily. 'Our Lady of Fatima' is one of the names of the Virgin Mary (who is said to have appeared in Fatima, Portugal, in 1917) and red in Stevens is usually the colour of the world and sun. Rouge-Fatima is perhaps the miraculous red lady of reality, its presiding genius or muse, chilled by the mind's cold.[17] Like the gesture of the swans, Rouge-Fatima is deliberately unexplained. Here, as throughout his poetry, Stevens creates his own modes of statement, his own set of symbols and equivalences, in order to discover the origins of his feelings. the obscurity, such as it is, is part of his meaning and a response to amorphousness. The mysterious nature of the poem's events is one of the things that he is try to communicate. For him they need to be acted out again; poetry is a theatre, the actors are the unique agents of his meaning – hence the necessity of Rouge-Fatima. As a result of the cold, the casino and its park are an empty stage. Desolation means loneliness, decadence is the impairment or decay of a thing, especially of something rich. Winter has invaded a summer place.

The third part, the longest and central section of the poem, contrasts the earlier richness with the later decadence and suggests why one changed into the other.

III

The swans . . . Before the bills of the swans fell flat
Upon the ground, and before the chronicle
Of affected homage foxed so many books,
They warded the blank waters of the lakes
And island canopies which were entailed
To that casino. Long before the rain
Swept through its boarded windows and the leaves
Filled its encrusted fountains, they arrayed
The twilights of the mythy goober khan.
The centuries of excellence to be
Rose out of promise and became the sooth
Of trombones floating in the trees.
The toil
Of thought evoked a peace eccentric to
The eye and tinkling to the ear. Gruff drums
Could beat, yet not alarm the populace.
The indolent progressions of the swans
Made earth come right; a peanut parody
For peanut people.

Before the change, the swans guarded the lakes and islands of the park that were the inalienable heritage of the casino, the fountain worked and the leaves were on the trees. *Warded, entailed* and *arrayed* insist on the order of that earlier time when the evenings were full of swans. Since then 'the chronicle of affected homage', decadent rhetoric and mannered emotion, has discoloured many books with its damp, the rain now sweeps through the boarded-up windows and dead leaves fill the encrusted fountain. *Decadence, foxed, encrusted*: all suggest deterioration as a growth, like a disease or a damp stain or lichen – or a chronicle. It is as if some inner failure of poetry, the incapacity for genuine praise, true homage, has brought to an end the play at the casino.

The old times are summed up in the orderly procession of white swans upon the blank and as yet pristine waters of the lakes at dusk, in the 'twilights of the mythy goober khan'. Myth comes before history. The earlier period is one in which differentiating imagination and reality is not a problem. The 'goober khan' is Coleridge's Kubla Khan. *Goober*, a dialect word of the American South meaning peanut, echoes *Kubla*, as the whole of 'Academic Discourse at Havana' echoes 'Kubla Khan'. The differences mark the transformation of a British into an American sensibility. For both poets the ground of the imagination is exotic: Stevens' Cuba, Coleridge's China. A casino is a pleasure-dome and the pleasure-dome that Kubla Khan decreed in Xanadu was a park running with water, with 'gardens bright with sinuous rills', a 'mighty fountain' and a 'sacred river'. Coleridge's *mazy* may have suggested Stevens' *mythy*; the tumult of the waters that Kubla heard, the voices (Stevens speaks of 'ornatest prophecy'), the playing and the singing may be compared to the resonant music and circus-parade in Stevens, the unexpected 'caves of ice' in the 'sunny pleasure-dome' to the decadent cold in Havana, and the Abyssinian maid to the vaguely Asiatic Rouge-Fatima. Stevens' notion that the poet's repetitions reconcile us to our selves, enabling us to repossess the sea-song and moon-speech, and that the casino perhaps defines 'An indefinite incantation of our selves' is a restatement of the idea in 'Kubla Khan' that, if the poet could revive within himself the Abyssinian maid's 'symphony and song', that inner music would enable him to build the dome in imagination.[18]

For both poets the imagination is a dream music that re-establishes the harmony of the inner world, a barely remembered harmony, now lost and recoverable only from the shadows of memory. Coleridge explains at the start of his poem how it issued from a twilight, mythy state and he subtitles it 'A Vision in a Dream'. Stevens closes his poem with the poet awake on his balcony in the half-day of the moonlight and everyone else asleep. This is a return to the swans, who, in the speaking silence of their mobile, white beauty, ordered 'The twilights of the mythy goober khan', their floating presence, a poem. The heyday of the casino was a time of the mutuality of the imagination and reality, when the inner and outer worlds were at one – a time that the poet seeks to restore. The ruler of this twilight realm was the 'mythy goober khan', *mythy* because his territory was largely fantasy and because he lived so long ago in our development that his existence can only be postulated. A 'khan' is a chief. Kubla Khan was all-powerful, rich and ruthless, the absolute master of all China. Ready and able to realise his fantasies, to establish gardens and build pleasure-domes at will, he was what the poet desires to be.

The 'goober khan', moreover, appears to stand for the kernel of the self. This idea seems implicit, as its title suggests, in 'Homunculus et La Belle Etoile', and Crispin, in 'The Comedian as the Letter C', in becoming 'an introspective voyager' as the result of his ocean crossing, is reduced to the 'merest minuscule in the gales' (I. 56) and in Yucatan he found that his vicissitudes had made him moody:

> He was in this as other freemen are,
> Sonorous nutshells rattling inwardly.
>
> (II. 26–7)

Stevens refers in 'The Dwarf' to the mind as 'the final dwarf of you', and his metaphors of the world as fat and thought as thin are variations on this idea, as are his notions of major and minor feeling. He states in the final section of 'Esthétique du Mal',

> The greatest poverty is not to live
> In a physical world, to feel that one's desire
> Is too difficult to tell from despair. Perhaps,
> After death, the non-physical people, in paradise,
> Itself non-physical, may, by chance, observe
> The green corn gleaming and experience
> The minor of what we feel. The adventurer
> In humanity has not conceived of a race
> Completely physical in a physical world.
> The green corn gleams and the metaphysicals
> Lie sprawling in the majors of the August heat,
> The rotund emotions, paradise unknown.
>
> (xv. 1–12)

'The greatest poverty is not to live / In a physical world', and, in so far as our lives are non-physical, they are a parody, mimic motions of imagination, ghostly gestures out of touch with reality. The music of the casino, the progressions of the swans, are 'a peanut parody / For peanut people'. They belong to the fictive music of 'To the One of Fictive Music':

> Now, of the music summoned by the birth
> That separates us from the wind and sea,
> Yet leaves us in them, until earth becomes,
> By being so much of the things we are,
> Gross effigy and simulacrum . . . .

'Academic Discourse at Havana' seems also to refer to this birth that separates and joins. Thus the peanut khan is the original dwarf, the first form of ourselves, what we grow out of, and the time of the casino's prosperity is our childhood. The 'goober khan' is father of the man.

The excellence of the future started as a promise and then took shape as the soothing music of the trombones, which, martial, phallic and with their floating sound, are suggestive of the swans. This smooth, easy, air-borne harmony is set against the 'tinkling' of 'The toil of thoughts', and, although the 'sooth', the 'tinkling' and the beating of the 'Gruff drums' all combine to sound like a parading band, there is a hint of fundamental dissonance between thought and senses. They have different centres. They are eccentric, in an irregular relation to each other, and, consequently, this dissonance persists and grows, even though in the beginning it may be no more than the steady and unalarming gruffness of the drums. If we wish to make a comparison to 'Kubla Khan', the drums can be thought of as 'voices prophesying war' – or a different kind of peace.

> And serener myth
> Conceiving from its perfect plenitude,
> Lusty as June, more fruitful than the weeks
> Of ripest summer, always lingering
> To touch again the hottest bloom, to strike
> Once more the longest resonance, to cap
> The clearest woman with apt weed, to mount
> The thickest man on thickest stallion-back,
> This urgent, competent, serener myth

> Passed like a circus.
>   Politic man ordained
> Imagination as the fateful sin.
> Grandmother and her basketful of pears
> Must be the crux for our compendia.
> That's world enough, and more, if one includes
> Her daughters to the peached and ivory wench
> For whom the towers are built. The burgher's breast,
> And not a delicate ether star-impaled,
> Must be the place for prodigy, unless
> Prodigious things are tricks. The world is not
> The bauble of the sleepless nor a word
> That should import a universal pith
> To Cuba. Jot these milky matters down.
> They nourish Jupiters. Their casual pap
> Will drop like sweetness in the empty nights
> When too great rhapsody is left annulled
> And liquorish prayer provokes new sweats: so, so:
> Life is an old casino in a wood.

The halcyon days of the casino were under the aegis of 'serener myth'. As myth-making is a habit of mind that disappears with the keeping of chronicles and the writing of history, they are thus a period of fulfilment before the beginning of the sense of time. This is completion that none the less promises more development and is itself temporary, passing like a procession of swans or a circus. The absolute completeness of 'serener myth' is denoted by the reduplication 'perfect plentitude', and the six successive superlatives: 'the hottest bloom', 'the longest resonance', 'the clearest woman', 'the thickest man' and the 'thickest stallion-back', one of which is super-superlative: 'more . . . than . . . ripest summer'. The dynamic character of the myth is shown by *conceiving, lusty, fruitful, ripest, bloom* and *urgent*, as well as by the comparison to June and summer, and by its power to make things happen: 'always lingering to touch . . . to strike . . . to cap . . . to mount . . . '. This is its competence; it appears to *make* 'earth come right', like the swans. Myths are stories that the imagination tells in order to explain the world, to make it meaningful. Although 'serener myth' appears as a joyous, effective and genuine ordering in contrast to the time-bound 'chronicle / Of affected homage', it is, nevertheless, only a season of the mind. Yeats' 'The Circus Animals' Desertion' (1939) is another poem using the metaphor of the circus for the passing of the mythy mode of the imagination.

The circus is followed by politics and sin. The rule of the 'goober khan' gives way to the new authority of 'Politic man', who is careful rather than fantastic and who apparently considers his decisions with all the caution of self-awareness (that self-conscious lover Prufrock describes himself as 'politic, cautious and meticulous') and his pragmatism establishes a law-giving state of mind. A change is *ordained*. Imagination becomes 'the fateful sin', the transgression that decides our destiny. 'Grandmother and her basket of pears' is the old Eve with enough fruit to tempt us all. Who else can she be if one of her daughters is Helen of Troy? Stevens reverses Marlowe in thinking of Helen as responsible for the building instead of the falling of the topless towers of Ilium, seeing her as a muse tempting us to acts of imagination. To *peach* is to accuse formally, to impeach (1460) and to inform against (1570). 'Peached and ivory wench' gives us both the rosy blush of ripe fruit and the imputation of sin and wrongdoing. Recently a slangy word, like *wench*, it sounds a humorous note, and the two words, together with the echoes of Marvell's 'To his Coy Mistress' and Marlowe's *Doctor Faustus*, make the language of this passage particularly archaic, as if old words were needed for any true discussion of origins. Before Stevens, Augustine substituted the pear for the apple in his myth of the fall (*Confessions*, II). If the apple suggests the breast, the pear suggests the woman's body. Pears are the food of temptation in 'Sunday Morning' where death:

> causes boys to pile new plums and pears
> On disregarded plate. The maidens taste
> And stray impassioned in the littering leaves.

The poet in Marvell's poem tells his mistress that, if they had world enough, her coyness would be no crime, bringing together love and crime as Stevens brings together love and sin. Stevens' subject, however, is poetry and not love, and his logic is obscure. He places two statements – imagination is the 'fateful sin', and 'Grandmother and her basket of pears / Must be the crux of our compendia' – side by side, as if the one followed from the other. The 'must be' adds a strange urgency to an argument in which the poet confesses his own bafflement. A *crux* is an enigma or riddle, the hard word that nobody knows, the place where the text is difficult to interpret and where the meaning is problematic. A *compendium* is an epitome, a summary, a large subject collected in a small space, a form of academic discourse; *compendia* is the plural. According to Stevens, the puzzle presented by grandmother and her basket of pears is necessarily the difficulty or discontinuity in all our formal thinking. If every daughter of Eve to Helen of Troy is included in the puzzle, this is more than enough to think about, all the problems we need in the world. So defined, the crux belongs to the very earliest period of our history; Helen, although not so mythy as the 'goober khan', is herself a mythical figure. It is as if the basic purpose of thought were to understand the muse. The poem describes the transition from the casino in the full bloom of its summer to the boarded-up casino in the moonlight; from swans, trombones, the 'goober khan' and the circus to love, sin, the burgher's breast' and 'liquorish prayer'; from serener myth to poetry. The change is a change in the mode of the imagination, in the attitude to imagination. Somehow, in a way the poet does not completely understand – this is the crux – the temptations of love and knowledge alter the nature of our imagination. Perhaps it can be said that he is aware of the change but cannot explain it, except with a myth.

The sentence following the one about Helen of Troy suggests that all this happens inside us. The burgher is *l'homme au moyen sensuel*, a solid citizen whose presence testifies that the world is real. The poet rejects the realms of fantasy whose atmospheres are so insubstantial that they can be pierced by starlight, for the 'not so elemental air' of part I of the poem. *Burgher* suggests old-fashioned manners, and *ether*, ancient cosmologies. They are archaic words denoting old orders. By his choice of words Stevens seeks to evoke the quality of times gone by, and, by his combination of old and new worlds, to communicate the texture of memory where the past is always subsumed into the present. Here the poet does not wish to be deceived or tricked. Genuine prodigies are part of the world, continuous with ourselves, and the world is neither dream – the imagination's toy – nor word. Reality does not have any comprehensive or absolute message (the *pith* is the core or essence of a thing) for Cuba, or any other place, which implies that its meaning like its objects is ever-changing and needs to be continually re-established, that the meaning of a process can only be another process.

The mention of the 'burgher's breast' leads on to the notion that the poem is like a breast:

> Jot these milky matters down.
> They nourish Jupiters. Their casual pap
> Will drop like sweetness in the empty nights
> When too great rhapsody is left annulled . . . .

'Burgher's breast' can be seen as a half-hidden autobiographical reference to the situation of the poet, who in 1923 was a member of the Hartford Accident and Indemnity Company and a director of the Hartford Live Stock Insurance Company. Stevens appears to have relished his identity as a businessman, and to have enjoyed being both a businessman and a poet. Thus he lived the double life of imagination and reality that constitutes the main subject of his poetry. As every child builds up its notion of reality upon its image of its mother's breast, the nature of reality is indeed a milky matter, cloudy and nuanced, whose elementary structures are established in our minds during the earliest period of our lives. The poem, or poetry, then becomes a recapitulation of, and substitute for, the experience of the mother's breast, and the poet takes over from the mother the formation of his own identity. This is alluded to in the original title of the poem, 'Discourse in a Cantina at Havana' – a cantina is a place to drink – and in the reference to the manna of Exodus and the lakes and the fountains (that have dried up) of the park. An abundance of running water, including, almost invariably, a spring or fountain, is a characteristic of the topos of the *locus amoenus*, and in 'Kubla Khan', which Stevens' poem echoes, there is a breast-shaped 'pleasure-dome', and at the close those who see the poet cry,

> For he on honey-dew hath fed,
> And drunk the milk of Paradise.

Paradise is where we feed without working.

The metaphor of the breast reminds us that perception is a taking-in. At Havana, as in Eden and in the dream of Kubla Khan's garden, knowledge is food and can make us god-like. The milk of paradise produces ecstasy; poetic knowledge nourishes Jupiters. The baby Jupiter, hidden by his mother so that he would not be eaten by his father, Saturn, grew up to overthrow his father and usher in a golden age. He is a veritable 'goober khan' and like him has disappeared. The poet states that the milky matters of the poem will sweeten the emptiness of when the music stops. There is no greater emptiness than the absence of the breast and there is a point at which hunger in the baby destroys identity. Poetry makes the memory of this silence tolerable. A rhapsody is an extravagant expression of unordered feeling, most commonly an instrumental composition of indefinite form and improvisatory character. This seems to refer to the exuberant feeling of serener myth embodied in the music from the casino. When this disconnected outpouring of emotion is reduced to nothing, the nights are empty and 'liquorish prayer' provokes only new fears, then these anxieties can be answered by the elementary and primitive food of the poem. Myth is manna. Poetry is a voice that fills up the space of loneliness. This suggests that it is specifically knowledge of the nature of hunger than can gratify that hunger, as if, in the psyche, consciousness of the problem is its solution. Thus inner failures can be resolved by interpretation, through their restatement or reformulation, and thus language changes us and what we apprehend of the world.

Liquorish means pleasing to the palate, fond of delicious food, fond of liquids and lecherous; it is one of a series of words denoting liquids: *milk, pap, drop, liquorish, sweats*. That the rhapsody was 'too great' suggests that it was too rhapsodic to last. When the sustaining power of the rhapsody has been abolished, the eager desire for tactile, palatable delight results in previously unknown fears. The 'so, so' has this change taking place in the now of the poem, and, as the final line of the section shows, this is a change in our way of seeing the world. Life becomes an old casino, not in a park, but a wood – dark, closed, obscure and complicated, like Dante's *selva oscura*.

The final section of the poem defines the function of the poet. It begins by asking whether poetry is mere sound to stuff the ear, another metaphor suggesting eating. This question, drawing attention to poetry as an elaborate and nuanced structure of sounds, as if sound were meaning or meaning insignificant when compared to sound, is answered neither immediately nor directly. This makes for a certain slackness in the ordonnance of the argument, but as the poem proceeds it becomes clear that the poet's answer is 'no'. The sharp focus of the question is in contrast to the rambling, expanding openness of the answer, which in its meditative freedom gathers to itself the details of the poem's setting: cantina, balcony, moonlight and vanished swans.

IV

Is the funcion of the poet here mere sound,
Subtler than the ornatest prophecy,
To stuff the ear? It causes him to make
His infinite repetition and alloys
Of pick of ebon, pick of halcyon.
It weights him with nice logic for the prim.
As part of nature he is part of us.
His rarities are ours: may they be fit
And reconcile us to our selves in those
True reconcilings, dark, pacific words,
And the adroiter harmonies of their fall.
Close the cantina. Hood the chandelier.
The moonlight is not yellow but a white
That silences the ever-faithful town.
How pale and how possessed a night it is,
How full of exhalations of the sea . . .
All this is older than its oldest hymn,
Has no more meaning than tomorrow's bread.
But let the poet on his balcony
Speak and the sleepers in their sleep shall move,
Waken, and watch the moonlight on their floors.
This may be benediction, sepulcher,
And epitaph. It may, however, be
An incantation that the moon defines
By mere example opulently clear.
And the old casino likewise may define
An infinite incantation of our selves
In the grand decadence of the perished swans.

   The poet, Stevens tells us, says the same thing over and over again.
His work is never-ending and consists of making alloys, amalgams
of a baser metal mixed with a nobler. Here, in a poem about a split, is
an intimation of reconcilation. *Ebon* is ebony, a heavy black wood;
halcyon is calm, quiet, undisturbed. The combination of the two
contrasts the tangible with the intangible, heaviness with lightness,
black with brightness. The halcyon is a fabulous bird said to breed at
the winter solstice in a nest floating in the sea and to charm the
waves and wind so that the sea is especially calm (which reminds us
that the 'indolent progressions of the swans' floating on the casino's
lakes 'Made earth come right'). Stevens has derived the terms of his

image from Marvell's description in 'Upon Appleton House' of how the shadows at evening creep underneath the river bank:

> And on the river as it flows
> With eben shuts begin to close;
> The modest halcyon comes in sight,
> Flying betwixt the day and night;
> And such an horror calm and dumb,
> Admiring Nature does benumb.[19]

Here 'halcyon' has its other meaning of *kingfisher* as well as magic overtones. Stevens' poet on his balcony is like the halcyon, betwixt day and night, between waking and sleeping, the summer sun and the moonlight, reality and imagination. His choice of the best of ebon and the best of halcyon 'weights him with nice logic for the prim', makes him as solid as the 'burgher's breast' and equipped to deal with repressive propriety and formality. Poems as alloys are *compendia*, a weighing-together, and, however rare, they are part of nature and, when successful, reconcile us to ourselves in a true, deep and important way. *Dark* is *ebon*, *pacific* is *halcyon* and also the name of the biggest ocean. *Adroit* is the old meaning of *nice*; *fall* follows *drop*. That we need to be endlessly reconciled to ourselves indicates the elemental nature of the split that the poem describes.

Then the scene shifts. The change is marked by the two imperatives. The cantina is closed and we go outside into the town. The poem is opened up to the moonlight. The poet confronts the imagination. The peace of the town ever-faithful to the moon is an example of how those true reconcilings feel. The moonlight is white, transparent, imposing silence on the town. The night is full of the deep breathing of the sea, salt-scented and vaporous, a sound of the beginning of time, older than any poetry. All of this has a meaning like food, but tomorrow's bread is no more than a promise; only today's bread can be eaten. This situation is transformed by the speech of the poet. He changes moonlight to manna, to the 'bread of faithful speech' of 'Notes Toward a Supreme Fiction'. He moves us with the power of our dreams and causes us to awake to the power of the imagination. The poem may be a blessing, tomb or the inscription upon a tomb, but in Havana, at night, he does not insist.[20] The nature of poetry is to be evoked by a series of particular metaphors rather than by any single decisive abstraction (and this is his procedure in all his long poems), because in a world of change there can be no final statement or activity. Poetry is an infinite incantation (note that the word contains *cantina* and is related to *canto*), an everlasting, never-ending creation of the self, words spoken to produce a magic effect, rich with the memory of loss, full of the halcyon days and mythy twilights of the vanished past.

PETER QUINCE'S CLAVIER

Stevens was always evasive about his reading of other poets. To Bernard Heringman, who had asked him about Hi Simons' essay, 'Wallace Stevens and Mallarmé',[21] he writes,

> And Mallarmé never in the world meant as much to me as all that in any direct way. Perhaps I absorbed more than I thought. Mallarmé was a good deal in the air when I was much younger. But so were other people, for instance, Samain. Verlaine meant a good deal more to me. There were many of his lines that I delighted to repeat. But I was never a student of any of these poets; they were simply poets and I was the youthful general reader. (3 May 1949)

There is nothing more misleading than this final sentence. Stevens, a poet of genius, was never 'the youthful general reader', and, although he may not have read the French poets as 'a student' in the strictest sense of that word, he certainly studied them as a poet. They were as much in his bones as in Eliot's, and one reason why it is difficult to be precise about their effect is that it was total; it cannot be located because it is everywhere – and he indicates as much to Simons when commenting upon his essay:

> I have read something, more or less, of all the French poets mentioned by you [Mallarmé, Verlaine, Laforgue, Valéry and Baudelaire], but if I have picked up anything from them, it has been unconsciously. It is always possible that, where a man's attitude coincides with your own attitude, or accentuates your own attitude, you get a great deal from him without any effort. This, in fact, is one of the things that makes literature possible.
> (8 July 1941)

Stevens in his letter to Heringman was similarly evasive about his reading of philosophy:

The same thing is true about philosophers. I have never studied systematic philosphy and should be bored to death at the mere thought of doing so. I think that the little philosophy that I have read has been read very much in the spirit in which Henry Church used to read it. He said that he had read philosophy for forty years. It seemed to me that he read it as a substitute for fiction. He could sit up in bed until two or three o'clock in the morning the Nietzsche. I could never possibly have any serious contact with philosophy because I have not the memory.

Again his examples negate his disclaimer. 'To sit up in bed until two or three o'clock in the morning with Nietzsche' is 'serious contact with philosophy', as is reading it for forty years in any spirit whatever. He is at pains to make clear that he has never studied philosophy systematically or as a philosopher; rather he has read it as a poet, and for Stevens, of course, there could be nothing more serious than this.

Stevens knew that he was evasive about his reading of other poets and it caused him to consider his own motives. To Richard Eberhart (significantly, a fellow poet) he writes,

Why do poets in particular resent the attribution of the influence of other poets? The customary answer to this is that it gives them the appearance of being second-hand. That may be one of the aspects of what seems to me the true answer. It seems to me that the true answer is that with a true poet his poetry is the same thing as his vital self. It is not possible for any one else to touch it.

(20 Jan 1954)

This not only helps us to interpret Stevens' comments on other poets but also offers a definition of poetry: with a true poet it is 'the same thing as his vital self', that which continuously makes him what he is; as a projection of the essential processes of the inner world, its purpose is self-repair. Poetry – in the terms of 'Academic Discourse at Havana' – restores the serener myth of the vanished swans, thereby producing pap to sweeten empty nights and reconcile us to ourselves. This, however, is new creation as well as re-creation (which is no more than to say that neither projection nor representation are simple acts). Poetry discovers, and makes, a part of the poet's self that which has no existence elsewhere; hence the need to protect it against all comers.

Stevens is, I believe, indebted to a French poet for the basic metaphor of his beautiful poem 'Peter Quince at the Clavier', and the poem can be seen as a synthesis of French and English poetic ideas. The poem is presented as a piece played on a clavier:

> Just as my fingers on these keys
> Make music, so the selfsame sounds
> On my spirit make a music, too.
>
> Music is feeling, then, not sound;
> And thus it is that what I feel
> Here in this room, desiring you,
>
> Thinking of your blue-shadowed silk,
> Is music. It is like the strain
> Waked in the elders by Susanna.

Peter Quince is the poet and playwright in *A Midsummer Night's Dream*, who says of one of the characters in his play, 'You must understand he goes but to see a noise he has heard', and to whom Bottom thinks of turning when he wakes in Titania's bower:

> I have had a more rare vision. . . . Methought I was – there is no man can tell what. . . . The eye of man hath not heard, the ear of man hath not seen, man's hand is not able to taste, his tongue to conceive, nor his heart to report, what my dream was. I will get Peter Quince to write a ballad of this dream: it shall be called 'Bottom's Dream', because it hath no bottom . . . .[22]

Synaesthesia in the life of the imagination is not an actual event but a metaphor. Bottom's dream is what the imagination apprehends which is beyond the reach of words but towards which words reach, sometimes accessible to music and to the music of language, poetry. Susanna and the elders, Titania and Bottom, beauty and ugliness – Peter Quince could make a song of this; and song is order for Stevens, as he states clearly in 'The Idea of Order at Key West'. The poet touches the keys as he wishes to touch the body of his beloved.

The clavier reminds us that the title of Stevens' first book is *Harmonium*, a word that suggests the ordering-power of music (as in the harmony of the spheres) as well as being the name of a keyboard instrument akin to the clavier.[23] The word – and the metaphor – meant enough to Stevens for him to want to call the 1954 collected edition of his poems 'The Whole of Harmonium'.[24] There are grounds for supposing that Peter Quince's instrument is of the manufacture of Baudelaire. In 'Salon de 1846', Baudelaire cites with approval a passage by Hoffman on the relation of colour and feelings:

> It is not only in dream and in the slight delirium that precedes sleep, it is on hearing music while still awake that I discover an analogy and intimate union between colours, sounds and perfumes. To me it seems that all these things are engendered by the same ray of light, and that they must come together in a marvellous concert.[25]

This idea informs Baudelaire's poem 'Correspondances', as it does 'Peter Quince at the Clavier', and in 'Exposition Universelle de 1855' Baudelaire returns to the idea of correspondences when he considers the effect on 'a man of the world, a thinker' if he is transported to a far-away country. 'It will', he says, 'create in him a new world of ideas, a world that will be an integral part of himself and will accompany him, in the form of memories, until death'. This is a description of Crispin in his new world in 'The Comedian as the Letter C', of the planter on his 'blue island' in 'Notes Toward a Supreme Fiction' (2. v) and of the value of Florida and Mexico in the poems of Stevens. Baudelaire then complains of what would be the unreceptiveness in that situation of one of those professors of aesthetics: 'who has forgotten the colour of the sky, the form of vegetation, the movement and smell of animality and whose clenched fingers, paralysed by the pen, are unable to run with agility on the immense clavier of *correspondences*!'[26] This is Peter Quince's instrument, and its music is the vivid sensuality of Stevens' poetry – a music that comes from the combination of English and French, of Shakespeare's rustic poet and Baudelaire's pensive *homme du monde*, a combination that perhaps only an American, the inhabitant of a new world, could make.

Stevens in *Adagia* makes the bold and startling assertion: 'French and English constitute a single language' (*OP*, p. 178). This very comprehensive statement of the relation of French and English poetry has baffled students of Stevens, and his explanation in a letter to Heringman does not make the matter any clearer:

I still think that English and French are the same language, not etymologically nor at sea level. But at sea level it is not possible to communicate with many people who speak English in English. You have to take my statement as applying only in areas in which it would in fact apply. What a great many people fail to see is that one uses French for the pleasure that it gives. (21 July 1953)

This remark about the pleasure of using French echoes what he wrote to René Taupin in reply to Taupin's inquiry about his knowledge of French symbolist poetry. (Taupin does not specify whether he has translated the letter or whether Stevens wrote in French.) Note that the influence is attributed to the language not the poets: 'La légèreté, la grâce, le son et la couleur de français ont eu sur moi une influence indéniable et une influence précieuse' ('The lightness, grace, sound and colour of French have had on me an undeniable influence and a precious influence').[27]

Consideration of all of Stevens' work suggests that French and English constituting a single language meant that he could introduce French words, phrases, sentences at will into any English text. This was his lifelong practice. The journal that he kept from 1898 until 1912 shows him speaking French to a cat:

Yesterday afternoon I lay in the orchard near the barn-yard gate tantalizing the barn-kitten which I have named 'Petit Gris' from its size & color. It was like a plaything for a Cyclop but I tried to lighten the fury of its handling by chattering in my softest French, 'N'ayez pas peur de moi, petit chat. Venez ici – sur ma jambe, ma main. Vous avez le bleu du ciel dans vos yeux – eh bien, jolie chose – n'ayez pas peur – montez – descendez – est-ce que vous pouvez atteindre cette pièce d'herbe – ah mon petit bleu, mon petit gris – soie de la couleur – songe d'une chose – jolie chose' etc etc keeping it up for a quarter of an hour at least, perhaps with countless mistakes in the French, but certainly with no flaw in the pleasure. (*SP*, p. 53)

He notes 'a sauvagerie of polk, elderberries, huckleberries, Virginia creeper', 'a deep ravine – *deep* en vérité', exclaims 'Voila',' *En effet*' and '*Mon Dieu!*' and refers to a fish that got away as ''Sieur Trout' (*SP*, pp. 53, 109, 110, 115, 118, 122). 'There's gold for the digging: j'en suis sur', he says of writing something every night (*SP*, p. 112). Camping in British Columbia, he amuses himself with a characteristic gamut of linguistic registers: 'Got back at six & bathed in the glacier stream & changed my duds. Maintenant, la lune se lève'; and, again:

Overhead in the *clair de crépuscule* lay a bright star. I've grown such a hearty Puritan & revel in such coarse good health that I felt scarcely the slightest twinge of sentiment. But tonight I've been polite to a friend – have guzzled *vin ordinaire* & puffed a Villar y Villar.... (*SP*, pp. 118, 127)

The down-to-earth spontaneity of the American slang 'duds' is set against the formality and measured elegance of the French, 'Maintenant, la lune se leve.' The physicality of 'coarse good health', bathing 'in the glacier stream', guzzling and puffing is in marked contrast to the studied refinements of European culture: wine, the cigars with their Spanish name, and the shadowy transparencies of *'clair de crépuscule'*. The Old World, where he has never been (and chose never to go) becomes the other world of the imagination, of twilight, moonlight and romance, as when his wife-to-be seems *'une vrai princess lointaine'* (*SP*, p. 146). (His mistakes – it should be 'une vraie princesse lointaine' – make French and English even more one language.) Stevens seeks in his description to use all the notes in the scale, and French provides another scale, doubling his range and enabling him to find two equivalents for every English expression, one in the world, the other in the man-made world of French, so that English can be at once the second and the first term of a metaphor. This second language incorporated in the first also facilitates movement back and forth between Stevens' seriousness and comedy; it is a sign of the essential playfulness of his poetry ('one uses French for the pleasure that it gives') as well as creating greater possibilities of irony. Stevens' French in his journal is usually ironic, a refuge from tragedy, as when, wondering whether life is worth living and success worth a struggle, he decides, *'ça depend de cas'* (*SP*, p. 170).

The habit of talking to himself in French became part of the ordinary process of his thinking from the time he seriously considered becoming an author (and studied French) at Harvard; that is, as he discovered his need to write, he developed a second language, or rather, adopted a foreign speech – as his native tongue. French phrases are scattered through his letters as they are through his journal. His letter to his wife on 4 September 1913 is a good example of how he used and absorbed things French. He had just returned from a visit to Reading, Pennsylvania, where he grew up, and he had found it 'unsympathetic':

> The trouble is that I keep looking at it as I used to know it. I do not see it as it is. I must adjust myself; because I do not intend to shut myself off from the heaven of an old home. How thrilling it was to go to the old church last Sunday! I had no idea I was so susceptible. It made me feel like Thackeray in the presence of a duke.... The nobility of my infancy, that is: the survivors, all in the self-same rows.... For me, a mirror full of Hapsburgs.... Je tremblais.... Well, again, I do not intend to shut myself off from the heaven of an old home. And so, I keep recalling Du Bellay's sonnet in the Book of Regrets; for, when all is said and done, there is more for a common yellow dog like me in our Pennsylvania Anjou than in the 'fronts audacieux' of New York. Only I never intend to admit that I'm a common yellow dog.... Indeed, tonight I'd like to be in Paris, sipping a bock under a plane-tree, and listening to Madame's parrot from Madagascar.

His old home is as far away as heaven – the connection evoked perhaps by his visit to the local church – and the people whom he sees in church are described as reflections, as images in a mirror, and he trembles like an image in a mirror, shifting to French to note his emotion. Moreover, the mirror's contents were described in French when he employed the metaphor over six-and-a-half years earlier, in his journal entry of 5 February 1906: 'Fancy the Ego looking into that mirror – *plein de Hapsburgs'* (*SP*, p. 159). All foreign places, especially those to which he had never been, were for Stevens landmarks of the imagination. 'Du Bellay's sonnet' is 'Heureux qui, comme Ulysse, a fait un beau voyage', in which the poet in Rome longs for 'ma pauvre maison', in 'mon petit village':

> Plus me plaist le sejour qu'ont basty mes ayeux,
>   Que des palais romains le front audacieux,
>   Plus que le marbre dur me plaist l'ardoise fine[28]
> (The dwelling that my ancestors built pleases me more
>   Than Roman palaces with bold fronts,
>   More than hard marble, I am pleased by the delicate slate)

or, in Stevens' version,

The little house my father built of old, doth please
More than the emboldened front of Roman palaces:
More than substantial marble, thin slate wearing through.

He had spent 25 July 1909, 'a gorgeous, blue day', reading 'the French poets of the sixteenth century', and the afternoon making his translation, enclosing a copy that evening with his letter to Elsie Moll. Now, four years later, one old home suggests another. Again memory is French; Stevens remembers his translations *and* du Bellay remembering his French home. He identifies with the French poet (a fragment of du Bellay's poem is included in the text of Stevens' letter) and uses French form to order American experience: Pennsylvania is Anjou, New York, Rome – the far-away is imaginary. This, however, is not the end of the matter. There is one more declaration of nostalgia, and that too is French. The ordinary is what he is ('a common yellow dog'), yet he yearns to be in Paris, to go home to where he has never been. For a moment he exists in the exotic of its *vie quotidienne* – the bock, Madame and Malagasy parrot suggesting the complacencies of the coffee, oranges, woman and bright green cockatoo of 'Sunday Morning', the record of another imaginative journey.

Paris for Stevens was one of the capital cities of the imagination and the freedom of the city was the freedom to be a poet. As he writes to Heringman, who had gone to Paris to study,

> I suppose that if I ever go to Paris the first person I meet will be myself since I have been there in one way or another for so long. . . . The great thing in Paris, I imagine, is to be able to walk from one end of the place to another over and over again in every direction and somehow to try to partake of its life as a concitoyen and to the most intense degree possible from the inside.
>
> (10 Feb 1950)

From 1935 until his death he maintained a correspondence first with Anatole Vidal and then with his daughter, Paule, from whom he bought books and pictures, creating for himself the illusion of being a *concitoyen*. 'One of the real pleasure of my life', he declares to Paule Vidal (15 Dec 1950), 'is to have such an agreeable correspondent in Paris' ('one uses French for the pleasure that it gives'), and, when he learned that she might have to give up her shop, he writes to Barbara Church in the strongest terms: 'But I shall keep in contact with her whatever happens because to have no contact in Paris is like having no contact anywhere' (25 July 1951).

To be without Paris is to cease to exist. For Stevens, Paris is a supreme fiction whose existence provides both an outer limit to the imagination that saves it from madness and an inexhaustible space within which it can thrive. That boundary is a condition of its thriving, and every word of French, not simply the words of the poets, renewed his sense that the inner world is a cosmos, an ordered world. This idea emerges as he describes to Paule Vidal the arrival of his French newspaper after a long delay:

> After waiting for FIGARO a long time, several numbers came at the same time. This has brought Paris close to me. When I go home at night after the office, I spend a long time dawdling over the fascinating phrases which refresh me as nothing else could. I am one of the many people around the world who live from time to time in a Paris that has never existed and is composed of the things that other people, primarily Parisians themselves, have said about Paris. That particular Paris communicates an interest in life that may be wholly fiction, but, if so, it is precious fiction.
>
> (2 Apr 1953)

Paris is sacred because he has never been there; and so it stands for everything that is imaginary, made-up, artificial (made of and by art), and its language, French, is the language *par excellence* of the imagination. Having found reading the poems of Léon-Paul Fargue 'far more exciting than I could have foreseen', Stevens tells Thomas McGreevy,

> The French understand poetry, as they understand all the arts, so much more naturally, easily and thoroughly than other people do or seem to do. But there is something incredibly satisfying in what they have to say. Not that they have a monopoly. I mean what I say in the same sense that I would mean if I said that it means more to one to live in Paris than to live in New York. Both places are much alike, but the accents of one are not the accents of the other and, however much alike they may be, there is a difference and the difference is not to be bridged.   (5 Nov 1950)

French is admitted into Stevens' English on equal terms to bridge this unbridgeable difference between Paris and New York. French

and English are the same language because the poet lives in the
indivisible double world of imagination and reality.

The French in Stevens' poems is usually no more than an
occasional word or phrase, but in 'Sea Surface Full of Clouds' he
uses it systematically, employing a French refrain. The poem is
Stevens' first major work in blank-verse triads, one of his favourite
forms and the one he comes to prefer for his long poems, a result
apparently of thinking through his unsuccessful 1918 experiment
with *terza rima*, the unfinished 'For an Old Woman in a Wig'. He
uses these triads in two of the poems (I and V) of 'Lettres d'un Soldat'
in 1918 and then in a number of shorter poems in 1921, 'Palace of the
Babies', 'The Doctor of Geneva', 'Tea at the Palace of Hoon',
'Hibiscus on the Sleeping Shores' and 'The Bird with the Coppery,
Keen Claws'. The virtue of Dante's form is interconnection, the
continuous interweaving of the meaning that follows from the
interlocking triple rhymes – the form must be broken in order to stop
the poem. Stevens re-forms *terza rima* to allow more autonomy to
each triad, making starting and stopping easier. This changes the
nature of the repetition, although, for him as well as for Dante, the
form is a way of promoting repetition, of dwelling on certain
elements, making them linger. His are repetitions of phrase and
image – at their maximum in 'Sea Surface Full of Clouds'.

The poem is divided into five equal sections, each at once a new
act of vision and a memory, a working through of the previous
image, showing how the past impinges on and turns into the
present.

I

In that November off Tehuantepec,
The slopping of the sea grew still one night
And in the morning summer hued the deck

And made one think of rosy chocolate
And gilt umbrellas. Paradisal green
Gave suavity to the perplexed machine

Of ocean, which like limpid water lay.
Who, then, in that ambrosial latitude
Out of the light evolved the moving blooms,

Who, then, evolved the sea-blooms from the clouds
Diffusing balm in that Pacific calm?
C'était mon enfant, mon bijou, mon âme.

The sea-clouds whitened far below the calm
And moved, as blooms move, in the swimming green
And in its watery radiance, while the hue

Of heaven in an antique reflection rolled
Round those flotillas. And sometimes the sea
Poured brilliant iris on the glistening blue.

II

In that November off Tehuantepec
The slopping of the sea grew still one night.
At breakfast jelly yellow streaked the deck

And made one think of chop-house chocolate
And sham umbrellas. And a sham-like green
Capped summer-seeming on the tense machine

Of ocean, which in sinister flatness lay.
Who, then, beheld the rising of the clouds
That strode submerged in that malevolent sheen,

Who saw the mortal massives of the blooms
Of water moving on the water-floor?
C'était mon frère du ciel, ma vie, mon or.

The gongs rang loudly as the windy booms
Hoo-hooed it in the darkened ocean-blooms.
The gongs grew still. And then blue heaven spread

Its crystalline pendentives on the sea
And the macabre of the water-glooms
In an enormous undulation fled.

III

In that November off Tehuantepec,
The slopping of the sea grew still one night
And a pale silver patterned on the deck

And made one think of porcelain chocolate
And pied umbrellas. An uncertain green,
Piano-polished, held the tranced machine

Of ocean, as a prelude holds and holds.
Who, seeing silver petals of white blooms
Unfolding in the water, feeling sure

Of the milk within the saltiest spurge, heard, then,
The sea unfolding in the sunken clouds?
Oh! C'était mon extase et mon amour.

So deeply sunken were they that the shrouds,
The shrouding shadows, made the petals black
Until the rolling heaven made them blue,

A blue beyond the rainy hyacinth,
And smiting the crevasses of the leaves
Deluged the ocean with a sapphire blue.

IV

In that November off Tehuantepec
The night-long slopping of the sea grew still.
A mallow morning dozed upon the deck

And made one think of musky chocolate
And frail umbrellas. A too-fluent green
Suggested malice in the dry machine

Of ocean, pondering dank stratagem.
Who then beheld the figures of the clouds
Like blooms secluded in the thick marine?

Like blooms? Like damasks that were shaken off
From the loosed girldes in the spangling must.
C'était ma foi, la nonchalance divine.

The nakedness would rise and suddenly turn
Salt masks of beard and mouths of bellowing,
Would – But more suddenly the heaven rolled

Its bluest sea-clouds in the thinking green,
And the nakedness became the broadest blooms,
Mile-mallows that a mallow sun cajoled.

V

In that November of Tehuantepec
Night stilled the slopping of the sea. The day
Came, bowing and voluble, upon the deck,

Good clown . . . One thought of Chinese chocolate
And large umbrellas. And a motley green
Followed the drift of the obese machine

Of ocean, perfected in indolence.
What pistache one, ingenious and droll,
Beheld the sovereign clouds as jugglery

And the sea as turquoise-turbaned Sambo, neat
At tossing saucers – cloudy-conjuring sea?
C'était mon esprit bâtard, l'ignominie.

The sovereign clouds came clustering. The conch
Of loyal conjuration trumped. The wind
Of green blooms turning crisped the motley hue

To clearing opalescence. Then the sea
And heaven rolled as one and from the two
Came fresh transfigurings of freshest blue.

The form is more than blank-verse triads; it consists of the same
arrangement of data in each section, of a repetition of syntactical

elements and vocabulary such that a rhythm is established in the events narrated. They become a process rather than a chaos; change is measured by the form. The ocean is described as a machine: total fluidity is reduced to a mechanism, a system of particular, definite moving parts, and the reductiveness of the metaphor helps us to understand the rigidity of the form. This is a poem about perception that conceives of perception as an unending flow of sense data, as an infinite number of small gradations – like the differences between *Paradisal, sham-like, uncertain, too-fluent* and *motley* green – and this is not an abstract matter, but the poet's life, everybody's life, what consciousness is made of, another name for being. To be mastered by perception is madness. This is the unspoken threat of the chaos of the senses. The rigidity of the form is a response to the fear of amorphousness. Repetition and similarity are protection against excessive change.

Each section has the following structure:

```
1   In that November off Tehuantepec
2   The slopping of the sea grew still     night          (v   stilled)
3                                the deck

4   And made me think of [adjective] chocolate
                             (v   Good clown..., One thought)
5   And [adjective] umbrellas [adjective] green
6                      the [adjective] machine

7   Of ocean
8   Who                                                   (v   What)
9

10  Who                          (iii   Of the milk; iv   Like blooms)
11
12  C'était mon/ma

13  The
14
15

16
17  And
18                              blue.    (ii   fled; iv   cajoled)
```

The poem works like a sestina where the repeated words used in place of rhymes generate patterns of syntax and subject. Unlike a sestina, however, the repeated words occur somewhat at random, at both beginnings and ends of the lines (with more at the beginnings than the ends) and a repeated first line that acts as a refrain. The form includes two recurrent rhymes, one in each of the first two triads: *Tehuantepec*/*deck*, and *green*/*machine*, the first marking and connecting the only two solid locations in the poem: the land-mass of Mexico and the deck of the ship, the second fixing the ever-changing ocean. (The poem refers to the cruise that Stevens and his wife took in October – November 1923 from New York to California by way of the Panama Canal. The isthmus of Tehuantepec is the narrowest part of Mexico; the city of that name is on the Pacific coast on the Gulf of Tehuantepec.) Each stanza, in addition, has its own rhymes, their arrangement showing the *terza rima* still echoing in Stevens' ear, with, in each case, the French sentence carefully integrated by rhyme:

balm (internal	sheen*	sure	marine*	jugglery
rhyme)	blooms	clouds	*divine**	sea
calm	floor	*amour*	rolled	*l'ignominie*
âme	or	shrouds	green*	hue
green*	booms	blue	cajoled	sea
hue	blooms	blue		two
blue	spread			blue
	glooms			
	fled			

The asterisk indicates additional repetitions of the recurrent rhymes; note that it is only the one that refers to the changing sea that is repeated. *Blue* is the last word of every other section and the *hue*/*blue* rhyme marks the close of both the first and the last section.

There is more repetition in the first two triads, so as to establish the situation in which change takes place, and the amount of repetition makes us particularly aware of the many small variations between the sections. Because the world is irregular and because our experience is always incomplete, the structure is imperfect. Nothing is immutable. Stevens introduces small gradations, variations (noted on the right-hand side of the first table) in elements where we might expect constancy. Ending the second section with *fled* rather than *blue* is a good example of this anti-symmetry (using *blue* instead near the end of the next-to-last triad), and substituting *what* in the fifth section for *Who*, weakening the repetition by changing the word without changing the grammar. There are, in addition, repetitions of no fixed location: *clouds* and *blooms* appear in every section, which has particular force as the clouds are blooms; and *sea* is repeated at least twice, in line 2 and then in the second half of each section. *Night* occurs in the second line of every section, but its position and grammar are changed in sections IV and V, while line 12 in each section is French (although only the first two words are the same in every section).

The poem – and each section – begins with the noisy motion of the sea unexpectedly stilled; night becomes morning and thoughts of breakfast are mingled with the image of the clouds reflected in the sea like gigantic white flowers. At the centre of the poem is the idea of the mirror and the question: where does the image in the mirror come from? This question is answered in French, the kaleidoscope turns, and the image changes. There is no story, no *dénouement*. No particular meaning is assigned to the various memamorphoses in the poem; what is significant is that they have no particular meaning, that each section is the same as every other section, and yet different. The poem moves from a specific location in time and space – 'that November off Tehuantepec' – as close to pure sensation as language allows: to brilliant iris poured on glistening blue, crystalline blue brightness dispersing blue glooms, blue-black deluged with sapphire blue, bluest sea-clouds rolling in thinking green, and clearing opalescence suffused with freshest blue. The poet's subject is perception and, therefore, surfaces: deck, umbrellas (miniature man-made heavens), sea-surfaces, cloud-surfaces, sky-surfaces – we perceive only the outside of objects. This is their mystery, their otherness. The many colours are the poet's attempt to express the intensity of his sensations, a statement of wonder, pleasure and anxiety at such intensity. His preoccupation with colour is a preoccupation with distinguishing shades of feeling. The poem is a celebration of the vividness with which the world appears to him. The anxiety is in being so profoundly moved by something that is so inexpressibly what it is that it has no meaning, or, alternatively, is a totally alien, unintelligible mode of discourse. Moreover, any state approaching pure sensation is a source of anxiety in so far as it reminds us of the formation of the self, of the creation of a centre for our perceptions, the time of our first primitive discovery of who we are. This is why there is a coherent effort in the poem to go beneath the surfaces, a yearning for the depths that produces three-dimensional images: 'crystalline pendentives', 'the crevasses of the leaves' and 'Sambo . . . tossing saucers'. This is the function of the clouds: to bulk large in sky and sea, to be massive and voluminous so as to show us the fullness of the world and to denote the shaping processes. Flatness is sinister, the sham-like green sheen is malevolent, and a too-fluent, too-smooth green suggests malice. The superficial is mere seeming, a threat to reality, identity. Thus, each image of the clouds in the sea expresses a tension: for example,

> And then blue heaven spread

> Its crystalline pendentives on the sea
> And the macabre of the water-glooms
> In an enormous undulation fled

where *spread* and *on* emphasise the two dimensions of the sea mirror, *crystalline*, *pendentives*, *glooms* and *undulation*, the three dimensions of the world. The poem is a demonstration that perception is a continuous struggle between appearance and reality, in which the elusiveness of reality is indicated by the fantastic, evanescent nature of the three-dimensional images. Reality comes and goes.

To the poet, the world as he apprehends it appears as a creation, a work of art, which prompts him to ask who the creator is, and knowing that his perceptions are no one's but his own and recognising that the daydreams that inform them are his prompts him to answer that he is himself the creator. The question 'Where does the world come from?' thus becomes in the poem the question 'Who am I?' The clouds first become blossoms when the poet seeks to find who transformed the reality of the sky into the metaphor of the reflection:

> Who, then, in that ambrosial latitude
> Out of the light evolved the moving blooms

> Who, then, evolved the sea-blooms from the clouds
> Diffusing balm in the Pacific calm?

The question is asked twice: 'Who?', 'Who?' This is the hoo-hooing that echoes throughout Stevens' poetry. The data of the senses is so multitudinous, so alien, so potent, that it challenges the existence of the self, and the integration of this data creates self-knowledge, calling forth the poet in every man. For Stevens, moreover, every order is personal, idiosyncratic. The mirror demands a face. The clouds are an identity in the process of formation, of detaching itself from the matrix of the sea. This is why the poem is full of personifications and impersonations and why they are more numerous in the final two sections, where 'the figures of the clouds' show their faces:

> The nakedness would rise and suddenly return
> Salt masks of beard and mouths of bellowing

and where, at last, the day that brings the light of consciousness comes upon the deck, 'bowing and voluble', a good clown, and the sea is another comedian:

> What pistache one, ingenious and droll
> Beheld the sovereign clouds as jugglery
>
> And the sea as turquoise-turbaned Sambo neat
> At tossing saucers – cloudy-conjuring sea?

Reality is a comedy. The world is created for our entertainment, a trick that we play on ourselves, an ever-changing image, very much a matter of the eye of the beholder. We are self-observers. The question throughout is, 'Who is there?' Who is the actor–witness, the author–onlooker? 'Turquoise-turbaned Sambo' is a covert allusion to Stevens himself. *Sambo* is how he signed himself in his letter to Elsie Moll postmarked 3 December 1908 (*SP*, p. 199) and the character he assumed in an imaginary dream in which he took her parasol – recounted to her in a letter of 7 December 1908. *Juggler*, the Old French *jogleor*, is one of the oldest European words for poet.

The poem demonstrates the workings of the mind, and its central metaphor was present in Stevens' mind long before his ocean voyage. He writes to Elsie Moll on 12 January 1909,

> From one of many possible figures – regard the mind as a motionless sea, as it is so often. Let one round wave surge through it mystically – one mystical mental scene – one image. Then see it in abundant undulation, incessant motion – unbroken succession of scenes, say. – I indulge in heavenly psychology – I lie back and drown in the deluge. The mind rolls as the sea rolls. –

Bo-Peep passes with her crook tending only young lambs with silver bells around their necks, – a golden valley sparkles through me – twilight billows in a dark wave – and the foam of the next motion is all starlight, or else the low beam of the rising moon. – The mind rolls as the sea rolls! I must save that for a rainy Sunday. It is preposterous on a Tuesday evening, and while one is so white awake.

'Bo Peep' is one of his names for Elsie (the letter begins, 'My dear Bo') and her presence here, like that of the pilgrim and dancing maidens who follow, shows clearly how figures, *personae*, keep emerging from the surge of the waves.

– The magic-lantern show continues: (that 'white awake' up there ought to be 'wide awake' – you see it back a line or two – it is so learned to be correct) – What's this (We concern ourselves only with the marvellous.) A yellow mountain-side in the background, its outlines dissolving in soft sunlight. In the foreground, sits a pilgrim, resting and gazing at the mountain before him. Near-by, on quiet feet, a group of maidens dance, as yet unseen. It is the *Pays du Plaisir* – the Country of Good Pleasance.

Thought is a 'magic-lantern show', a succession of virtually disconnected (or connected) images, the ordering of which is beyond ordinary grammar, so that Stevens in his letter resorts to interjections and dashes to hold everything together – and when it comes to naming the country of the imagination, that name is French, '*Pays du Plaisir*'; as if thought is French ('One must keep in touch with Paris, if one is to have anything to think about'). Thus, the beholder in 'Sea Surface Full of Clouds' is identified in French and the inner world is separated from the outer world. This is the poet's way of showing us how foreign his perceptions sometimes feel to him. He is split by the existence of the world, like the clouds divided between sky and sea. The imagination speaks another language. The self is an inner stranger who changes with every perception, always strange because always changing, and who, therefore, can never be definitively named and is, as a result, faceless, an obscure reflection in a vague mirror. Question and answer change as the image of the clouds in the sea changes. The changes are slight, minor rather than major. Identity is a refrain, but not a constant.

The French sentence always has at least two nouns in apposition and in the first two sections it has three: the beholder who was my child, my jewel, my soul (I. 12) and my brother of the sky, my life, my gold (II. 12). Each set in the first two sections contains one noun making the apprehending power another person, but of the poet's immediate family (*enfant, frère*); one making it identical with the poet himself (*âme, vie*), with *âme* clearly suggesting that it is his inner *vie*; and one treating it as a precious substance (*bijou, or*), although *mon bijou* is also an ordinary term of endearment that like *enfant* and *frère* suggests deep affection. After this the poet's creation becomes wholly an affair of intangibles, a product of his emotion – and the number of nouns is reduced to two. The third section refers the image of the sea surface to his *extase* and his *amour*, the conjunction making the emotion double where in sections I and II the apposition suggests a single agent with many names. The syntax is altered again and the words chosen so that the second part of the phrase elucidates the first rather than providing a series of identities. The beholder in section IV is the poet's faith (*foi*) defined as divine nonchalance (*la nonchalance divine*). Belief becomes a freedom in keeping with the shaking-off of damasks, loosed girdles and nakedness; the certainties of faith take on an insouciant randomness. Finally, the darker forces in the poem come to the fore: the agent is my bastard spirit or mind, *ignominie*. *Esprit*, like *âme*, locates the poet's power unambiguously in the inner world; *bâtard*, like the French refrain, emphasises its alien nature. The spirit is his, but somehow other; his child, but not a legitimate one. the poem as a whole suggests that the ignominy is related to the pistache one's ingeniousness. The shame is in the sham. The poet feels dishonoured by his fluency in falsehood. For the reasons that Plato expelled the poets from his republic, he turns away from himself. Perhaps also there is ignominy, as well as sadness and fear, in feeling divided. However, the self-obloquy passes, and these misgivings of disloyalty to reality are short-lived, even if recurrent. They are dispersed by the trump of loyal conjuration, by the white magic of poetry, a new profession of faith in the changing world, and a renewed allegiance to its inconstancy under the sovereignty of the amorphous clouds. The reward is immediate:

Then the sea
And heaven rolled as one and from the two
Came fresh transfigurings of freshest blue.

The new blues reshape the world, transforming the identity of the
perceiver, and the immediacy of their beauty is itself an assertion of
meaning, of unity, more satisfying than the figures of fantasy that
they evoke.

For his French again Stevens is indebted to Baudelaire. 'Sea
Surface Full of Clouds' is a reworking of some of 'L'Invitation au
voyage'. This a poem of three stanzas that starts,

> Mon enfant, ma soeur,
> Songe à la douceur
> D'aller là-bas vivre ensemble!
> Aimer à loisir,
> Aimer et mourir
> Au pays qui te ressemble!
> Les soleils mouillés
> Des ces ciels brouillés
> Pour mon esprit ont les charmes
> Si mystérieux
> De tes traîtres yeux,
> Brillant à travers leurs larmes.

> (My child, my sister,
> Dream of the sweetness
> Of going down there to live together!
> To love at leisure,
> To love and die
> In a country that resembles you!
> The moist suns
> Of those blurred skies
> For my spirit have the charms
> So mysterious
> Of your traitorous eyes,
> Shining through their tears.)

and each stanza is followed by a refrain:

> Là, tout n'est qu'ordre et beauté,
> Luxe, calme et volupté.

> (There all is only order and beauty,
> Luxury, calm and voluptuousness.)

Stevens adapts a single feature of Baudelaire's poem. His refrain is a series of variations on the haunting, incantatory 'Mon enfant, ma soeur', set within, rather than at the end of, each section. Although Baudelaire's voyage is imaginary and Stevens' real, both poems are exercises in the imagination. Baudelaire depends on the contrast between the particulars of his stanzas and the five reiterated abstractions of his refrain; Stevens makes order out of change by repeating the form of his particulars and demonstrating a rich sensuousness, rather than a voluptuous sensuality. Baudelaire concentrates on the destination, Stevens on the journey. Baudelaire describes the room that he and his beloved will inhabit and the dream landscape of the far-away country, and only in the final stanza does he focus, and then only briefly, on the changes of the light:

> – Les soleils couchants
> Revêtent les champs,
> Les canaux, la ville entière,
> D'hyacinthe et d'or;
> Le monde s'endort
> Dans une chaude lumière.[29]

> (– The setting suns
> Clothe the fields,
> The canals, the entire city,
> With hyacinth and gold;
> The world falls asleep
> In a warm light.)

The colour hyacinth occurs in both poems. The comparison with Baudelaire brings out the elaborateness and specificity of Stevens' description and his greater concern with formlessness.

The child–sister of Baudelaire becomes the child–soul of Stevens, his sky brother as well as his ecstasy and his love, and is a response to this formlessness. This figure, both masculine and feminine, like 'the softest woman' in 'Esthétique du Mal' who has a 'vague moustache', is one of the many transformations of 'the interior paramour' who inhabits so many of Stevens' poems. The change in sex (or double sex) in this poem indicates how completely she has been appropriated, and that this inner personage has a different name in each section of the poem shows us that the self is a process. the interior paramour is the idea of order in the chaos of perception. The poet defines himself – his self – in relation to her. The French in this poem makes her of the imagination, yet outside the processes of the senses and other than the poet: intimately foreign, part of him, someone else, and masculine and feminine (and French, unlike English, marks the gender of all its nouns). She is the inner–outer model from which the poet builds his identity, the sea-surface reflecting, shaping his unformed cloudiness. Her presence provides the continuity – the voice or fictive music – of being. As the poet is in some respects a child in spirit, he reverses their roles, making her a child. The many references to food and words associated with eating in 'Sea Surface Full of Clouds' – *chocolate, ambrosial, breakfast, jelly, chop-house, milk, saltiest, obese, pistache* and *saucers*, while *mile-mallows* and *mallow* recall the confection *marshmallows* – suggest that the poem refers to the early period of identity formation. Perception is nourishment; the world of November off Tehuantepec is good enough to eat.

'Sea Surface Full of Clouds' marks the end of a period of which 'Sunday Morning' marks the beginning. Stevens has, for the moment, worked through myth and religion to a concern with the intimate, moment-to-moment data of the mind. His perspective is not the 1900 years since the Crucifixion, Palestine as seen from Connecticut, but a single day. He is wholly in the present of the New World, at sea in the paradise of sensation, without a destination and face to face with the disintegrating power of perception. Sound has been restored to the wide water and he abandons himself to the machine of his stanzas as a response to the 'machine / Of ocean'. Out of this will eventually come, after he resumes in 1930, a fully developed theory of poetry. With 'Sea Surface Full of Clouds' the luscious luxury of *Harmonium* disappears from Stevens' work. The exuberant, saucer-tossing Sambo is replaced by the more thoughtful, more heroic, brooding musician of the blue guitar. Stevens' poems incorporate an increasing power of abstraction as the sky-coloured pigeons that sink downward to darkness are replaced by 'fresh transfigurings of freshest blue'.

4

'My Reality–Imagination Complex'

There is a sense in which all of Stevens' poetry is about a single subject, and this is true of his work in a way that it is not true of the poetry of Whitman, Yeats, Hardy, Eliot or Williams. His discovery of this subject – the relation between imagination and reality – was infinitely fruitful. The more he wrote about it the more he had to say, and he saw it as distinguishing him from all other poets. As he writes to Bernard Heringman,

> While, of course, I come down from the past, the past is my own and not something marked Coleridge, Wordsworth, etc. I know of no one who has been particularly important to me. My reality – imagination complex is entirely my own even though I see it in others.   (21 July 1953)

That he describes it as a *complex* suggests that he was aware of the obsessive, almost pathological quality of his interest, and recognised this all-absorbing concern as fundamental to his psychology and an irresistible force of his nature.

For each individual the imagination comes first and the world afterwards. The baby, with its powerful but undeveloped and imprecise senses and without any experience or understanding of the world, dwells in a fantasy realm that is transformed only gradually into reality. This mutually enriching interplay between the imagination and reality is the process that creates the self – and art. For Stevens, the world, even when conceived as a whole, is a 'total double-thing', as he says in 'An Ordinary Evening in New Haven' (x). 'We do not know what is real and what is not', he declares, and tells of the man of bronze 'whose mind was made up and who, therefore, died'. 'We are not men of bronze and we are not dead.' He is constantly changing his mind, as if in the hope of being continuously reborn, and he accepts this process as his destination. To Sister Bernetta Quinn he writes,

133

I don't want to turn to stone under your very eyes by saying 'This is the centre that I seek and this alone.' Your mind is too much like my own for it to seem to be an evasion on my part to say merely that I do seek a centre and expect to go on seeking it. I don't say that I shall not find it or that I do not expect to find it. It is the great necessity even without specific identification.   (7 Apr 1948)

Winnicott considers this phenomenon in a series of talks to mothers on the BBC:

If you listen to philosophical discussions you sometimes hear people using a lot of words over the business of what is real and what is not real. One person says that real means what we can all touch, see, and hear, while another says that it is only what feels real that counts, like a nightmare, or hating the man who jumps the bus queue.

He asks, 'What relevance can these things have for the mother looking after her baby?' and 'why is it that the ordinary healthy person has at one and the same time a feeling of the realness of the world, and of the realness of what is imaginative and personal?' His answer is 'that we do not grow like that, not unless at the beginning each one of us has a mother able to introduce the world to us in small doses'.[1] This capacity for living simultaneously in their own imaginative worlds and in the outside world, especially marked in children of two, three or four, he refers back to the mother's early feeding of the child: 'the way in which the mother makes her breast available (or the bottle) just as the baby is preparing to conjure up something, and then lets it disappear as the idea of it fades from the baby's mind'. Thus the baby comes into contact with the world and the world validates his ideas. The mother will give 'about a thousand feeds' in nine months as well as performing innumerable other actions in caring for the child 'with the same delicate adaptation to exact needs':

For the lucky infant the world starts off behaving in such a way that it joins up with his imagination, and so the world is woven into the texture of the imagination, and the inner life of the baby is enriched with what is perceived in the external world.

Winnicott then returns to the people talking about what is *real*: 'If one of them had a mother who introduced the world to him when he was a baby in the ordinary good way ... then he will be able to see that real means two things, and he will be able to feel both kinds of reality at once.' For those whose mothers have not made a success of it all, 'either the world is there and everyone sees the same things, or else everything is imaginary and personal. We can leave these two people arguing'.[2]

This, of course, does not *explain* the poetry of Wallace Stevens, any more than it enables us to make any statement about his upbringing. What it does indicate is the area of experience to which his poetry refers and the psychological structures or processes involved, and, in showing the primary nature of these concerns, it helps us to understand the very powerful creative energies that they generated and the necessity of his poetry to him. Stevens knew 'that the real means two things', and yet, so it would appear from the poems, he was not able all the time 'to feel both kinds of reality at once'; rather he felt first one and then the other. The two people arguing are him. His poetry grows out of this tension, this dynamic antithesis. This argument, often poignant, sometimes painful, never rancorous, is conducted with great resourcefulness, gusto, vigour, spontaneity and – especially remarkable in view of its subject – self-effacement. Cassirer in his biography of Kant observes,

> From the earliest childhood and youthful memories of most great men there radiates a peculiar glow, illuminating them from inside as it were, even in cases where their youth was oppressed by need and harsh external circumstances. The magic is, as a rule, especially characteristic of great artists.[3]

Stevens is not an exception to this rule. His poetry is alive with the magic of his reality–imagination complex.

The desire to have a single subject is present in Stevens' work from beginning to end, apparent in his wish to call his first book, *Harmonium*, 'THE GRAND POEM: PRELIMINARY MINUTIAE', and *The Collected Poems* 'THE WHOLE OF HARMONIUM', and it is difficult to escape the conclusion that this need for his poems to form a whole is the need for them to express a unified self. As he writes to Richard Eberhardt on 20 January 1954, 'with a true poet his poetry is the same thing as his vital self', and so the poet does not merely describe what he feels, he creates and rebuilds his inmost being. As a poet Stevens was not interested in personal psychological analysis. while he understood that the subject of a poem is in a way only a pretext for the poem, and that there is another subject, he resisted anything other than a poetic interpretation.

He makes all this clear in 'The Irrational Element in Poetry', a talk that he gave at Harvard in 1936, the year before 'The Man with the Blue Guitar' was published. He explains the 'transaction between reality and the sensibility of the poet' by recounting something that had happened to him in Hartford a 'day or two before Thanksgiving'. There had been 'a light fall of snow' that had 'melted a little by day and then froze again at night, forming a thin, bright crust over the grass'. He had awakened 'several hours before daylight' – all of these details demonstrate the value of reality to the poet (his thought is shapeless without them) and only in reality does perception form a time sequence, so that if we do not live in the world, we have no history, no individuality. Stevens continues, 'as I lay in bed I heard the steps of a cat running over the snow under my window almost inaudibly. The faintness and strangeness of the sound made on me one of those impressions which one so often seizes as pretexts for poetry' (*OP*, p. 217).

Thus the choice of subject happens. There is within the poet lying awake an energy stirring, a text that demands a pretext and the intervening half-conscious thought that what he perceives now is related to some lost, or somehow unknown, set of perceptions. The poem is the establishment of a connection between otherwise unrelated events, or, as Stevens puts it, 'One is always writing about two things at the same time in poetry and it is this that produces the tension characteristic of poetry. One is the true subject and the other is the poetry of the subject.' In his example the 'thin bright crust over the grass' and the almost inaudible running footsteps of the cat are 'the poetry of the subject'; 'the true subject' is unstated. The tension between the two makes the course of the poem problematic, 'just as the choice of subject is unpredictable, at the outset, so its development, after it has been chosen, is unpredictable'. Stevens calls this unpredictability 'irrational'. This is his way of denoting the unconscious.

The advantages to the poet of having an idea of his true subject are considerable:

The difficulty of sticking to the true subject, when it is the poetry of the subject that is paramount in one's mind, need only to be mentioned to be understood. In a poet who makes the true subject paramount and who merely embellishes it, the subject is constant and development orderly. If the poetry of the subject is paramount, the true subject is not constant nor its development orderly. This is true in the case of Proust and Joyce, for example, in modern prose. (*OP*, p. 221)

The disadvantages of not knowing his subject were such that they appear, at least in part, to have prevented Stevens from collecting his poems any earlier than he did. On 9 April 1918 he writes to William Carlos Williams, apropos Williams' *Al Que Quiere!*, a letter that he almost did not send, because 'it is quarrelsomely full of my own ideas of discipline':

> What strikes me most about the poems themselves is their casual character. . . . Personally I have a distaste for miscellany. It is one of the reasons I do not bother about a book myself. . . . Given a fixed point of view, realistic, imagistic or what you will, everything adjusts itself to that point of view; and the process of adjustment is a world in flux, as it should be for a poet. But to fidget with points of view leads always to new beginnings and incessant new beginnings lead to sterility.[4]

Harmonium might be described as work in which the poetry of the subject is paramount. The poems represent many new beginnings, fruitful until 1924, then leading to a period of silence if not sterility. *Ideas of Order*, as the title suggests, is a deliberate searching for a constant subject and orderly development, for the fixed point of view that is fully achieved in *The Man with the Blue Guitar*. After 1937 everything adjusted itself to this point of view, and the process of adjustment was a world of poetry in flux in which the true subject – 'my reality–imagination complex' – is paramount.

As hard as Stevens worked to discover his true subject and as a decisive as that knowledge was, he resisted analysing it. This was his 'negative capability'. However far we think through an idea, there is always a point at which we stop, as if, however conscious we become, the unconscious always imposes a limit to our consciousness. A man is a poet, says Stevens in 'The Irrational Element in Poetry', 'because of his personal sensibility', and he flatly refuses to take the matter any farther: 'What gives a man his personal sensibility I don't know and it does not matter because no one knows.' Moreover, he implies that this is knowledge no one needs. He feels such knowledge to be a threat to his existence as a poet, because it might empower us to predetermine poets and 'if they could be predetermined, they might long since have become extinct' (*OP*, p. 217). 'There is', he tells Simons, 'a kind of secrecy between the poet and his poem which, once violated, affects the integrity of the poet'(8 Aug 1940).

The title of *Ideas of Order*, and what can be called the title poem of the collection, 'The Idea of Order at Key West', show Stevens on his way to the major discovery of 'The Man with the Blue Guitar': 'Poetry is the subject of the poem' (xxii). Trying to find 'the fixed point of view' that he spoke about to Williams, he recognises that there are many possible orders, potentially as many as there are persons, and that every order is provisional – and yet (this lingering, persisting *'and yet'* is ever present in Stevens) he feels that there is an order beyond the personal, a feeling that might be described as between a belief in science and a belief in the possibility of religion. Writing to Ronald Latimer on 15 November 1935, he defined the change from his first book to his second as follows:

In THE COMEDIAN AS THE LETTER C, Crispin was regarded as a 'profitless philosopher'. Life, for him, was not a straight course; it was picking his way in a haphazard manner through a mass of irrelevancies. Under such circumstances, life would mean nothing to him, however pleasant it might be. In THE IDEA OF ORDER AT KEY WEST life has ceased to be a matter of chance. It may be that every man introduces his own order into the life about him and that the idea of order in general is simply what Bishop Berkeley might have called a fortuitous concourse of personal orders. But still there is order.

He will not commit himself to any 'fixed philosophic proposition'; such a statement would be as destructive to poetry as an explanation 'in personal terms'.[5] Freedom is the life of poetry: 'These are tentative ideas for the purposes of poetry.' To establish a point of view is, none the less, to establish where and who you are; it means an end to omnipotence, entering into space and time. To be at a particular point in space and time is to be a particular person – it is a way of confirming or validating one's existence, of locating one's self in every sense. Stevens' search for his own subject takes him to the end of the mind – and beyond, producing a number of poems full of a strange, harsh music like the 'jangling' and 'buzzing' song of the blue guitar.

The primary idea of order is the idea of the self. This emerges in 'Autumn Refrain', published in 1931, in which there is, as in 'Sea Surface Full of Clouds' and 'The Man with the Blue Guitar', a continuous repetition of certain words and phrases, suggesting that the self is a refrain, the burden of perception, harmonising to a varying degree the separate items of sense data by connecting, associating, them. Music, or a persisting sound or noise, occurs as a metaphor with this meaning throughout Stevens' poetry, and autumn is a time of truth when the world reveals its essential form and we can see our condition in the changing, falling, disappearing leaves, 'the leaves / Of sure obliteration'.

> The skreak and skritter of evening gone
> And grackles gone and sorrows of the sun,
> The sorrows of sun, too, gone . . . the moon and moon,
> The yellow moon of words about the nightingale
> In measureless measures, not a bird for me
> But the name of a bird and the name of a nameless air
> I have never – shall never hear. And yet beneath
> The stillness that comes to me out of this, beneath
> The stillness of everything gone, and being still,
> Being and sitting still, something resides,
> Some skreaking and skrittering residuum,
> And grates these evasions of the nightingale
> Though I have never – shall never hear that bird.
> And the stillness is in the key, all of it is,
> The stillness is all in the key of that desolate sound.

Skreak is one of the many unusual words in Stevens that appear to be made up, but are in *The Oxford English Dictionary*, a copy of which was on Stevens' shelves. A *screak* is 'A shrill cry; a shrill grating sound', and '*Screak of day*' is daybreak. Stevens has modified the spelling slightly and used it to describe the other twilight of the dawn. *Skritter*, however, appears to be of his making, a combination of *scritch* (to screech) and *twitter*, with perhaps connotations of the American *skitter* ('A light skipping movement or the sound caused by this') and the more common *skittish* (capricious, high-spirited, playful) – a word appropriate to the final, unstable flickerings of the sun as well as to birdsong, for, although *skreak* and *skritter* can describe the raucous call of grackles, they are ascribed to the evening. The music and the light are merged in this phrase, in the 'yellow moon composed of words about the nightingale / In measureless measures' and in the pun on *air*, a merging that endows poetry virtually with the power of creating the world. The 'words about the nightingale' are Keats' 'Ode to a Nightingale', where the poet's meditation on the bird's singing recalls him to his 'sole self', and where, as the song dissolves, he becomes uncertain of its reality, uncertain whether he wakes or sleeps. Stevens opposes the American grackle to the British nightingale. There are no grackles in Europe, no nightingales in America and his 'I have never – shall never hear that bird' is like a declaration that he will never forsake his home ground. He rejects the murmurous surfeit and verdurous sweetness of Keats' poem for the native 'skreak and skritter'. The 'Ode to a Nightingale' is so much moonshine, wonderful, but inappropriate – 'not a bird for me'. His is a harsher desolation.

The poem opens with the statement of three absences. The phrase 'the moon and moon' after the ellipsis causes us to wonder whether the moon has gone as well. Perhaps it is that the moon in the sky reminds him of Keats' 'Queen-Moon' and that Keats' poem is like a moon, the sustaining light of the imagination in the mind's dark, yet none the less inadequate in the present circumstances. Putting it in this way ('the moon and moon') so as to emphasise the moon's doubleness (existing in the sky as well as the mind) introduces into the poem the *idea* of metaphor. The poet discovers – and the purpose of the poem is to commemorate this discovery – that beneath his thoughts, the 'stillness of everything gone' and his own being still, there is a something that exists and that harmonises the stillness. As the fading of the nightingale's song in Keats' 'Ode to a Nightingale' returns him to 'my sole self' with a bitter-sweet feeling of disillusionment, the disappearance of evening's 'skreak and skritter' in 'Autumn Refrain' causes the poet to discover that there is within him a desolate sound that is the key to everything else, the lowest note in the poem's scale of sounds – and stillnesses (which are not exactly silences), a sound that establishes a relation between all the other sounds, making their most discordant notes into a system of tonalities.[6] This is something that is left over when everything has gone and that apparently participates in, and partakes of, everything when everything is there. It is like a memory, a residue of previous events, 'Some skreaking and skrittering residuum', harsh, painful, lonely, desolate, but enduring and with the power of combining everything, a *tertium quid* between presence and absence. This is a statement of what it is to be, a definition of the self. Stevens separates 'being still' into 'Being and sitting still'. He desires greater authenticity than any 'name' can offer, a need that forces him beyond speech (names) to the language of music, but almost beyond language, as his 'desolate sound' is music at its most primary, most shapeless, virtually a cry – and is almost beyond him, as if personality is secondary. He does not say, *I think*, *I feel* or *I believe*. His formulation is impersonal: there exists, 'something resides'.

The idea is similar to that of Valéry –

Our history, our moment, our body, our hopes, our fears, our hands, our thoughts – everything is foreign to us.

Everything is exterior (in brusque meditation) to the indescribable something that is *me*, – and that is a myth; – for there is no quality, sensation, passion, remembrance . . . of which it does not feel itself independent when its life might depend upon it[7]

– only Stevens emphasises the saving, ordering and, by implication, consoling power of this essentially melancholy *it is*. The phrase 'grates these evasions of the nightingale' is slightly ambiguous: suggesting both that what remains of the many stillnesses that the poet inhabits, and that inhabit him, produces the poem ('these evasions of the nightingale') – the grating being like the playing of an instrument, the bow rubbing on the strings – and that the residue of being in the world grates on, clashes with, these poetic evasions because the imagination is always slightly out of phase with reality. This is one of the purposes of the poem, to tell us that our unity with the world, such as it is, is a function of this disharmony; and for Stevens any sound in nature, however discordant, is harmonious enough (most of the time) to have meaning, to provide at least intimations of order, although this meaning, this order, is still recognised as created.

'Autumn Refrain' is another demonstration that 'Americans are not British in sensibility'. It also shows that this declaration is a very self-conscious, poetry-conscious one – in fact, a statement of Stevens' involvement with British poetry. He defines his poem in terms of Keats' ode – 'these evasions of the nightingale' – which suggests that throughout the poem Stevens is opposing or (more neutrally) rethinking Keats, choosing his words with reference to Keats, which means that, however much aggression there may be in this process, Keats' poem, like any form, a metre or rhyme scheme, supports and guides Stevens, and is, in a sense, predictive in that it helps him decide what to do next. What 'Autumn Refrain' reveals is that the world for Stevens is charged with poetry, with language, that there is no simple perception of the world, that the poem from the beginning is involved with Keats, with poetry – it is in the nature of language that it can never be separated from perception; it is Stevens' nature that he is acutely aware of language, of perception as language (the world is constantly speaking to him) and of other poems.

His poem, Stevens states, is a set of evasions of a bird that he has never heard and shall never hear, the negation of a negation where the elimination of past and future is used to empty the present. The present is a space from which everything (skreak, skritter, grackles, sorrows) has gone – except some elusive residuum that is specified by evading the never-heard absent nightingale. This evasion can be said to be represented by the shift of subject from one clause to another across the two very long connected ('And yet') sentences of the poem, with the old words constantly repeated, brought forward into new contexts. Uncertainty about what if anything exists in the present is created by marking the difference between 'sorrows of the sun' and 'The sorrows of sun' and 'the moon and moon', as well as distinguishing the many kinds of stillness ('The stillness that comes to me out of this', 'The stillness of everything gone', 'being still', 'sitting still'), so that nothing is what it appears, or, rather, appearance becomes extremely complex and problematic, its indeterminacy emphasised by such antithetical expressions as 'measureless measures', 'the name of a nameless air' and the idea of stillness being a sound – 'Some skreaking and skrittering residuum'. Where in Keats a real nightingale unknowingly evades the poet, here the poet knowingly evades a represented or imaginary nightingale – by insisting on his lack of experience. The present is filled with thoughts of absence. Perhaps it is at the beginnings of our lives, the beginnings of our consciousness, that disembodied voices sustain our reality and pose existence as a problem – a problem that the poet solves by creating a space (the poem) in which voice and body can be united so as to form a real world.

'The Idea of Order at Key West', published in 1934, explores this same metaphor. The poet and a friend (one of the many couples in the poems) walking on the beach at nightfall hear a woman singing beyond the 'mimic motion' and 'constant cry' of the primeval, elemental, ever-changing ocean. Her voice and the voices of her surroundings intermingle and separate in a process that changes the world for the poet:

> It was her voice that made
> The sky acutest at its vanishing.
> She measured to the hour its solitude.
> She was the single artificer of the world
> In which she sang. And when she sang, the sea,
> Whatever self it had, became the self
> That was her song, for she was the maker. Then we,
> As we beheld her striding there alone,
> Knew that there never was a world for her
> Except the one she sang and, singing, made.

Despite their coexistence, the poet concludes that song and sea are essentially independent –

> The water never formed to mind or voice,
> Like a body wholly body,

– and yet he finds that what he heard was not sound alone:

> But it was more than that,
> More even than her voice, and ours, among
> The meaningless plungings of water and the wind,
> Theatrical distances, bronze shadows heaped
> On high horizons, mountainous atmospheres
> Of sky and sea.

The poet's function in this poem is to listen rather than create, a version of the old (inescapable) notion that the muse sings within the poet and that poetry is the notation of that song; and, as in 'Autumn Refrain', the song is both performance and residuum. The poet asks his companion why, when the woman stopped singing and they turned back toward the town, the lights in the fishing-boats at anchor there:

> Mastered the night and portioned out the sea,
> Fixing emblazoned zones and fiery poles,
> Arranging, deepening, enchanting night.

Order – the self – is a lingering music. The need for order is a passion as urgent and strong as anger, a rage that confers a blessing:

> Oh! Blessed rage for order, pale Ramon,
> The maker's rage to order words of the sea,
> Words of the fragrant portals, dimly-starred,
> And of ourselves and of our origins,
> In ghostlier demarcations, keener sounds.

Perhaps the rage exists because the desire is for ever unsatisfied, because there can be no final order – because the waves are inhuman and never form to mind or voice, although it is not the sea, or sky, but 'words' that are to be ordered. The world even in its disorder is conceived of as language, made and unmade in words. 'The fragrant portals' suggest Keats'

> Charmed magic casements, opening on the foam
> Of perilous seas, in faery lands forlorn.

and Tennyson's

> Yet all experience is an arch wherethrough
> Gleams that untravelled world, whose margin fades
> For ever and for ever when I move.[8]

The world is a window on the self. The words to be ordered are of the sea, the portals, ourselves and our origins, all of which refer the poem back to our very beginnings, our coming into being and entry into the world. Our knowledge of this remote past is like the shining of a far-away star, as elusive and ineffable as a fragrance, but ineluctably there, the memory of a voice, an underlying, inner music, a residuum. The deep need to come to terms with it is the source of the blessed rage. As in 'Autumn Refrain', the poet discovers the nature of the self in the interrelation between the person and the world. This is Stevens' way of asking and answering the question 'Who am I?' Here he asserts that, the ghostlier the distinctions, the sharper, the more exact and the more poignant: grey words embody the truth of a black and white world, by combining and merging its antithetical elements as well as indicating that much of the power of this world is in its mystery. 'Nuance' means cloudy, *nuageux*.

'Botanist on Alp (No. 1)' and 'Botanist on Alp (No. 2)', also composed in 1934, state clearly Stevens' desire to make some kind of comprehensive statement about existence. Wordsworth chooses the Simplon Pass as the setting for his discussion of the nature of the imagination; similarly, Stevens locates these poems in the Alps. As a botanist his protagonist can be expected to observe the small, hardy alpine plants capable of enduring very low temperatures (the cold is frequently a metaphor in Stevens for the uncompromising essentiality of things); as a man on an alp he will take in the view and look as far as he can. 'Botanist on Alp (No. 1)' begins, 'Panoramas are not what they used to be', and its third stanza celebrates the ordered world of Claude:

> But in Claude how near one was
> (In a world that was resting on pillars,
> That was seen through arches)
> To the central composition,
> The essential theme.

Stevens makes do with the *idea* of order. He creates poems by asserting an order and then analysing how the world evades it. He feels himself to be in a period between certainties. The gods have departed: 'Claude has been dead a long time' and 'Marx has ruined Nature, / For the moment', but he is continually looking around for something to believe in, seeking the vantage point for a new panoramic view, one that brings us close (like Claude)

> To *the* central composition,
> *The* essential theme.

What he finds is disorder; the definite articles disappear. The poem asks one question to which the poet has no answer except his poem:

> What composition is there in all this:
> Stockholm slender in a slender light,
> And Adriatic *riva* rising,
> Statues and stars,
> Without a theme?

Stockholm and the Adriatic, north and south (like Bordeaux and Yucatan, Connecticut and Florida), stand for the entire earth.

Statues are monuments to outmoded dogmas; stars are solitaries, sources of light in a world in which they do not participate. The botanist, who like all botanists is committed to system, sees only unconnected objects. The old orders are no longer available: Claude's pillars have collapsed, his arches are 'haggard', our old home (Stevens repeats the metaphor of 'Academic Discourse at Havana') is no longer habitable: 'The hotel is boarded and bare'. That it is a hotel marks it as a temporary dwelling – nevertheless, his response is not despair:

> The pillars are prostrate, the arches are haggard,
> The hotel is boarded and bare.
> Yet the panorama of despair
> Cannot be the specialty
> Of this ecstatic air.

This is a major characteristic of Stevens work: the profound feeling of the world's disorder and man's loneliness keeps company with a profound pleasure in apprehending the world. Perception is sweet, vivid to the pitch of ecstasy, and this pleasure informs all his metaphysics.

'Botanist on Alp (No. 2)' restates the same problem in slightly different terms. Above and below are the past; 'last night's crickets, far below' are as past as 'all the angels are' above. The alp is the present. Again the speaker feels himself to be alone in a time of ineffective orders. The faithful exist but without a faith. He calls on them to chant the 'poem of long celestial death', the poem of the passing of Christianity, shoring the fragments against the ruin:

> For who could tolerate the earth
> Without that poem, or without
>
> An earthier one . . . ?

'An earthier one', he suggests, might be composed of the glittering of the crosses on the convent roofs below in the sun, merely this, 'A mirror of a mere delight'. Again, the poem ends on the deep pleasure of perception, the glittering of objects in the sun, 'mere delight'. Even so, as his question suggests, this pleasurable earth is intolerable without some all-inclusive poem. this is the desperation that makes the need for order a rage.

Another pair of very short poems published in October 1934,

'Nudity at the Capital' and 'Nudity in the Colonies', each only two lines, discuss what poetry can disclose, a discussion that depends on the communication of opposites: the black servant addresses the white master at the centre of the old world; the white man speaks to the black in an outlying district of the new. The master in the first poem is like Freud's superego concerned with repression, he is covered up, *woolen*. His servant questions his policy:

> But nakedness, woolen massa, concerns an innermost atom.
> If that remains concealed, what does the bottom matter?

'Autumn Refrain' finds that there is something in each of us composed or formed of our first experiences that survives the subtraction of all subsequent experience and make it possible for us to order our perceptions. This idea of order in a number of Stevens' poems is presented as a song or poem, more or less harmonious music or more or less intelligible speech – as if communication were order and our first communication with the world the basis of all our understanding. 'Nudity in the Capital' assumes that in each of us there is a concealed *innermost* (note the superlative) atom, an invisible centre that is a constituent element (an atom) in a universal order (all matter being composed of atoms) – that being has a capital. These are definitions of the self. That the term is not used in these poems is indicative of Stevens' sense that what he is cannot be named in other people's words and that to discover himself he needs to go beyond what has been said before – even by himself. He feels that his subject is so amorphous that perhaps it cannot be named, or that in the process of naming it becomes something else and therefore demands continuous naming – poem after poem in which the terms are constantly changed. Throughout Stevens' writing (including his letters) the effort to name is balanced by a desire for impersonality. He keeps his self to himself. 'I have the greatest dislike for explanations', he tells Latimer (15 Nov 1935); 'there is nothing that kills an idea like expressing it in personal terms' (5 Nov 1935).

Winnicott, in his essay 'On Communication', comments on the behaviour of a patient who told him she kept a private book in which she copied poems and sayings. Her mother found and read the book and asked her about it, and the patient explained that it would have been all right if the mother had read the book but said nothing. Winnicott observes,

> Here is a picture of a child establishing a private self that is not communicating, and at the same time wanting to communicate and to be found. It is a sophisticated game of hide-and-seek in which *it is joy to be hidden but disaster not to be found.*

This ambivalence of motive characterises all art and is a way of explaining its symbolic or metaphoric structure. The success of the novel as a form can be attributed not only to the way in which it balances the real and the imaginary but also to the way in which it enables private truths to be hidden in public fictions. The use of the *persona* in poetry develops after Wordsworth for the same reasons. Art is the realm in which disclosures can be at once made and concealed (hidden even from the artist), in which the disaster can be averted and the joy obtained, a mode of communication that does not violate the innermost secrecy of the individual.

Winnicott concludes,

> I suggest that in health there is a core to the personality that corresponds to the true self of the split personality; I suggest that this core never communicates with the world of perceived objects, and that the individual knows that it must never be communicated with or be influenced by external reality. . . . I would say that the traumatic experiences that lead to the organization of primitive defences belong to the threat to the isolated core, the threat of its being found, altered, communicated with. The defence consists in a further hiding of the secret self, even in the extreme to its projection and to its endless dissemination. Rape, being eaten by cannibals, these are mere bagatelles as compared with the violation of the self's core, the alteration of the self's central elements by communication seeping through the defences.[9]

Thus, the black man in 'Nudity in the Capital', an incarnation, if we like, of the savage, repressed id, reassures his master that their secrets are safe, that the capital is secure. This is also a justification for a greater freedom and openness in poetry. Such nudity will not give away or expose anything that matters. The white man's reply, 'Nudity in the Colonies', concerns the state of things a long way from the capital:

> Black man, bright nouveautés leave one, at best,
>   pseudonymous,
> Thus one is most disclosed when one is most anonymous.

The 'bright nouveautés' that attract the black man (as opposed to plain wool?) may be a disguise, a *persona*, but at best they still require that one assume a name; they create an identity as a writer, a pen name. The white man declares that the greatest anonymity produces the greatest revelation. Perhaps this is because the very foreignness of the new (indicated by the French word) is an intimation of the self's dark, alien inexpressible centre, and because this core is nameless.

'Re-statement of Romance', which Stevens placed immediately after these two poems in *Ideas of Order*, and which was first published in March 1935, offers another solution, another reworking of the problem, raised in 'Autumn Refrain' and 'The Idea of Order at Key West', of the self's relation to the world:

> The night knows nothing of the chants of night.
> It is what it is as I am what I am:
> And in perceiving this I best perceive myself
>
> And you. Only we two may interchange
> Each in the other what each has to give.
> Only we two are one, not you and night,
>
> Nor night and I, but you and I, alone,
> So much alone, so deeply by ourselves,
> So far beyond the casual solitudes,
>
> That night is only the background of our selves,
> Supremely true each to its separate self,
> In the pale light that each upon the other throws.

This is a poem about the loneliness of love. The world's music – 'The skreak and skritter of evening', 'the chants of night' – is an imaginary music about which the night knows nothing. The 'night is only the background to our selves', as the sea in 'The Idea of Order at Key West' 'was merely a place by which she walked to sing'. The world is a place of 'casual solitudes'. Any notion of communication with it is only wishful thinking, a daydream that interferes with self-knowledge and the knowledge of any deep relation we may have with others. Order is in the song of the perceiver; meaning is wholly an affair of the mind. This is why the couple's relation is precious. Each object of the world is incommunicably what it is, everlastingly separate, except for the two lovers who are one, even though separate: 'Supremely true each to its separate self'. They are limited to their own resources, giving of themselves ('what each has to give') not of the world, an 'interchange' rather than 'exchange', and its location '*in* the other' makes this a matter of private rather than public processes. Similarly, 'the pale light that each upon the other throws' – the pallor of the imagination's moonlight – suggests an interchange of auras, that the contiguity of presences is decisive and that unspoken is as important as spoken communication. Certainly there is no reference to speech – nor to feeling. It is the word 'romance' and the description of the closeness of the couple that cause us to accept this as a love poem, showing the power that ideas of proximity and mutuality have over us – as well as their source.

On 17 March 1937 Stevens writes to Latimer,

> During the winter I have written something like 35 or 40 short pieces, of which about 25 seem to be coming through. They deal with the relation or balance between imagined things and real things which, as you know, is a constant source of trouble to me. I don't feel that I have as yet got to the end of the subject.

He hopes, he says, in the next few months to double the number of poems, but is finding the task of composition more difficult than usual: 'Apparently, only the ones over which I take a great deal of trouble come through finally. this is contrary to my usual experience, which is to allow a thing to fill me up and then express it in the most slap-dash way.' He completed a series of thirty-three poems to his satisfaction, and the sequence was published as 'The Man with the Blue Guitar' in October 1937.

The work is Stevens' first full diagnosis of his 'reality – imagination complex' and the first of his three great poems on poetics (the other two are 'Notes Toward a Supreme Fiction' and 'An Ordinary Evening in New Haven'). The point of departure for the poem was probably Picasso's painting *The Old Blind Guitar Player* (1903), which Stevens could have seen in the Zervos 'Picasso, Blue and Rose Periods' exhibition at the Seligman Gallery in New York in 1936.[10] The guitartist is the poet and his guitar is blue because poetry is an instrument of the imagination. The poem is the occasion for Stevens' discovery that any statement of the relation of imagination and reality is a statement of the nature of poetry, and that the poetic process reduplicates that of the growth of the self, so that in creating a poem he is re-creating or composing himself. This is a view of poetry that, according to Marcel Raymond, originated after the criticism of the Church by the *philosophes* when people turned to art (although not to art alone) to meet many of the demands previously exorcised by religion:

Poetry from then on tended to become an ethic or indefinable, irregular means of metaphysical knowledge, tormented by the need to 'change life', as Rimbaud desired, to change man and to put him in touch with being (*de lui faire toucher l'être*). What is new in this is less the fact than the intention, that gradually freed itself from the unconscious, to regain possession of obscure powers and to attempt to overcome the duality of the *me* and the universe.[11]

The phychological reality of these obscure powers and of the need to change life and touch existence is why Stevens tells Latimer that he does not want him to think that the poems comprising 'The Man with the Blue Guitar' are abstractions:

Actually, they are not abstractions, even though what I have just said about them suggests that. Perhaps it would be better to say that what they really deal with is the painter's problem of realization: I have been trying to see the world about me both as I see it and as it is.

'Realization' in every sense is Stevens' aim. For him the poem is where doubt is brought to a successful (artistic) conclusion. Both a creation of mind and an object in the world, and composed of signs marked by contact, at some stage, with reality, the poem is itself the sign of the reality–imagination complex. 'Poetry is the subject of the poem' (xxii. 1) and 'the theory / Of poetry is the theory of life'. Twelve years later, in 'An Ordinary Evening in New Haven', Stevens affirmed that he was never going to get 'to the end of the subject':

This endlessly elaborating poem
Displays the theory of poetry,
As the life of of poetry. A more severe,

More harassing master would extemporize
Subtler, more urgent proof that the theory
Of poetry is the theory of life . . . .

                                   (XXVIII. 10–15)

'The Man with the Blue Guitar' consists of thirty-three numbered sections, or 'poems' as Stevens repeatedly calls them in his letters to Poggioli, each composed of from four to eight two-line stanzas. (There are two with four stanzas, seven with five, fourteen with six, six with seven, and four with eight.) The whole poem is characterised by a certain limited freedom: variation in the length of the sections, variation in the length of the lines (a basic octosyllabic line varied to include as many as twelve syllables), occasional rhyme and a lack of connection between sections that is a consequence of Stevens' making each one virtually independent. This apparent looseness of structure, together with all the repetition, creates the feeling that the poem could go on indefinitely and that any end is arbitrary. Certainly the end that Stevens provides (poem XXXIII) is no more conclusive or final then many of the others. The emphasis is on the continuing activity of the guitarist–poet and the impression is of a man improvising a world in which to live. The short lines, terse, epigrammatic statements, the independence of the individual sections and the repeated words balance this looseness. They are all part of the poet's insistent concentration on his subject, and it is this concentration, the effort to make a definitive statement in every section, that makes Stevens' point: that every conclusion is temporary because the interrelations of the imagination and reality are beyond words. The whole poem can be said to be a development of Stevens' rhyming of 'things as they are' with 'blue guitar'; only in poetry, in the momentary harmony of rhyme, can their antithetical separateness be reconciled. The rhyme creates as much order as is possible in these intractable circumstances in which reality is incommensurate with the mind. By defining the situation the poem prevents it from becoming intolerable.

Again and again Stevens repeats the words *blue guitar* or *guitar*, reminding us that imagination is an activity and that this activity is continuous. The guitar and its music are our only stability. These repetitions function as a refrain and as a substitute for thoroughgoing rhyme. Because the same words are repeated, there is no suggestion of any elaborate pattern or order, but rather of the solipsistic loneliness of the guitarist. This is the monotony of stability in a changing world and a constant reaffirmation of the poet's existence. Stevens, in addition to repeating the same words, employs many words closely associated with them: a set of words referring to the playing of the guitar and music generally, and another set denoting shades of blue and blue objects. The nature of this order can be seen in the following table. The roman numbers stand for the individual sections or poems. The arabic numbers in parentheses indicate the number of times each word is repeated; a word that is not followed by a number in parentheses occurs only once in that section. The repetitions of *guitar* and *blue guitar* are noted first and then words ordinarily associated with playing the guitar and blue. This does not begin to show the subtlety of the order (especially as a poem is a machine for maximising the connections between words, and every word in a successful poem is in a vital relation to every other word). To simplify the table, many words where the association is extra-ordinary (for instance, *hi and ho* and *tick it, tock it* – III) or less explicit than with the words cited (for example, *A fat thumb beats out ai-yi-yi* – XXV), are somewhat arbitrarily excluded. Similarly, *choirs* (VIII), *bell, trombones* (X) and *orchestra* (XII) are excluded because they refer to instruments other than the guitar, and so is the allusion, in *Good-bye, harvest moon* (XV), to the popular song 'Shine On, Harvest Moon', which has no particular association with the guitar, although all these expressions obviously belong to the set of words about music. Limited as it is to words most easily and obviously associated with the instrument of the title, the blue guitar, the scheme takes no account of other tropes, the associations created by the poem itself or the effects of the position of the words within the section; however, even this very rudimentary listing shows the order to be all-pervasive.

I	III	IV
guitar	play	blue guitar (2)
blue guitar (3)	strike	picks
play (2)	bang	string
tune (2)	jangling	
	strings	
II	savage blue	
blue guitar		V
serenade (2)		guitar
		music

VI
guitar
blue guitar (3)
tune (3)
play
composing

VII
blue guitar

VIII
turgid sky
drenching thunder
chords
twang (2)

IX
blue guitar
color (2)
overcast blue
shadow
strings

X
blue guitar
prelude

XI
sea (2)
chord
discord

XII
blue guitar
strum

XIII
pale intrusions into
blue
blue buds
pitchy blooms
of blue, blue sleek

XIV
blue guitar
sky
sea
chiaroscuro
plays

XV
blue guitar

XVI
chop the sullen psaltery

XVII
blue guitar (2)
composing

XVIII
blue guitar
strumming
sea

XIX
player
lutes
play
lute

XX
pale guitar

XXI
shadow (2)
shadows

XXII
sky

XXIII
duet
song
playing

XXIV
play

XXV

XXVI
music

XXVII
sea (6)
gloom

XXVIII
blue guitar

XXIX
song

XXX

XXXI
blue guitar
compose
player
rhapsody (2)

XXXII
blue guitar

XXXIII
play
jay

The phrase *blue guitar* itself is repeated twenty times in thirty-three sections, seventeen of the repetitions are in the first eighteen sections, while the other three are in the final six. The poem is generated by a single, static situation: the man playing the blue guitar, and is given form by the poet continuously reminding us of that situation. Most of the repetitions of *blue guitar* are in the first half of the poem. There are three in the first section, nine in the first six sections, and the third section contains probably more of the guitar's sound than any other; in this way the situation is established clearly and unambiguously at the start (other ambiguities are more important). The poem is built on this foundation. The infrequency of the repetition towards the end also shows us that the poet enters into the world through the process of the poem. Everyday reality is there at the end in a way it is not at the beginning.

The repetitions of the older type of poetic form (metre, rhyme, stanza) establish a formal and regular boundary between the poem and the world. They help to change poetry into another and special language and came to be thought of by many poets as exterior to the words of the poem and as imposed upon the words. Stevens, in so far as he employs these older types of form, uses them irregularly in an unpatterned way. He does not believe in a symmetrical reality. For him form is an approximation. He fears that the world is formless and that his identity (as the word implies) depends on his finding an ordered counterpart to himself. Chaos is looking into the mirror and not seeing your reflection. His forms reveal his doubts – and, because he is uncertain, he doubts even this, and so imagines a world in which everything corresponds to something else as the baby corresponds to the mother or the first term of a metaphor to the second. This would be a wholly intelligible world – and his poetry is predicated on the longing for such a home. It vacillates between illusion and disillusionment, rich in the consciousness of its predicament. The keenness of Stevens' sense of disorder causes him to find new methods of ordering his poems and, like most poets since *Leaves of Grass*, he searches for techniques of inner order. Instead of repeating the same sounds at the edge of the text, thereby creating a frontier, he repeats the same words at various points throughout the text. He works from within to achieve greater integration. The Spenserian stanza can be used for many different poems; the order of 'The Man with the Blue Guitar' is unrepeatable and cannot be copied, and, as the table above shows, is too complicated to be abstracted simply from the poem. It is a unique order composed of unique elements, unalterable and, like history, irreversible. Stevens' order is an anti-plot, a system that connects without allowing any pattern to be formed. A more or less static situation is constantly transformed so as not to produce a narrative. The repetition, however, makes us feel that each section is somehow the equivalent of every other section. The order is analogous to that of 'Thirteen Ways of Looking at a Blackbird'.

The man with the blue guitar is a solitary figure, but he is alone in a world full of other people and in the poem they speak first:

I

> The man bent over his guitar,
> A shearsman of sorts. The day was green.
>
> They said, 'You have a blue guitar,
> You do not play things as they are.'
>
> The man replied, 'Things as they are
> Are changed upon the blue guitar.'
>
> And they said then, 'But play you must,
> A tune beyond us, yet ourselves,
>
> A tune upon the blue guitar
> Of things exactly as they are.'

Those who hear the man with the blue guitar state that he does not play things as they are. The day is green, the guitar is blue – this disparity is the poem's subject. Poetry cannot reproduce the world as it is. The reality it offers is different, changed, unlike the world we know by living in it. The people, however, if they cannot have 'things *as* they are', demand 'a tune . . . *Of* things *exactly* as they are', where the *of* allows for the disparity and *exactly* insists on fidelity and accuracy. They want as much reality as possible in the interests of self-knowledge. They desire the elucidation of a world whose existence is ambiguous because it is inseparable from their own consciousness. Their sense of who they are includes an element that is foreign, radically other, not-them. As Stevens puts it in a letter to Simons, 'The poet was required to express people beyond themselves, because that is exactly the way they are' (8 Aug 1940).

It is, however, the audience rather than the performer who find it difficult to accept that the day is green and the guitar blue, and the presentation of all this as a dialogue between the artist and his public shows us that meaning is a shared creation. That the poetic mind is envisaged as an instrument and that the making of poems is seen as a manual activity is a way of depersonalising and externalising the poems. Throughout the poem, feeling where possible is presented as action. Similarly, clipped, aphoristic assertions and neutral reporting of the dialogue (*They said, The man replied, They said then*) enable Stevens to keep himself out of the poem. This dispassionate tone is his way of avoiding sentimentality on an intensely personal matter.

Stevens tells Poggioli that his description of the guitar is as 'A shearsman of sorts' 'refers to the posture of the speaker, squatting like a tailor (a shearsman) as he works on his cloth' (25 June 1935). This image of the poet as a tailor is developed in the next section, where the player speaks of patching the world. His thoughts are presented in the first person without quotation marks, although they are a continuation of his reply in the previous section – thus we enter the inner world.

II

> I cannot bring a world quite round,
> Although I patch it as I can.
>
> I sing a hero's head, large eye
> And bearded bronze, but not a man,
>
> Although I patch him as I can
> And reach through him almost to man.
>
> If to serenade almost to man
> Is to miss, by that, things as they are,
>
> Say that it is the serenade
> Of a man that plays a blue guitar.

That his search for reality leads the poet to sing of the hero shows us the anthroprocentric nature of Stevens' view. He cannot imagine a world without imagining its creator or perceiver. Every thought contains the image of its thinker. Things as they are depend on man as he is. The poet's goal is reality, but he abstracts and idealises so much, is so self-centred, that the result is a round head rather than a round world and a mythic figure instead of man himself. The song reaches only *almost* to man.

The large-eyed, bronze-bearded hero is the first in a series of idealised images of human nature that appear intermittently throughout the poem and from which the poet tries to disengage himself – often violently. He fights to free himself. There is no consciousness without a self. Every thing is a mirror that reflects a face. Attempting to represent the day's stormy weather (VIII and IX), the guitarist thinks of himself as merely 'a shadow hunched' over the guitar's strings, the 'maker of a thing yet to be made', then he finds himself taking shape in the thought of the overcast blue sky:

> The color like a thought that grows
> Out of a mood, the tragic robe
>
> Of the actor, half his gesture, half
> His speech, the dress of his meaning, silk
>
> Sodden with his melancholy words,
> The weather of his stage, himself.

> (IX. 7–12)

He is half his perceptions, half the weather of the world – the ever-changing reality – and without it he is incomplete, an actor without a role. As Stevens comments to Poggioli,

> The imagination is not a free agent[.] It is not a faculty that functions spontaneously without references. In IX the reference is to environment: the overcast blue: the weather = the stage on which, in this instance, the imagination plays. The color of the weather is the role of the actor, which, after all, is a large part of him. The imagination depends on reality.   (12 July 1953)

Our every thought is derived from the world; it is of necessity (there is nothing else) the substance of our most insubstantial thoughts. As Stevens remarks in 'Notes Toward a Supreme Fiction', 'We are the mimics. Clouds are pedagogues' (1. IV. 16).

The song of the large-eyed bronze-bearded hero is followed by an imagined scene of violence:

III

Ah, but to play man number one,
To drive the dagger in his heart,

To lay his brain upon the board
And pick the acrid colors out,

To nail his thought across the door,
Its wings spread wide to rain and snow,

To strike his living hi and ho,
To tick it, tock it, turn it true,

To bang it from a savage blue,
Jangling the metal of the strings . . . .

Stevens' image is one of ordinary country life, as he explains to Simons: 'On farms in Pennsylvania a hawk is nailed up, I believe, to frighten off other hawks. Here in New England a bird is more likely to be nailed up merely as an extraordinary object to be exhibited; that is what I had in mind' (8 Aug 1940).

'His living hi and ho. This means', he tells Poggioli, 'to express man in the liveliness of lively experience, with pose; and to tick it, tock it, etc. means to make an exact record of the liveliness of the occasion' (25 June 1953). Paradoxically, the man dies in order that the essence of his liveliness can be expressed. The poet murders to dissect. He tries to achieve all his purposes at once by a direct and total assault upon the man who is another version of the hero, both *alter ego* and ancestor. 'Man number one' is, in the terms of 'Notes Toward a Supreme Fiction', major man, the thinker of the first idea – the first cause personified and the problem of origins solved in human terms. The dissection emphasises that the truth of life is to be found within, and it is almost as if the man's power is taken from him by an act of cannibalism. The violence of its appropriation is matched by the savageness of its substance: it is *acrid*, bitter to the taste, stinging to the eyes, and banging, jangling discord to the ear.

The hawk reappears in xxiv, where Stevens says that he thinks of a poem that will contain at least one phrase that is 'A hawk of life' (XXIV. 6): 'one of those phrases that grips in its talons some aspect of life that it took a hawk's eye to see. To call a phrase a hawk of life is itself an example', he writes to Poggioli (25 June 1953). The metaphor indicates the aggression in seeing and knowing, as well as suggesting that for Stevens seeing is the major mode of knowing (this emphasis on seeing is also revealed in the statement that man number one's brain is full of 'acrid *colors*'). Seeing, moreover (including reading), is equated with eating: the poem is a book to be devoured by the 'brooding-sight' of the young scholar 'hungriest for that book'. Poet and scholar are joined by a kind of talion principle; the making and comprehension of each phrase are the products of rapacious acts of vision.

XXIV

A poem like a missal found
In the mud, a missal for that young man,

That scholar hungriest for that book,
The very book, or, less, a page

Or, at the least, a phrase, that phrase,
A hawk of life, that latined phrase:

To know; a missal for brooding-sight.
To meet the hawk's eye and to flinch

Not at the eye but at the joy of it.
I play. But this is what I think.

'To know a thing', Stevens writes to Simons, 'is to be able to seize it as a hawk seizes a thing. The sort of scholar to whom one addresses oneself for all his latined learning finds in "brooding-sight" a knowledge that seizes life, with joy in his eye'; and he concludes with another metaphor of savagery: 'A paraphrase like this is a sort of murder' (8 Aug 1940).

Despite the violence that it brings, the possibility of a hero continues to attract Stevens as if entry into reality involves an initiation that could only be effected by another person. He tells Poggioli, 'If we are to think of a supreme fiction, instead of creating it, as the Greeks did, for example, in the form of a mythology, we might choose to create it in the image of man: an agreed-on superman' (12 July 1953). This is the man who is mocked in x, where Stevens imagines him and finds him unbelievable. His scepticism makes him a mock Caesar in a mock Roman triumph:

X

Raise reddest columns. Toll a bell
And clap the hollows full of tin.

Throw papers in the streets, the wills
Of the dead, majestic in their seals.

And the beautiful trombones – behold
The approach of him whom none believes,

Whom all believe that all believe,
A pagan in a varnished car.

Roll a drum upon the blue guitar.
Lean from the steeple. Cry aloud,

'Here am I, my adversary, that
Confront you, hoo-ing the slick trombones,

Yet with a petty misery
At heart, a petty misery,

Ever the prelude to your end,
The touch that topples men and rock.'

When the hero is in the present he is the poet's adversary, because he usurps the poet's function (this is implied rather than clearly stated) and because he is unbelievable, he is unable to perform his function of creating meaning. Stevens tells Poggioli why he rejects 'an agreed-on superman':

He would not be the typical hero taking part in parades, (columns red with red-fire, bells tolling, tin cans, confetti) in whom actually no one believes as a truly great man, but in whom everybody pretends to believe, someone completely outside of the intimacies of profound faith, a politician, a soldier, Harry Truman as god. *This second-rate creature is the adversary.* I address him but with hostility . . . I deride & challenge him and the words hoo-ing the slick trombones express derision & challenge.   (12 July 1953)

The 'petty misery' is 'the cheap glory of the false hero, not a true man of imagination' that 'made me sick at heart. It is just that petty misery, repeated in the hearts of other men, that topples the worthless.' The imagination depends on reality, society, on imagination. The supreme fiction is the unprovable axiom from which is derived the system of meaning without which society topples and the individual life has no value. Stevens perceives from within his virtual if intermittent solipsism that meaning is the shared creation of a group, and his search for faith is the desire for a sense of solidarity with other men and women. He can only imagine belief, and the imagination *as imagination*, self-conscious, knowing what it is doing, is necessarily sceptical, only temporarily whole-hearted. This is why the poet in Stevens is comedian, actor, sleight-of-hand man, acrobat and juggler, always *playing*:

> He held the world upon his nose
> And this-a-way he gave a fling.
>
> His robes and symbols, ai-yi-yi –
> And that-a-way he twirled the thing.

> (xxv. 1–4)

Keeping the world going, balanced, requires continuous effort, poem after poem, like the sections of 'The Man with the Blue Guitar'. To Poggioli, Stevens writes, 'A personage regards the world and revolves it this way and that, a great personage, as his vestments show. He conceives that it is fluid, its changes like generations, but there is an eternal observer – man' (22 July 1953); who is he? 'Any observer: Copernicus, Columbus, Professor Whitehead, myself, yourself' (12 July 1953). *Any observer*: everyone who looks at the world, not the poet alone, has to undertake to keep it balanced, in order; perception is work, poetry, a mode of perception, and again the perceiver is presented as a figure – symbol, notation, personage – a hero.

The poem's view of the violence of the act of knowledge is entirely in keeping with Picasso's definition cited in xv of a painting as a 'hoard / Of destructions', which leads Stevens in xvi to consider the earth as 'an oppressor' and in xvii and xix to think of the poet's task as a struggle between the fierce animality of human nature and the monstrous force of nature. Our aggression is at the formless core of what we are:

> The person has a mould. But not
> Its animal. The angelic ones
>
> Speak of the soul, the mind. It is
> An animal. The blue guitar –
>
> On that its claws propound, its fangs
> Articulate its desert days.
>
>   (XVII. 1–6)

To Simons, Stevens comments, 'The person has a mould = the body has a form. All men have essentially the same form. But the spirit does not have a form' (8 Aug 1940). Stevens converts the Latin word for soul, *anima*, into the English *animal*. The curving fingers of the guitarist and the hawk's talons become the predatory *claws* and *fangs*, and this predator is within. This is our savage centre. We are inhabited by a violent inner voraciousness, a hunger that makes the world a desert. Similarly, the world confronts us like a wild animal of overwhelming strength. The poet attempts to cope with this power by taking it in to himself. He tames it through imagination, by giving it a form; thus the inner and outer world become opposing monsters and almost simultaneously are immobilised, in the lute and in stone:

XIX

> That I may reduce the monster to
> Myself, and then may be myself
>
> In face of the monster, be more than part
> Of it, more than the monstrous player of

> One of its monstrous lutes, not be
> Alone, but reduce the monster and be,
>
> Two things, the two together as one,
> And play of the monster and of myself,
>
> Or better not of myself at all,
> But of that as its intelligence,
>
> Being the lion in the lute
> Before the lion locked in stone.

He says, again to Simons,

The monster is what one faces: the lion locked in stone (life) which one wishes to match in intelligence and force, speaking (as a poet) with a voice matching its own. One thing about life is that the mind of one man, if strong enough, can become the master of all the life in the world. To some extent, this is an everyday phenomenon. Any really great poet musician, etc. does this. (8 Aug 1940).

To Poggioli he sums up the section in this way:

Monster = nature, which I desire to reduce: master, subjugate, acquire complete control over and use freely for my own purpose, as poet. I want, as poet, to be that in nature, which constitutes nature's very self. I want to be nature in the form of a man, with all the resources of nature = I want to be the lion in the lute; and then, when I am, I want to face my parent and be his true part. I want to face nature the way two lions face one another – the lion in the lute facing the lion locked in stone. I want, as a man of the imagination, to write poetry with all the power of a monster equal in strength to that of the monster about whom I write. I want man's imagination to be completely adequate in the face of reality.

These two long glosses show how completely Stevens thought through his metaphors. The images of the lions in their respective cages are of great forces brought under control, of the kinetic become static. The nature of the antagonism between the poet and the various figures of authority is made specific here. Stevens' comments make this combat a struggle with the father (the lion is the *king* of beasts). The desire to 'be his true part' is analogous to the desire 'to play man number one' that in III resulted in a dismemberment.

The violence of xvii and that of xix are connected by a moment of supreme delicacy. To face reality the poet needs a dream:

> A dream (to call it a dream) in which
> I can believe, in face of the object,
>
> A dream no longer a dream, a thing,
> Of things as they are, as the blue guitar
>
> After long strumming on certain nights
> Gives the touch of the senses, not of the hand,
>
> But the very senses as they touch
> The wind-gloss.

(xviii. 1–8)

This dream (or music, or poem) must be one in which he can believe. The poet does not so much desire certainty as desire to mobilise the totality of his energy once and for all, and to commit himself absolutely in a single act of faith. The dream, as it is believed, fills with reality, and the imagined world becomes tangible. Poetry produces belief. When previously the guitarist attempted to play the weather he was only half-successful; now his success 'on certain nights' is given and becomes the metaphor for the greater achievement of belief in what is imagined. The status of this new possibility is problematic, not only because it is a 'dream no longer a dream' (an indeterminate state), but also because neither of the two statements in the poem is a sentence: there is no subject, object or principal verb. The tenses shift the events gradually, almost imperceptibly, into the world. The poem moves from possibility ('in which / I can believe') to actuality ('the blue guitar . . . gives'; 'as daylight comes').

'After long strumming on certain nights', the blue guitar gives the touch not of the hand, but of the senses, as they touch the shiny-smooth surface of the wind. This is the most that is possible. The object can never be known wholly or purely in its own terms, only through and along with the touch of the senses as they free themselves from the memory of past events:

> Or as daylight comes,

> Like light in a mirroring of cliffs,
> Rising upward from a sea of ex.

(xviii. 8–10)

The world comes to us like the morning, a great bulwark that rises from the realm of what has been (now *ex*) and shining with the reflected light of this past. The *mirroring* in this example gives us the gloss of the senses and the object in the shimmering uncertainty of all our knowledge, an uncertainty that is maintained by our being to various degrees, absorbed by our fantasies.

XXVI

> The world washed in his imagination,
> The world was a shore, whether sound or form

> Or light, the relic of farewells,
> Rock, of valedictory echoings,

> To which his imagination returned,
> From which it sped, a bar in space,

> Sand heaped in the clouds, giant that fought
> Against the murderous alphabet:

> The swarm of thoughts, the swarm of dreams
> Of inaccessible Utopia.

> A mountainous music always seemed
> To be falling and to be passing away.

The swarms of thoughts and dreams threaten to overwhelm the

world, which, subject to the imagination, appears an ever-varying reality: shore, rock, acrobats' bar and shifting sand heaped on dream clouds. To the senses the world is a 'mountainous music' always on the verge of fading away, – *mountainous* to stand for its physicality, *music* to indicate that perception is creation and that the harmony that we find in the world is imaginary, *falling* and *passing* because the poet feels that he can only maintain his contact with the world through the unending struggle of his poetry.

'The Man with the Blue Guitar' does succeed at this task, after the long strumming of the poem, and the poet, with new faith, does enter into reality. The final sections, however nuanced, are of affirmation, of which the most clear-cut and obvious example is XXVIII:

> I am a native in this world
> And think in it as a native thinks,
>
> Gesu, not native of a mind
> Thinking the thoughts I call my own,
>
> Native, a native in the world
> And like a native think in it.
>
> It could not be a mind, the wave
> In which the watery grasses flow
>
> And yet are fixed as a photograph,
> The wind in which the dead leaves blow.
>
> Here I inhale profounder strength
> And as I am, I speak and move
>
> And things are as I think they are
> And say they are on the blue guitar.

There is nothing like this earlier in the poem. The world is accepted in all the imperfections of its perception and the poet feels new strength in having made his peace with the imagination's absolutes, a sense of integration.

This change transforms Stevens' protagonist–antagonist:

XXX

From this I shall evolve a man.
This is his essence: the old fantoche

Hanging his shawl upon the wind,
Like something on the stage, puffed out,

His strutting studied through centuries.
At last, in spite of his manner, his eye

A-cock at the cross-piece on a pole
Supporting heavy cables, slung

Through Oxidia, banal suburb,
One-half of all its installments paid.

Dew-dapper clapper-traps, blazing
From crusty stacks above machines.

Ecce, Oxidia is the seed
Dropped out of this amber-ember pod,

Oxidia is the soot of fire,
Oxidia is Olympia.

To Poggioli, Stevens explains,

Man, when regarded for a sufficient length of time, as an object of
study, assumes the appearance of a property, as the word is used
in the theatre or in a studio. He becomes, in short, one of the
fantoccini of meditation or, as I have called him 'the old
fantoche'.... As we think about him, he tends to become
abstract. We cannot think of him as originating in Oxidia. We go
back to an ancestor who is abstract and being abstract, that is to
say, unreal, finds it a simple matter to hang his coat upon the
wind, like an actor who has been strutting and seeking to increase
his importance through centuries, whom we find, suddenly and
at last, actually and presently, to be an employee of the Oxidia
Electric Light & Power Company.   (12 July 1953)

Fantoche is a French word for puppet or marionette. The Italian is *fantoccio*, of which the diminutive, *fantoccini*, is in the *OED*. The bronze-bearded hero, man number one, the actor in his tragic role, the juggler are all versions of 'the old fantoche', who, as a result of Stevens' successful struggles with the world, suddenly appears as a telephone linesman, a citizen and wage-earning member of the community whose vocation is communication. His shabbiness and ordinariness are the marks of a disillusionment (more obvious in the Charlie Chaplin figure in 'his old coat, / His slouching pantaloons', in 'Notes Toward a Supreme Fiction', 1. x). He is poorer for being stripped of the glamour of dreams, and this poverty is the banality of Oxidia, with its 'clapper-traps' and 'crusty stacks'. Oxidia (so called perhaps because oxygen is the element in which we live, and oxidisation is a process through which things lose their shine when they come in contact with the oxygen-filled, real world) is on the periphery rather than at the centre. It is a 'suburb' rather than the capital, 'the soot of the fire' (another effect of combining with oxygen), all of Olympia or Utopia that we shall ever know; it is things as they are: a compound of our perceptions and imagination, which is why exactly one-half of its instalments have been paid. As Stevens tells Poggioli,

> if I am to 'evolve a man' in Oxidia and if Oxidia is the only possible Olympia, in any real sense, then Oxidia is that from which Olympia must come. Oxidia is both the seed and the amber-ember pod from which the seed of Olympia drops. The dingier the life, the more lustrous the paradise. But if the only paradise must be here and now, Oxidia is Olympia.   (12 July 1953)

The compound nature of things as they are appears not only in the contrast between 'the old fantoche' and the employee of the Oxidia Electric Light and Power Company, the soot and the fire, and Oxidia and Olympia, but also in the contrast between *dew-dapper* and *clapper-traps*, *blazing* and *crusty*, and *amber* and *ember*. For Poggioli, Stevens drew a small diagram and wrote,

> This is a dew-dapper clapper-trap. It goes up and down or is fixed at an angle. Dew-dapper is merely an adjective. Clapper refers to the noise as this opens and shuts. Obviously not a modern piece of equipment. When flame pours out at white heat it looks dew-dapper.

Along with the dew-dapper clapper-trap, other new metaphors
enter the poem in its concluding sections. As is often the case in
Stevens, the world exists as if under the aegis of a bird, but, instead
of the hawk (III, XXIV), the humdrum cock pheasant wakes up from
its sleep, and, instead of the struggles of the self, 'The employer and
employee contend'. These are the activities of things as they are, of
an ordinary morning in Oxidia:

XXXI

> How long and late the pheasant sleeps ...
> The employer and employee contend,
>
> Combat, compose their droll affair.
> The bubbling sun will bubble up,
>
> Spring sparkle and the cock-bird shriek.
> The employer and employee will hear
>
> And continue their affair. The shriek
> Will rack the thickets. There is no place,
>
> Here, for the lark fixed in the mind,
> In the museum of the sky. The cock
>
> Will claw sleep. Morning is not sun,
> It is this posture of the nerves,
>
> As if a blunted player clutched
> The nuances of the blue guitar.
>
> It must be this rhapsody or none,
> The rhapsody of things as they are.

Again this is an emphatically American new world – established in
terms of its British counterpart and progenitor. Shelley's skylark is
rejected. There is no place for any lark from the mind's sky museum,
and, instead of the unsurpassed music of its 'unpremeditated art', 'a
crystal stream' of divine rapture, the thickets are racked by the
abrupt, disturbing, discordant shriek of the awakened pheasant.[12]
The pheasant is real:

Occasionally I put something from my neighborhood in a poem. We have wild pheasants in the outskirts of Hartford. They keep close to cover, particularly in winter, when one rarely seeks them. In the spring they seem to reappear, although they have never really disappeared, and their strident cry becomes common. Thus, toward the end of winter one can say how long and late the pheasant sleeps.   (Stevens to Simons, 9 Aug 1940)

The pheasant's stirring is a sign of spring, an indication of the possibility of renewal through renewed contact with the world as it exists. The poet (like each of us) has perennial difficulties in responding to this challenge. 'I want man's imagination to be completely adequate in the face of reality', Stevens declares to Poggioli (12 July 1953). 'I want, as a man of imagination, to write poetry with the power of a monster equal in strength to that of the monster about whom I write.' The problem of the pheasant in the guitar is that of the lion in the lute, and in the above letter to Simons, he goes on to say, 'This poem deals with a moment of reaction when one is baffled by the nuances of the imagination and unable to attain them.' His point is that things *are* a certain way, that we can neither choose our reality nor escape from our inadequacies; all our rhapsodies are fumbled – clutchings at straws, rhapsodies of failure.

The universe for Stevens is dark with our ignorance. Our definitions of it are wisping torches (v. 2) and 'rotted names'. He urges us to discard our distorting lights and corrupt, worn-out nomenclature and to make our peace afresh with uncertainty, to accept the dark because it is real:

XXXII

Throw away the lights, the definitions,
And say of what you see in the dark

That it is this or that it is that,
But do not use the rotted names.

How should you walk in that space and know
Nothing of the madness of space,

Nothing of its jocular procreations?
Throw the lights away. Nothing must stand

Between you and the shapes you take
When the crust of shape has been destroyed.

You as you are? You are yourself.
The blue guitar surprises you.

The hoped-for moment is one of unmediated contact (the touch not
of the hand, but of 'the very senses as they touch / The wind-gloss').
Its reward is the freedom of self-discovery, as if we could choose
who we are, a moment in which we are surprised by the identity
between the many shapes we take and our self. The final section
allows us to believe that the moment has occurred in the poem.
Stevens writes to Simons that it is hypothetical. 'Being oneself' is, he
says,

being . . . not as one really is but as one of the jocular procreations
of the dark, of space. The point of the poem is, not that this can be
done, but that, if done, it is the key to poetry, to the closed garden,
if I may become rhapsodic about it, of the fountain of youth and
life and renewal. This poem depends a good deal on its
implications.   (10 Aug 1940)

It is worth noting that the other side of the jocular is madness.
    The poem concludes with thoughts not of Sunday but of dingy,
workaday Monday morning. The dream in which the poet desired
to believe is emphatically a 'dream no longer a dream'. The dreamer
has come down to earth, to the mud and messiness of living. 'Time
in its final block' is the present, here and now, four-square in the
world, no longer a wrangling of impossible and possible futures.

XXXIII

That generation's dream, aviled
In the mud, in Monday's dirty light,

That's it, the only dream they knew,
Time in its final block, not time

To come, a wrangling of two dreams.
Here is the bread of time to come,

Here is its actual stone. The bread
Will be our bread, the stone will be

Our bed and we shall sleep by night.
We shall forget by day, except

The moments when we choose to play
The imagined pine, the imagined jay.

When Pierre is imprisoned during the occupation of Moscow in *War and Peace*, he is struck by the prayer of one of his fellow captives, a peasant soldier, Platon Karataev. Before he falls asleep, Karataev prays, 'Lay me down like a stone, O god, and raise me up like a loaf.'[13] The bread in the poem has been on the table with the fruit, wine and book (xiv. 11–12), 'things as they are', our ordinary life in all its ordinariness; and the metaphor of the earth as a stone, the indubitable rock on which our belief rests, occurs in a number of places (xi, xvi, xxvi). As a dream, 'the bread of time to come' is as simple as Karataev's prayer or the single candle that lights the world (xiv. 8). Our daily bread is what sustains us and it can only be consumed in the here and now. We shall go to sleep in reality and waking, forget our dreams, except when we choose to play upon the blue guitar the green pine and the blue jay. Poetry provides us with an alternative to our Monday world; it is that world transformed.

No statement is more important for the understanding of Stevens' work than his declaration, 'Poetry is the subject of the poem'. This, however, is only the first part of the description of a process:

XXII

Poetry is the subject of the poem,
From this the poem issues and

To this returns. Between the two,
Between issue and return, there is

An absence in reality,
Things as they are. Or so we say.

But are these separate? Is it
An absence for the poem, which acquires

> Its true appearances there, sun's green,
> Cloud's red, earth feeling, sky that thinks?
>
> From these it takes. Perhaps it gives,
> In the universal intercourse.

The description emphasises the degree to which we inhabit the imagination. The world is conceived as somewhere other and at a remove from us. The phrase 'absence in reality' endows the poem with a life of its own separate from the poet and appears to reverse the ordinary values of absence and presence. The poem fills with reality when it is absent so that it can be said to come into existence when it is not there. This paradox causes the poet to question his formulation: 'Is it / An absence for the poem . . . ?' Moreover, he wants to believe in wholeness for his own reasons. This preoccupation with the processes of art is an attempt to discover the nature of self-consciousness and find himself; it is a working-through of his feelings of separation – from the world and between parts of himself. His model of wholeness is one of communication ('universal intercourse'). The strength of his need is the logic of his categories. As he feels the poem changing him, he thinks of it as changing the world as well. The questions and the *perhaps* show this to be a hope rather than a conviction.

Of these lines, Stevens writes to Simons, 'Poetry is the spirit, as the poem is the body. . . . The purpose of writing poetry is to attain pure poetry' (10 Aug 1940). Pure poetry for Stevens was not only (as he states to Latimer, 31 Oct 1935) 'the idea of images and images alone, or images and the music of verse together', but also (as he tells Simons, 28 Aug 1940) a belief in the imagination as, 'at least potentially, as great as the idea of God, and . . . greater, if the idea of God is only one of the things of the imagination'. 'The validity of the poet', he continues (10 Aug 1940), 'is wholly a matter of' his ability to make a comprehensive statement about the meaning of everything – making it clear that he writes because his life depends on it. The poet, he says:

> adds to life that without which life cannot be lived, or is not worth living, or is without savor, or, in any case, would be altogether different from what it is today. Poetry is a passion, not a habit. This passion nourishes itself on reality. Imagination has no source except in reality, and ceases to have any value when it departs

from reality. Here is a fundamental principle about the imagination: It does not create except as it transforms. There is nothing that exists exclusively by reason of the imagination, or that does not exist in some form in reality. thus, reality = the imagination, and the imagination = reality. Imagination gives, but gives in relation.

Absence creates presence; his two antagonists, imagination and reality, turn out to be the same person. Using his equations, we might say that reality (or imagination) is the subject of poetry. Poetry makes life worth living by keeping imagination and reality in relation; poetry is the subject of the poem because this integration nourishes the poet.

The imagination 'ceases to have any value when it departs from reality'. Stevens rejects any idea of poetry's self-sufficient greatness, or grand or glamorous remoteness:

V

Do not speak to us of the greatness of poetry,
Of the torches wisping in the underground,

Of the structure of vaults upon a point of light.
There are no shadows in our sun,

Day is desire and night is sleep.
There are no shadows anywhere.

The earth, for us, is flat and bare.
There are no shadows. Poetry

Exceeding music must take the place
Of empty heaven and its hymns,

Ourselves in poetry must take their place,
Even in the chattering of your guitar.

Stevens paraphrases this to Simons as: 'We live in a world plainly plain. Everything is as you see it. There is no other world. Poetry, then, is the only possible heaven. It must necessarily be the poetry of ourselves; its source is in our imagination (even in the chattering, etc.)' (8 Aug 1940).

'The structure of vaults upon a point of light' is an image of the imagination's elaboration of wonderfully intricate, self-contained systems. The metaphor recurs when Stevens describes the discoveries of science radiating light like a thousand stars:

> One says a German chandelier –
> A candle is enough to light the world
>
> (xiv. 7–8)

The chandelier's flashing patterns are beautiful in themselves, but the plain candle shows the chiaroscuro truth of our plain world. For poetry to take the place of religion, we in all our plainness must enter the poem. As Stevens says in xxi, it is 'This self' here and now in the world, 'not that gold self aloft' that is 'A substitute for all the gods'; it is Chocorua in New Hampshire not the shadow mountain of the imagination:

> One's self and the mountains of one's land,
>
> Without shadows, without magnificence,
> The flesh, the bone, the dirt, the stone.
>
> (xxi. 10–12)

Near the end of the poem, after he has affirmed, 'I am a native in this world', and before he evolves 'the old fantoche' as an employee of the Oxidia Electric Light and Power Company, the poet is in a great church. The vaults of light have been translated into real vaults. The poet is enclosed in the church and further enclosed by his reading; none the less, he is conscious of his reading and attempts to establish a relation between it and what is going on around him:

XXIX

> In the cathedral, I sat there, and read,
> Alone, a lean Review and said,
>
> 'These degustations in the vaults
> Oppose the past and the festival.

What is beyond the cathedral, outside,
Balances with nuptial song.

So it is to sit and to balance things
To and to and to the point of still,

To say of one mask it is like,
To say of another it is like,

To know that the balance does not quite rest,
That the mask is strange, however like.'

The shapes are wrong and the sounds are false.
The bells are the bellowing of bulls.

Yet Franciscan don was never more
Himself than in this fertile glass.

The imagination's distillations are tasted like wines and savoured as a counterpoise both to the past (things as they were) and to the marriage festival (of things as they are). Similarly, the world beyond the cathedral is a counterweight to these nuptial celebrations. This balancing of inside and outside is less frenetic than the acrobat holding the world upon his nose (xxv) and more enduring than sand heaped in the clouds (xxvi). Every poem is such a balancing, a wedding of imagination and reality; even though any given combination may be unstable, strange, wrong, false or discordant, the activity serves its purpose, which is for the poet to be himself.

When asked by Renato Poggioli to explain the conclusion of this poem, Stevens replied, 'You have me up a tree on this one', but his answer is none the less clear and positive:

I imagine that I chose a Franciscan because of the quality of liberality and of being part of the world that goes with the Franciscan as distinguished, say, from a Jesuit. I have no doubt that I intended to use the word don with reference to a clerical figure. (25 June 1953)

The poet who earlier (xxiv) is to create a 'poem like a missal' (the book containing the service of the mass for a year – that is, the text of a ceremony in which the spirit enters into a body, a marrying of the word with the bread and wine of reality) is now compared to a Franciscan as he is compared to that other 'clerical figure', the rabbi, in 'Le Monocle de Mon Oncle', 'The Sun This March' and a number of other poems. His task is priest-like, his knowledge sacramental. He is generous and 'part of the world'. The poet is at one with himself although his reflections are continually changing. The poem is the fixation of a single point of view, and, consequently, a mask that, however good the resemblance, is always strange when compared to the face. The metaphor of marriage is more outward-looking than the self-regarding one of the glass, although here fruitfulness is only implicit in the former, while explicit in the latter. Poetry is a mirror capable of producing an endless series of approximate self-images, and, for all its limitations and shortcomings, there is no better means of self-knowledge – the knowledge necessary in order to live fully in the world as it is. Significantly, it is *after* the function of poetry has been settled that the poem is most down-to-earth, that we have Stevens' rhapsody of the world's banality; nevertheless, the last words are of 'The imagined pine, the imagined jay'.

5

Parts of a World

The sound of the guitar lingers on in Stevens' poetry virtually until the end. Of the several men who make up chaos and destroy each other in 'Extracts from Addresses to the Academy of Fine Ideas' (1940),

> He that remains plays on an instrument
>
> A good agreement between himself and night,
> A chord between the mass of men and himself,
>
> Far, far beyond the putative canzones
> Of love and summer.
>
> (v. 10–14)

There is 'repetition on / One string', in 'Montrachet-le-Jardin' (1942) and 'thin music on the rustiest string' in 'God is Good. It is a Beautiful Night' (1942) (although here the instrument is a zither), while in 'Jouga' (1945) the guitarist and the guitar are 'two conjugal beasts' and in 'Madame La Fleurie' (1951):

> The black fugatos are strumming in the blackness of black ...
> The thick strings stutter the final gutturals.
> He does not lie there remembering the blue-jay, say the jay.

Thought in Stevens turns into music as a way of entering consciousness without words, as if only thus can the poet establish a relation with the unspeaking world. The inanimate objects that surround him are at once the reality in which he must nourish himself, nuclei of projected fantasies and components of the languages in which he is obliged to interpret everything, including language itself. These objects are uncertain, because perception, fantasy and language are dynamic systems constantly exchanging values, and there is a permanent instability, because, as Stevens

179

states in 'The Pure Good of Theory', 'It is never the thing but the version of the thing'. All our knowledge is a makeshift. The metaphor of music represents this instability of perception and fantasy as a harmonious flow, unified and unifying, single despite endless changes in emphasis. Any irregularity can be expressed in terms of the system, accommodated as a *discord*. Music stands for the deeper accord between ourselves and the world where each of us is virtuoso and listener, the moment Eliot describes in 'The Dry Salvages' of:

> Music heard so deeply
> That it is not heard at all, but you are the music
> While the music lasts.[1]

Guitarist and guitar are at the centre of Stevens' attempt to define exactly the tradition to which he and his contemporaries belong, 'Of Modern Poetry' (1940):

> The poem of the mind in the act of finding
> What will suffice. It has not always had
> To find: the scene was set; it repeated what
> Was in the script.
>   Then the theatre was changed
> To something else. Its past was a souvenir.
>
> It has to be living, to learn the speech of the place.
> It has to face the men of the time and to meet
> The women of the time. It has to think about war
> And it has to find what will suffice. It has
> To construct a new stage. It has to be on that stage
> And, like an insatiable actor, slowly and
> With meditation, speak words that in the ear,
> In the delicatest ear of the mind, repeat,
> Exactly, that which it wants to hear, at the sound
> Of which, an invisible audience listens,
> Not to the play, but to itself, expressed
> In an emotion as of two people, as of two
> Emotions becoming one. The actor is
> A metaphysician in the dark, twanging
> An instrument, twanging a wiry string that gives
> Sounds passing through sudden rightnesses, wholly
> Containing the mind, below which it cannot descend,

Beyond which it has no will to rise.
                                  It must
Be the finding of a satisfaction, and may
Be of a man skating, a woman dancing, a woman
Combing. The poem of the act of the mind.

The movement is from 'The poem of the mind in the act of finding/ What will suffice' to 'The poem of the act of the mind'. If we can never know any thing, only versions of things, then all our knowledge is an approximation; we can never know who we are or where we are. Each version will make us feel the falsity, artificiality and temporariness of all the other versions. The real and the unreal both will feel unauthentic. Modern poetry is a description of the mind in the act of making do in these circumstances, and it is this that suffices: the description of the problem is its solution. Becoming fully conscious of our predicament enables us to cope with it, and it must be coped with because the circumstances cannot be changed; they are inexorably given. This is the certainty of Stevens' uncertainty, and it is not surprising to find him writing to Ronald Latimer, 'A most attractive idea to me is the idea that we are all the merest biological mechanisms' (15 Nov 1935). For Stevens this is not a tragic conception. He, none the less, seeks momentary fulfilment and imperishable bliss. The poetry of the mind 'must / Be the finding of a satisfaction'; similarly, the final prerequisite of the poetry of supreme fiction is that 'It Must Give Pleasure', and to this end Stevens turns to the world rather than to himself. 'The poem of the act of the mind' is an escape from introspection, solipsism and autobiography. His examples are not at all intellectual: 'a man skating, a woman dancing, a woman / Combing'. The emphasis is on bodily action. All are ordinary activities without any precise exterior purpose, performed by a single person alone in a state analogous to daydreaming (or playing the guitar), each with its own particular rhythm. the body in each case describes a figure in harmony with an implied music.

According to the poem, the modern poet is in a different situation from previous poets in that he must reinvent his art. There is no question of the origin of this change or of locating it in time. *Modern* is unspecific; in the context of Stevens' work as a whole it would appear to refer, more or less, to the poets of his generation. As in 'The Man with the Blue Guitar', the poet is compared to actor and guitarist (both *players*), and Stevens uses all the meanings of *acting*:

doing, assuming a role, producing effects. The theatre is the world.
The idea, implicit in the shadows on the wall of the cave in *The
Republic*, is clearly stated by Augustine's Egyptian contemporary
Palladus: Σκηνή πᾶς ὁ βίος ('All life is a stage'). His epigram in the
Greek Anthology (by way of John of Salisbury's *Politcraticus*) is the
source of Ronsard's 'Le monde est un théâtre' and Shakespeare's
'All the world's a stage'.[2] The metaphor in Stevens' poetry
emphasises the rhetoric and sham in all our gestures. 'Authors are
actors, books are theatres', he states in *Adagia* (*OP*, p. 157).

Here, although the theatre has been changed to 'something else',
the poet cannot redefine his art by leaving the theatre. His task is to
construct a *new* stage and he must be 'like an insatiable actor' on that
stage. Where previously the office of the poet was well established
and new poems repeated old ones, so that poetry was a single
continuous discourse (a 'script'), now, for reasons that are not
discussed, these old stabilities and the continuity that they provided
have disappeared. The past no longer has any meaning; it is a
'souvenir', a dead memory. The poet is in a new situation, a place
and time discontinuous with the past. He needs to enter more fully
into the present. This means learning a new language ('the speech of
the place') and making his contemporaries his audience. As in the
final examples, gender matters. Poetry has to *face* the men and *meet*
the women. The men must be confronted more directly than the
women, but the women are approached more closely, and it is this
distinguishing of the sexes that causes us to think that the 'emotion
as of two people' is that between a man and a woman. Among these
emphases on the contemporary, the statement in a poem first
published in May 1940 (the month in which Germany invaded
Holland and Belgium) that poetry 'has to think about war' is
noteworthy as demonstrating the seriousness of Stevens' conten-
tion that everything in all his poems could be related to real events.

The poet is to speak slowly, deliberately, studiously, almost as if
he were speaking to induce a dream-like state. His speech in its
capacity to be indefinitely prolonged is like skating, dancing and
combing. His words are for the most sensitive and discriminating
area of the mind ('The delicatest ear of the mind'); his audience is
'invisible' and he seeks to bring about a unity of feeling. The play is
not the thing; it is, rather, the deeper communication, the self-
communion, that it makes possible. The poet's words establish a
bond between himself and the audience that expresses what *they*,
the audience, are. They hear themselves in terms of one emotion

shared by two people or of two emotions becoming one – all Stevens' poetic effort is directed to healing this fundamental duality, and for him it is a never-ending process (this is why the poet needs to be 'like an insatiable actor'). This is presented not as a personal manifesto, but as a description of the nature of all modern poetry.

Poetry is wish-fulfilment: it repeats exactly what the mind wants to hear. This exactness is its rigour, the law of its existence. Thus, everything about it is a response to inner need. That it is a repetition suggests already-formulated desire, and that it is the perfect satisfaction of that desire explains why, in Stevens' view, it is not a tragic art. The poet is a metaphysician, concerned with being and knowing. Poetry (in Richard Blackmur's reformulation of Marcel Raymond's phrase) is an 'irregular metaphysics', an unsystematic philosophy, and its irregularity is very apparent in 'Of Modern Poetry'.[3] The poet is not a philosopher; he is an actor who is a 'metaphysician in the dark', not practising any formal discipline, but twanging an instrument, engaged in an activity without any ostensible purpose, like skating, dancing or combing. What is significant is not any verbal expression, but an evocative, facilitating sound and the establishment of a rhythm, whose efficacy depends, perhaps, on its only suggesting language or speech. That dark is the irrational or inexplicable, the totality of our ignorance, and the slightly discordant twanging of the wiry string (its singleness emphasising the poverty of our means) indicates the degree to which we are off key, out of true, in all our perceptions. This music contains the mind, much as the curvature of light, according to the theory of relativity, closes the universe. The sounds establish a final limit – this is the idea of the palm at the end of the mind, the notion of an omega that follows from Stevens' search for an alpha of origins (compare 'An Ordinary Evening in New Haven', vi) – in this case it is a varying limit, a minimum so that the mind cannot disappear in itself, a maximum so that there is a restful check to its desire for omnipotence. Time, Blake says, is the mercy of eternity. The thought of a conclusion makes duration bearable, giving a direction to existence and ordering the intervening moments. The sounds pass 'through sudden rightnesses', as if these satisfactions were the unexpected discoveries of the process of playing; and, because the rightnesses are always passing, they always need to be rediscovered. The poem of the act of the mind is the poem of the mind committed to a self-sustaining process of composing itself, to action in support of being.

The poetry of Stevens is full of descriptions of moments of completion such as this one. Each description is both partial and temporary, at once an approximation and the achievement of this most wished-for state – we are the music while the music lasts. The feeling of endlessness in Stevens produces images of finality. The poem of the act of the mind takes him ever more into the world. Because in the last analysis the poem owes its existence to being in the world, its existence is an affirmation of the existence of reality. Poetic thinking, even with all its uncertainties, is the antithesis of solipsism; it is the 'way to life', as Stevens puts it in 'Extracts from Addresses to the Academy of Fine Ideas'. Musing on 'systematic thinking', and recognising that his imaginary protagonist, Ercole, in his cavern (a version of Plato's cave) may 'think the way to death', the poet prefers to follow another guide:

> That other one wanted to think his way to life,
> Sure that the ultimate poem was the mind,
> Or of the mind, or of the mind in these
> Elysia, these days, half earth, half mind
>
> (VI. 5–8)

Again, thinking sustains being:

> He, that one, wanted to think his way to life,
> To be happy because people were thinking to be.
> They had to think it to be. He wanted that . . . .
>
> (VI. 11–13)

Stevens' answer to 'being unhappy' is to 'talk of happiness' and to 'know that it means / That the mind is the end and must be satisfied' (VI. 20–2). When the mind is satisfied, even the doubleness of the world will be tolerable:

> It cannot be half earth, half mind; half sun,
> Half-thinking; until the mind has been satisfied,
> Until, for him, his mind is satisfied.
> Time troubles to produce the redeeming thought.
> Sometimes at sleepy mid-days it succeeds,
> Too vaguely that it be written in character.
>
> (VI. 23–8)

'What/ One believes is what matters' (vII. 9–10). The mind's greatest satisfaction is to believe – in anything. Wordsworth remarks, 'Archimedes said that he could move the world if he had a point whereon to rest his machine. Who has not felt the same aspirations as regards the world of his own mind?'[4] This is perhaps Stevens' most profound aspiration, and like Wordsworth he seeks for an answer in 'the world of his own mind', in the representation of mental events, and it is a question of belief rather than knowledge, not of truth but of *feeling* certain. The ultimate poem is to produce final belief:

> The prologues are over. It is a question, now,
> Of final belief. So, say that final belief
> Must be in a fiction. It is time to choose.

Thus Stevens begins 'Asides on the Oboe', using another solo instrument to present another set of metaphors of fulfilment, and introducing the notion that we can be certain only of our fictions, that all our ideas of order are of our own making. As Stevens develops the notion in subsequent poems, poetry becomes the object of final belief. He commits himself in this way to a process rather than to any fixed object, and it is, of course, a process of mental acts.

Every poem, therefore, is an act of faith, yet, even with this transformation, completion is for Stevens, as it is for Wordsworth, a matter of special moments, 'sudden rightnesses'. Wordsworth finds these 'spots of time' in his own history. He is renewed by remembering particular past instants. Stevens creates moments of fulfilment out of whatever comes to hand in the present. His comment to Simons on 'The Man with the Blue Guitar' applies to his poetry generally: 'Anyhow, one is trying to do a poem which may be organised out of whatever material one can snatch up' (9 Aug 1940). Only very rarely are such moments set in time, because they have occurred only as wishes, or in that most remote past, the mythic period before we began to apprehend our lives historically, the period in which the feeling of being originates – and this earliest period can only be recovered as form, or symbolically. This, I think, explains why Stevens' poems are as if removed from time, for ever present, and more fantastic than dreams.

'A Rabbit as King of the Ghosts', which Stevens liked very much, is a good example of these fantasies of completion or fulfilment. In the twilight, when the world is sufficiently shadowy to allow the imagination free play, the poet sees a rabbit on the lawn as the imagination's king. The opening lines might be spoken of any weary thinker at the end of his day until one comes to the exotic strangeness of 'your fur', and 'green mind':

> The difficulty to think at the end of day
> When the shapeless shadow covers the sun
> And nothing is left except light on your fur –
>
> There was the cat slopping its milk all day,
> Fat cat, red tongue, green mind, white milk
> And August the most peaceful month.

Summer is for Stevens when the world is most itself, and August the centre of the summer. It is this access of reality that makes it for poet – and rabbit – 'the peacefullest time'. The cat stands for the hot, bright day that nourishes us like mother's milk, and, in common with all Stevens' cats, is an emblem of the world's fluidity.

The third stanza begins, 'To be' (carefully marked off by a comma), and everything that follows is in elaboration of that phrase. In keeping with the subject of being, none of the final six stanzas, unlike the first two, can be separated from the others; punctuation or syntax ties each stanza to the next, to the end of the poem. The kingly power of the rabbit is shown by the way in which he grows before our eyes, exchanging magnitudes with the cat, becoming equally monumental, 'black as stone' 'like a carving in space'. His enlargement acts out the idea of fulfilment:

> To be, in the grass, in the peacefullest time,
> Without that monument of cat,
> The cat forgotten in the moon;
>
> And to feel that the light is a rabbit-light,
> In which everything is meant for you
> And nothing need be explained;
>
> Then there is nothing to think of. It comes of itself;
> And east rushes west and west rushes down,
> No matter. The grass is full

And full of yourself. The trees around are for you,
The whole of the wideness of night is for you,
A self that touches all edges,

You become a self that fills the four corners of night.
The red cat hides away in the fur-light
And there you are humped high, humped up.

You are humped higher and higher, black as stone –
You sit with your head like a carving in space
And the little green cat is a bug in the grass.

The rabbit uses the twilight as the audience in 'Of Modern Poetry' uses the actor's speech. Being is a feeling and introduces the notion of self. Fully to be is to feel that you are the purpose of everything and that consequently 'nothing need be explained'. Then the world happens and thought 'comes of itself'. This definition of 'the peacefullest time' implies that at all other times everything needs to be explained. Stevens' poetry is an unending explanation, the effort to make sense of this world in which we are all ghosts because we are never fully ourselves. Through the experience of completion the rabbit becomes a new self that is dark, a matter of tactility ('touching') and total (making contact with '*all* edges', filling all available space, 'the four corners of night') in keeping with the 'everything' and 'nothing' earlier in the poem.

There is similar description of completion in 'Description without Place':

There might be, too, a change immenser than
A poet's metaphors in which being would

Come true, a point in the fire of music where
Dazzle yields to a clarity and we observe,

And observing is completing and we are content,
In a world that shrinks to an immediate whole,

That we do not need to understand, complete
Without secret arrangements of it in the mind.

(III. 11–18)

Again there is the desire to know intuitively and totally without thinking, without the mind's 'secret arrangements'; the wish for understanding without explanation, for perception to be self-sufficient and to achieve in its every act the wholeness of the perceiver. The wished-for clarity is a 'rabbit-light', although in this case, rather than the perceiver growing, the world shrinks. Feeling poetry's power, the poet wants 'a change immenser than / A poet's metaphors' – greater than the metamorphosis of 'A Rabbit as King of the Ghosts' – such that the ever-changing world will offer him the fixed point of Archimedes and Wordsworth. He wants the supreme fiction to become the supreme truth so that he will be wholly true and truly whole.

These daydreams of the wholeness of perfect knowledge come and go in Stevens' poetry. Because, perhaps, our having such longings so perfectly defines our condition, and because, therefore, the poem dreams *are* the reality; they produce affirmation rather than disillusionment. Reality for us is impure, a compound, an assembly of parts: *things* as they are, where any one thing can stand, partially, imperfectly, for the whole. This view, as in 'The Poems of Our Climate', accords the greatest significance to the individual object (and, as the second stanza shows, the object conceals a person):

I

Clean water in a brilliant bowl,
Pink and white carnations. The light
In the room more like a snowy air,
Reflecting snow. A newly-fallen snow
At the end of winter when afternoons return.
Pink and white carnations – one desires
So much more than that. The day itself
Is simplified: a bowl of white,
Cold, a cold porcelain, low and round,
With nothing more than the carnations there.

The poet focuses with loving solicitude on the effect of the bowl of carnations. The coolness of the poem is the coolness of the imagination. The season is not stated; the light is '*like* a snowy air, / Reflecting snow', and the idea of wintry flowers is an oxymoron combining summer and winter. As the bare, grey jar in 'Anecdote of the Jar' opposes the wilderness of Tennessee and 'did not give of bird or bush, / Like nothing else in Tennessee', the equally austere porcelain bowl full of pink and white carnations simplifies its surroundings – and so the poet abstracts a climate from the weather of the world's changeableness. The jar and bowl are like containers for the world, ideas of order, but, very much more than their imaginary perfection, we desire what is excluded, the disordering wildness of what we feel when we are heated: anger and love:

II

Say even that this complete simplicity
Stripped one of all one's torments, concealed
The evilly compounded, vital I
And made it fresh in a world of white,
A world of clear water, brilliant-edged,
Still one would want more, one would need more,
More than a world of white and snowy scents.

III

There would still remain the never-resting mind,
So that one would want to escape, come back
To what had been so long composed.
The imperfect is our paradise.
Note that, in this bitterness, delight,
Since the imperfect is so hot in us,
Lies in flawed words and stubborn sounds.

So free, detached and under control is Stevens' poetry that it is something of a shock to encounter strong unambiguously stated emotions – torment, the evilness of the self, bitterness; but, as the poem suggests, these two *interiors* of the room and the self balance each other. The *raison d'être* of the day's white, cold, pure brilliance is to contain these powerful, complex feelings. The completeness and simplicity of the bowl of carnations creates a form in which they can be expressed. Again and again in the poem, as all through Stevens' work, antithesis is a figure of unity, like the bond of negative and positive that holds the nucleus of an atom together. Antithesis in its instability is also a figure of energy. The 'evilly compounded . . . I' is 'vital', unlike the cold perfume of order of the cut carnations. The second section restates *desire* and *need*. Even if pain and evil disappeared, the mind would not stop its never-ending consideration of the world, and ultimately we should want to come back, out of habit and nostalgia, to things as they had been, because the never-resting mind could not find peace in a static world. This return is bitter-sweet, a pungent satisfaction rather than a snowy scent. The imperfect earth is all the paradise that we shall know – the never-resting mind at home in its always-changing world – and this imperfect world demands an imperfect language, or rather 'flawed words and stubborn sounds': parts rather than a whole and entities that do not belong to any particular language. The final lines can be read as a justification of the idiosyncratic strangeness and eccentric dissonances of Stevens' vocabulary and of his penchant for onomatopoeic words, exclamations and words that verge on music, and that are the notation of almost meaningless sounds. There is the suggestion that all words are flawed in their incapacity to express things as they are, that language is not enough and all sounds are stubborn. Stubborn sounds are those that do not do what they are told, that resist the poet or refuse to yield up any meaning – like the banging, jangling, twanging tick-tock of the blue guitar. Stevens rejects mere euphony. Flawed words and obstinate sounds match the 'evilly compounded, vital I' defect for defect, a poetic correspondence that demonstrates yet again that for Stevens the texture of his poems – the poems of our climate of extremes of hot and cold – 'is the same thing as his vital self'.

The same antitheses are restated to the same purpose in 'The Well-Dressed Man with a Beard'. The well-dressed man with a beard is a 'figure of capable imagination'[5] who is named, like the protagonists of 'Mrs Alfred Uruguay' and 'Phosphor Reading by his own Light', only in the title of the poem, showing Stevens' recurring uneasiness with unattributed thoughts and his need to get outside himself. The man is a composition of antithetical forces, bearded like a giant, hero, rabbi or poet, and dressed with the decorum of a vice-president of Oxidia Electric Light and Power or a resident of the Waldorf. The 'western cataract' is where the 'west rushes down' in 'A Rabbit as King of the Ghosts'. The *no* and *yes* are the poet's constantly repeated disbelief and belief in the world's independent existence, that everlasting argument with himself that Stevens found infinitely fruitful. Characteristically, final disbelief is less attractive than final belief; it is the possibility of knowledge that sustains and enriches his doubts:

> After the final no there comes a yes
> And on that yes the future world depends.

No was the night. Yes is this present sun.
If the rejected things, the things denied,
Slid over the western cataract, yet one,
One only, one thing that was firm, even
No greater than a cricket's horn, no more
Than a thought to be rehearsed all day, a speech
Of the self that must sustain itself on speech,
One thing remaining, infallible, would be
Enough. Ah! douce campagna of that thing!
Ah! douce campagna, honey in the heart,
Green in the body, out of a petty phrase,
Out of a thing believed, a thing affirmed:
The form on the pillow humming while one sleeps,
The aureole above the humming house . . .

It can never be satisfied, the mind, never.

As always, the poet searches for a single fixed point; a thing can be a thought; thinking ('a thought to be rehearsed all day') maintains being; and the outer world is upheld by an affirmation in the inner world – 'a speech / Of the self'. The poem is a series of indentities (virtually all the phrases can be set equal to each other: 'one thing remaining' = 'douce campagna' = 'honey in the heart' = 'green in the body', and so on) in order to establish an identity. *Rehearsed* suggests the theatre in 'Of Modern Poetry', and, as in that poem, the self 'must sustain itself on speech' – or murmurous humming verging on both music and speech, a lullaby for doubt. The poet in 'Arrival at the Waldorf' hums and the orchestra hums in response, and the 'anti-master-man, floribund ascetic' in 'Landscape with Boat' concludes the rehearsal of his doubts by saying, 'The thing I hum appears to be / The rhythm of this celestial pantomime'. So the poet wishes that his speech were true and that the universe had a rhythm, were ordered, were meaningful, and again the theatrical metaphor reveals his doubt: his feeling that he may be performing only for his own benefit. The humming in all three poems is like that of a machine that keeps the world going when we are absent, the music of the spheres or 'never-resting mind'.

As the balanced lines show, there is a residual doubleness in the thing believed. Its attributes come two by two. It is campagna and honey; green and 'out of a petty phrase'; believed and affirmed; a form that hums and a form that encloses 'the humming house'. This 'form' with neither face nor body has only the most tenuous humanity and is no sooner mentioned than it is diffused as an *aureole*. That it hums 'while one sleeps' suggests the reassuring presence of another person who watches over us while we are asleep, yet there is something frightening in its featurelessness and in the barely adumbrated possibility that in sleep one part of the self could separate itself from the body. The collocation of elements makes us feel that there is a connection between this vestigal parental guardian figure and the separation, as if the fear of facelessness were the result of its absence (or insufficient presence) at some decisive period – which is perhaps why so many of Stevens' poems are about saying goodbye.

The deeper sources of this form are clearly stated in another poem composed at this time, 'The Woman that Had More Babies than That'. There an acrobat 'on the border of the sea' observes the waves as they wash over the sand:

> Berceuse, transatlantic. The children are men, old men,
> Who, when they think and speak of the central man,
> Of the humming of the central man, the whole sound
> Of the sea, the central humming of the sea,
> Are old men breathed on by a maternal voice,
> Children and old men and philosophers,
> Bald heads with their mother's voice still in their ears.
> The self is a cloister full of remembered sounds
> And of sounds so far forgotten, like her voice,
> That they return unrecognized. The self
> Detects the sound of a voice that doubles its own,
> In the images of desire, the forms that speak,
> The ideas that come to it with a sense of speech.
> The old men, the philosophers, are haunted by that
> Maternal voice, the explanation at night.
> They are more than parts of the universal machine.
> Their need in solitude: that is the need,
> The desire, for the fiery lullaby.

These yearnings are to an extent self-fulfilling in that they are haunted by the memory of the mother's presence. They are incarnations of what is for ever lost and their dissatisfaction is the mark of their authenticity. 'The Well Dressed Man with a Beard' comes to an analogous conclusion. After this visit to the douce campagna and humming house protected by its aureole, the poem closes with a rejection of finality that is an affirmation of the poet's argument with himself: 'It can never be satisfied, the mind, never.' The ultimate poem is the mind, because ultimately the poet can believe from day to day, continuously, in nothing else.

The increasing acceptance that his knowledge of the world is partial causes Stevens to focus more fully on the parts of the world: on individual objects, and, then, on the idea of metaphor. This invests the part with new meaning, with, in the words of one of the addresses to the Academy of Fine Ideas:

> the repeated sayings that
> There is nothing more and that it is enough
> To believe in the weather and in the things and men
> Of the weather and in one's self, as part of that
> And nothing more.

(VII. 14–18)

This acceptance of the final incompleteness of his knowledge is acknowledged in the title of Stevens' fourth collection of poetry, *Parts of a World*, and, as if in compensation, each object offers its own completeness, another idea of wholeness. The world disintegrates into truth, multiplicity becomes an idea of unity – and, to mark this new understanding, in the penultimate section of 'Landscape with Boat' the word *part* recurs as a refrain:

> He never supposed
> That he might be truth, himself, or part of it,
> That the things that he rejected might be part
> And the irregular turquoise, part, the perceptible blue
> Grown denser, part, the eye so touched, so played
> Upon by clouds, the ear so magnified
> By thunder, parts, and all these things together,
> Parts, and more things, parts. He never supposed divine
> Things might not look divine, nor that if nothing
> Was divine then all things were, the world itself,
> And that if nothing was the truth, then all
> Things were the truth, the world itself was the truth.

Reality is transformed in every sense of the word. The change is so profound that in 'On the Road Home' Aesop's fox takes a new interest in the unobtainable grapes. Like the fable, the poem is a demonstration of how our theories empower our perceptions. The poet and his companion speak and the world changes before their eyes:

It was when I said,
'There is no such thing as the truth',
That the grapes seemed fatter.
The fox ran out of his hole.

You ... You said,
'There are many truths,
But they are not parts of a truth.'
Then the tree, at night, began to change,

Smoking through green and smoking blue.
We were two figures in a wood.
We said we stood alone.

It was when I said,
'Words are not forms of a single word.
In the sum of the parts, there are only the parts.
The world must be measured by eye';

It was when you said,
'The idols have seen lots of poverty,
Snakes and gold and lice,
But not the truth';

It was at that time, that the silence was largest
And longest, the night was roundest.
The fragrance of the autumn warmest,
Closest and strongest.

Every poem is composed with the notion of an audience in mind. The purpose of every author is communication with an absent other, someone whose presence is re-created by the text. The audience is named in 'The Man with the Blue Guitar', 'Of Modern Poetry' and many other poems, so that Stevens can engage more fully in this dialogue. The relation of each person to the world is essentially a relation of two people: infant and mother, lover and beloved, I and you – an exchange of being; and the dialogue must occur for the exchange to take place. The speech in 'On the Road Home' enlarges the silence as the song of 'The Idea of Order at Key West' deepens the night, producing a three-dimensional world that holds the poet. The conclusion is an embrace: round, warm, close and strong, feminine in its fragrance. Even so, the poet's doubts linger in the reference to the fox and the grapes; in that we are only *on the road* home; and, perhaps, in the randomness and unconnectedness of the conversation, and the fact that the relation of the speakers is unspecified. 'To agree with oneself is to be without self-knowledge', Alain remarks:

> We are never unified by a thought. . . . We dream only before the awakening that is doubt. In this world of things where I try to find my way, there is not one in which I believe. Or rather it is in the totally familiar thing, such as my stair or my lock; but then I do not see them. Contrarily, the things that I see are the things that I do not trust, in which I never believe. They are denied and still denied, discussed and still discussed. . . . All our thoughts are disputes with ourselves.[6]

On the three occasions that he published them, Stevens followed 'On the Road Home' with 'The Latest Freed Man'. The latest freed man is at home. 'Tired of the old descriptions of the world' (the old theatre in 'Of Modern Poetry'), at six in the morning he sits on the edge of his bed, at the edge of sleep, and looks about him. His freedom is his capacity to believe in change. Suddenly, without explanation, the present moment and its weather is enough:

> 'I suppose there is
> A doctrine to this landscape. Yet, having just
> Escaped from the truth, the morning is color and mist,
> Which is enough: the moment's rain and sea,
> The moment's sun (the strong man vaguely seen),
> Overtaking the doctrine of this landscape . . . .'

Although he needs the idea of imprisonment to define his new liberty, he is like the sun that 'bathes in the mist / Like a man without a doctrine'. His freedom is 'being without description', a state in which 'nothing need be explained' ('A Rabbit as King of the Ghosts'), 'complete / without secret arrangements of it in the mind'

('Description without Place'), that came as 'the sun came shining into his room', enabling him:

> To be without a description of to be,
> For a moment on rising, at the edge of the bed, to be.

'The ant of the self' is 'changed to an ox' and this increase in the man's self-feeling produces an enhanced feeling of the reality of the world, outside and inside. This is an increase in his strength, in his own significance to himself. Like the rabbit king, the freed man feels himself changed into the centre of things:

> It was the importance of the trees outdoors,
> The freshness of the oak-leaves, not so much
> That they were oak-leaves, as the way they looked.
> It was everything being more real, himself
> At the centre of reality, seeing it.
> It was everything bulging and blazing and big in itself,
> The blue of the rug, the portrait of Vidal,
> *Qui fait fi des joliesses banales*, the chairs.

The idea that emerges from these poems affirming a world of parts is that the mere idea of chaos is an idea of order, as is stated in 'Connoisseur of Chaos':

> A.   A violent order is disorder; and
> B.   A great disorder is an order. These
> Two things are one. (Pages of illustrations.)

There is, however, a chaos of ideas as well as of things. 'Extracts from Addresses to the Academy of Fine Ideas', Stevens writes to Oscar Williams (18 Nov 1940), grows out of 'the Lightness with which ideas are asserted, held, abandoned, etc.' in 'the world today':

> The law of chaos is the law of ideas,
> Of improvisations and seasons of belief.
>
> (v. 1–2)

The mind's response to chaos is converted into a small drama from which the assassin emerges as a figure of capable imagination, someone who can imagine a self-sufficient truth:

Ideas are men. The mass of meaning and
The mass of men are one. Chaos is not

The mass of meaning. It is three or four
Ideas or, say, five men or, possibly, six.

In the end, these philosophic assassins pull
Revolvers and shoot each other. One remains.

The mass of meaning becomes composed again.
He that remains plays on an instrument

A good agreement between himself and night,
A chord between the mass of men and himself,

Far, far beyond the putative canzones
Of love and summer. The assassin sings

In chaos and his song is a consolation.
It is the music of the mass of meaning.

And yet it is a singular romance,
This warmth in the blood-world for the pure idea,

This inability to find a sound,
That clings to the mind like that right sound, that song

Of the assassin that remains and sings
In the high imagination, triumphantly.

                                                        (v. 3–22)

Such is the abstracting, comprehending power of naming that any
idea can compose, temporarily, the mass of meaning that the mass
of men make of the world. The assassin offers us single-
mindedness. He, outlaw and usurper, rules by force rather than
hereditary power and is as close as we can come to:

> a dark-blue king, *un roi tonnerre*,
> Whose merely being was his valiance,
> Panjandrum and central heart and mind of minds . . .

                                                        (iii. 10–12)

The poet is the assassin who eliminates all conflicting ideas. Love and summer are 'seasons of belief', the periods of our greatest knowledge of reality. Their commonly accepted and suppositious songs come far, far short of the assassin's song of unorganised multiplicity that is comprehensive enough, singular enough, to console us for not merely being, for a world made of ideas. The blood world needs the imagination, otherwise the dweller in reality cannot begin to satisfy the mind. The mind clings to the improvised mind-made sound, because this is what it knows and believes: this is the assassin's triumph.

As the world goes to pieces, the poet feels complete in his incompleteness – and says his piece. This is a movement in the direction of reality, epitomised by Stevens' 'Prose statement on the poetry of war'.[7] These three untitled paragraphs appeared as the last page of *Parts of a World*, which was published on 8 September 1942. The last poem in the collection is 'Examination of the Hero in a Time of War'. This was the only occasion on which he included any explanatory material with his poems, and it was never reprinted by him (he and his editor agreed to omit it from *The Collected Poems*).[8] The statement shows us Stevens' attempt to take in the tremendous and horrific changes and to define himself in the face of the Second World War, making clear his sensitivity to the specific events in the world around him. The repetition of *immense* demonstrates his sense of the magnitude of these events:

> The immense poetry of war and the poetry of a work of the imagination are two different things. In the presence of the violent reality of war, consciousness takes the plae of the imagination. And consciousness of an immense war is consciousness of fact.

Here, the poet is set equal to the soldier. At sixty-three Stevens was too old to fight in this war (as he had been in the First World War), so his poems are his contribution to the war effort. This is one reason why 'Notes Toward a Supreme Fiction', composed immediately after this prose statement, closes with an address to a soldier, and why in 'Esthétique du Mal'

At dawn,
The paratroopers fall and as they fall
They mow the lawn.

The war in Stevens' poetry during this period is simultaneously the Second World War and the 'war between the mind / And sky', as it is called in 'Notes Toward a Supreme Fiction'. The poet's struggle with imagination and reality is transformed by the advent of the World War, the conditions in the world becoming a metaphor for the condition of the poet. The metaphor represents Stevens' profound need to keep in touch with the world at all times, and especially in the most extreme conditions, at the moments of greatest violence of change, when the risk of losing touch is at its maximum; and his exceptional summary prose statement and the poetic statement that followed it, 'Notes Toward a Supreme Fiction', are as if called forth to comprehend the unimaginable violence of the world at war. Stevens' greatest theoretic poem was a response to his feeling, expressed in the prose statement, that everything was moving in the direction of fact:

> It has been easy to say in recent times that everything tends to become real, or, rather, that everything moves in the direction of reality, that is to say, in the direction of fact. We leave fact and come back to it, come back to what we wanted fact to be, not to what it was, not to what it has too often remained. The poetry of a work of the imagination constantly illustrates the fundamental and endless struggle with fact. It goes on everywhere even in the periods that we call peace. But in war, the desire to move in the direction of fact as we want it to be and to move quickly is overwhelming.
>
> Nothing will ever appease this desire except a consciousness of fact as everyone is at least satisfied to have it be.

The new focus on individual objects in *Parts of a World* is an attempt to create this makeshift 'consciousness of fact as everyone is at least satisfied to have it be'.

It is as if the integration of 'The Man with the Blue Guitar' makes a world in parts tolerable, allowing the poet to be a connoisseur of disorder instead of its victim. This focus on things is not simply to verify the world's solidity, but also to define the otherwise intangible relations of feeling between the poet and the objects of his perception. Consequently, the result is not a simple realism (if such a thing exists), rather, poems strange with the freshness of their vision, as if of a new world, where we suddenly do not know where we are. Such a poem is 'Anything Is Beautiful if You Say It Is', whose title asserts the power of language, the poet's power, to transform reality. The rest of the poem is a testing of the title:

> Under the eglantine
> The fretful concubine
> Said, 'Phooey! Phoo!'
> She whispered, 'Pfui!'
>
> The demi-monde
> On the mezzanine
> Said, 'Phooey!' too,
> And a 'Hey-de-i-do!'
>
> The bee may have all sweet
> For his honey-hive-o,
> From the eglantine-o.
>
> And the chandeliers are neat ...
> But their mignon, marblish glare!
> We are cold, the parrots cried,
> In a place so debonair.
>
> The Johannisberger, Hans.
> I love the metal grapes,
> The rusty, battered shapes
> Of the pears and of the cheese
>
> And the window's lemon light,
> The very will of the nerves,
> The crack across the pane,
> The dirt along the sill.

The poem is set in our demi-monde, the half-way house between imagination and reality that we all inhabit. The muse, the 'interior paramour', as Stevens calls her in a later poem, has prostituted herself to reality to become a 'fretful concubine'. She, in her compromised position, as an object of both admiration and devaluation, is a comic version of the Lady Macbeth of Baudelaire's 'L'Idéal' and the 'Mégère libertine' of his 'Sed non satiatia'. Words of rejection, 'Phooey! Phoo!', are incorporated into a text of affirmation. This is Stevens proving his title. Similarly, the slangy colloquial exclamations are merged with meditative statement, while the eglantine and chandeliers keep company with the cracked window, its dirty sill and the sweet–sour lemon light. Unified by the delicately irregular rhymes, the poem can be divided into two parts: the marked exuberance and linguistic playfulness of the first three stanzas with their shorter lines contrast with the more subdued, thoughtful longer lines of the last three stanzas, filled with objects. The chandeliers, like the 'German chandelier' of 'The Man with the Blue Guitar', (xiv. 7) stand for 'the brilliance of modern intelligence' that, although it irradiates us, 'may be just a bit of German laboriousness' (note the Johannisberger and Hans), so that one realises that, for all the brilliance, 'the secret of the world is as great a secret as it ever was' (Stevens to Simons, 10 Aug 1940). The chandeliers are elaborate constructions of the reason, too neat, too cold, too elegant, for the parrots, who prefer the exuberant vegetation of the jungle and the warm, tropical, lemon light. The poet dines comfortably and simply in the penultimate stanza: the world is real enough to taste, yet it is like dining from a Cubist still-life. The grapes are 'metal', the pears and cheese are 'rusty, battered shapes', as hard, cold and angular as the crystal pieces of the chandeliers. These are forms the mind imposes. Their angularity is the sign of this imposition. They are acts of the perceiver's will, battered, distorted, changed by things as they are. The nervous awareness of the window with which the poem closes (the sense of it being composed of parts: its light compared to a solid, the separating pane, the crack, the dirt and the sill) suggests that all vision is distorted by its own structure. Seen in this way, even the feeling, the 'very will of the nerves', is as if powdered, granulated, like 'The dirt along the sill'.

The exotic quality of Stevens' poetry is not merely the result of references to things foreign to our everyday experience ('raspberry tanagers in palms') and of unexpected combinations of things (lions and Sweden, St John and back-ache); it is also linguistic, the result of surprising combinations of words and exotic turns of phrase: 'The squirming facts exceed the squamous mind' or 'One's tootings at the weddings of the soul / Occur as they occur', or 'Unsnack your snood, madanna, for the stars / Are shining on all brows of Neversink'.[9] All his experience is to an extent outlandish. He is pervaded by a feeling of the strangeness of the world and as a consequence he feels strange to himself. The world is a dream and the dream is the world. In the face of this, he combines rather than juxtaposes, integrating the various elements, grammatically and concisely, with a tremendous and seemingly effortless power of concentration. The lions in Sweden are a fully developed metaphor; St John and the Back-ache engage in a sustained dialogue. His style is a new language, idiomatic, not a collage.

'A Weak Mind in the Mountains', which Stevens composed after 'Anything Is Beautiful if You Say It is', is similarly disorienting. The interchangeability of fantasy and reality enables him to combine a diverse range of feelings, and in this case to incorporate violent, murderous thoughts:

> There was the butcher's hand.
> He squeezed it and the blood
> Spurted from between the fingers
> And fell to the floor.
> And then the body fell.

The presence of the butcher's hand is unexplained; it is simply *there*, almost a disembodied object, as eerie as a bad dream, except that the next stanza makes it appear that this is an image of the day rather than a nightmare:

> So afterward, at night,
> The wind of Iceland and
> The wind of Ceylon,
> Meeting, gripped my mind,
> Gripped it and grappled my thoughts.
>
> The black wind of the sea
> And the green wind
> Whirled upon me.
> The blood of the mind fell
> To the floor. I slept.

The poet is of two minds, caught in the cross-currents of the cold wind of the darkness of the imagination without the world and the green wind of reality. Reality is flesh and blood – slices of meat, 'crude collops' coming together as one ('An Ordinary Evening in New Haven', I. 16), 'An abstraction blooded, as a man by thought' ('Notes Toward a Supreme Fiction' 1. VI. 21). Both the body's blood and 'The blood of the mind' fall as the body falls, with the force of gravity, according to the world's laws. The poet, however, is full of the feeling of his own potential. He imagines himself, as does the rabbit, as king of the ghosts – standing up as sharply as the butcher's knife and with the butcher's power of disposing of the world. Perhaps the implicit meaning of the first stanza is that this final resolution can only occur over another's dead body, that one king must die before another king can reign:

> Yet there was a man within me
> Could have risen to the clouds,
> Could have touched these winds,
> Bent and broken them down,
> Could have stood up sharply in the sky.

The next poem that Stevens completed, 'Parochial Theme', is the one he chose as the opening poem for *Parts of a World*. The scene is a somewhat exotic one, a French shooting-party:

> Long-tailed ponies go nosing the pine-lands,
> Ponies of Parisians shooting on the hill.

Stevens evades Simons' request for an explanation of this poem, saying that it is 'rather a long story':

It is an experiment at stylizing life and consequently the references to health are to be thought of in connection with the stylizing of life. This makes too long a story for a letter of this sort. The poem may be summed up by saying that there is no such thing as life; what there is is a style of life from time to time.

(12 Jan 1943)

The wind blows, absorbing the halloos of the hunters. The grunting, shuffling sounds of the pine branches 'Deepen the feelings to inhuman depths'. These are feelings of how the world resists and transforms us. The voices in the wind have 'shapes that are not yet fully themselves'. Stylised, like the grapes, pears and cheese in 'Anything Is Beautiful if You Say It Is', they are 'sounds blown by a blower into shapes, / The blower squeezed to the thinnest *mi* of falsetto' – only slightly false (as the pears and cheese are merely rusted and battered) because they embody only vestiges of the falsifying me (*mi*), the blower's efforts being overpowered by the inhuman wind. None the less, the 'halloo, halloo, halloo' of the hunters is heard over the cries of those who keep close to their firesides and whose lives are regulated by the rigid codes represented by official statues in public places. Their full-bodied shouts in the face of reality are a sign of their vigorous health:

> This health is holy, this descant of a self,
> This barbarous chanting of what is strong, this blare.

The descant is sung or played above the plainsong as counterpoint, a metaphor for the relation of imagination and reality. Here there is no diminution of the me, rather, if anything, a melodious enlargement. 'But salvation here?' the poet asks; what about the sound of the beaters closing in on the game, as relentless as a clock or heartbeat, what about death? He feels life passing and sees the hunters as the skeletons that they will become resting in the spring sunlight:

> The spring will have a health of its own, with none
> Of autumn's halloo in its hair. So that closely, then,
>
> Health follows after health. Salvation there:
> There's no such thing as life; or if there is,
>
> It is faster than the weather, faster than
> Any character. It is more than any scene:
>
> Of the guillotine or of any glamorous hanging.
> Piece the world together, boys, but not with your hands.

Salvation, it appears, is in the succession of apprehended moments. Life goes on, health following health, when the imagination takes hold of reality and pieces together a world. The violence in the choice of a shooting-party as a subject is hidden, but the guillotine and 'glamorous hanging', forms of premeditated judicial execution, are as conspicuous and almost as shocking as the butcher's hand in 'A Weak Mind in the Mountains'. The speed of life is the speed of perception, so that without the imagination our existence eludes us. Life is more than any sense, but even death does not make us whole – because our experience is fragmentary; even wholeness can only be achieved piecemeal. The individual object is, therefore, a microcosm of the problems of perception and completion, and its analysis is a first step toward wholeness and perhaps a recapitulation of the first step, a way of rebeginning at the very beginning. The power of these poems is the power of what is unexplained and repressed in our own lives. They have the force of half-understood, half-remembered dreams. A group of images is connected, or a single image developed, so as to narrate a mysterious, metaphoric story, or rather an episode from a longer, largely unknown and incomplete story, in which the objects present are charged with the values, the emotions, of those that are missing.

Perhaps the tendency of all perception is to form itself into stories, merging each thing with all other things even as it distinguishes them. Stevens plays with this idea so as to explore the nature of what it is to be (and metaphor) in his 'Study of Two Pears', which consists of a series of short, simple statements of what the pears are, and are not:

I

Opusculum paedagogum.
The pears are not viols,
Nudes or bottles.
They resemble nothing else.

II

They are yellow forms
Composed of curves
Bulging toward the base.
They are touched red.

III

They are not flat surfaces
Having curved outlines.
They are round
Tapering toward the top.

IV

In the way they are modelled
There are bits of blue.
A hard dry leaf hangs
From the stem.

V

The yellow glistens.
It glistens with various yellows,
Citrons, oranges and greens
Flowering over the skin.

VI

The shadows of the pears
Are blobs on the green cloth.
The pears are not seen
As the observer wills.

This poem, written after his still-life of pink and white carnations, 'The Poems of Our Climate', demonstrates how much Stevens learned about vision from French painting, in this case especially Cézanne. The year before, he had written to Ronald Latimer about 'The Man with the Blue Guitar'. Of its various sections he said, 'what they really deal with is the painter's problem of realisation: I have been trying to see the world about me both as I see it and as it is' (17 Mar 1937). 'Study of Two Pears' is a triumphant resolution of 'the painter's problem of realisation' (the 'stylising of life' of his later letter to Simons), and, in the manner of the painters whom he admires, he allows his brush-strokes to show: the touch of red, bits of blue, the various yellows. The bulky tactility of the pears is built up of many small, stylised touches just as the glistening yellow is composed of various yellows, citrons (the lemon light again), oranges and greens. The colour applied like paint, the 'Study' of the title, the Latin tag, the viols, nudes and bottles – the paraphernalia of innumerable paintings by Cézanne, Picasso, Braque and others of Stevens' contemporaries – create the presence of the painter–perceiver, so that, although the two pears are fully themselves, in the sense that they are 'composed' and 'modelled' they recall the 'battered shapes' of the pears in 'Anything Is Beautiful if You Say It Is', deformed in the struggle between the imagination and reality. Interestingly there are two pears – as if the poem expresses 'an emotion as of two people' – so that most of the nouns in the poems are plurals. The pears are singular in their plurality, stubbornly themselves: they 'resemble nothing else'; they 'are not seen / As the observer wills'. The object's power is recognised in 'Credences of Summer':

> Far in the woods they sang their unreal songs,
> Secure. It was difficult to sing in face
> Of the object. The singers had to avert themselves
> Or else avert the object.
>
> (VII. 1–4)

This is the difficulty, the pleasure and the necessity of living in the world. The pears are an indubitable point of contact with all that is other than the mind. They become in the poem the centre of reality. Their still life offers the experience of a world in which every thing is completely itself – including the poet. *Opusculum paedagogum*: two small works to teach us how to be.

'A Dish of Peaches in Russia' is the focus of a profound if undifferentiated nostalgia. Perhaps this is why the peaches are so far away – in Russia.

> With my whole body I taste these peaches,
> I touch them and smell them. Who speaks?
>
> I absorb them as the Angevine
> Absorbs Anjou. I see them as a lover sees,
>
> As a young lover sees the first buds of spring
> And as the black Spaniard plays his guitar.
>
> Who speaks? But it must be that I,
> That animal, that Russian, that exile, for whom
>
> The bells of the chapel pullulate sounds at
> Heart. The peaches are large and round,
>
> Ah! and red; and they have peach fuzz, ah!
> They are full of juice and the skin is soft.
>
> They are full of the colors of my village
> And of fair weather, summer, dew, peace.
>
> The room is quiet where they are.
> The windows are open. The sunlight fills

The curtains. Even the drifting of the curtains,
Slight as it is, disturbs me. I did not know

That such ferocities could tear
One self from another, as these peaches do.

'The moon', in 'Variations on a Summer Day', 'follows the sun like a French / Translation of a Russian poet'. The sun-red peaches, large, round and full of the colours of the speaker's village and its summer weather, are a poem in the rich, barbaric, vernacular of this Russian poet – and in this case they are also Anjou to the Angevine, a comparison that makes them a Russian version of a French poet. The reference is to du Bellay's famous sonnet on his homesickness, 'Heureux qui, comme Ulysse, a fait un beau voyage', which Stevens had translated thirty years earlier (and included in his letter to Elsie Moll, 25 July 1909) and whose metaphor of the return of Ulysses he reworked in 'The World as Meditation' (1952). Du Bellay declares that everything in his native province pleases him more than the grandeur that surrounds him in Rome:

Plus mon Loyre gaulois que le Tybre latin,
Plus mon petit Lyré que le mont Palatin,
Et plus que l'air marin la douceur angevine.[10]

Or, as Stevens translates:

More than the Latin Tiber, Loire of Angevine,
More, more, my little Lyré than the Palatine,
And more than briny air the sweetness of Anjou.

The location of the dish of peaches is ambiguous. Are they in Russia and present only in the poet's imagination or before him in the room? As a consequence the nature of his exile is obscure. The poem begins with unity and ends in separation, and the poet is uncertain who he is. Our impression is of the overwhelming reality of the peaches. Their taste, touch and smell produces in the speaker a feeling of wholeness – and a question. He does not recognise the sound of his own voice; it is as if his body and its feelings belong to someone else or many others: he absorbs the peaches like the

Angevine, a young lover and the black Spaniard, yet none of them is the speaker. The Spaniard, I suggest, is the one whom the woman blamed for life in 'The Woman Who Blamed Life on a Spaniard'. The speaker is another I: that anima, soul and anti-self, the exiled Russian whose heart teems with the sounds propagated by the chapel bells (presumably the chapel in his own village, although this too is left open). The poet discovers himself (his self) to be like the peaches, plural in a singular dish.

The peaches are a homeland experienced with the passion of *young* love. They are the past seen as a new beginning like 'the first buds of spring', and this budding also occurs within the poet's heart: the chapel bells pullulate sounds that appear to germinate as his speech. The various *personae* vanish as they have come with the description of the peaches. Fruition means the act of enjoyment and the pleasure arising from possession (and according to the *OED* is erroneously associated with fruit); for Stevens perception is fruition. The poet possesses the completeness of the peaches. They contain his entire world. The double 'ah' is the sign of his pleasure; like the bowl of carnations in 'The Poems of Our Climate', the dish of peaches establishes a simplicity and peace: 'The room is quiet where they are'. This is the 'visible and responsive peace' of 'Yellow Afternoon': 'A uniting that is the life one loves, / So that one lives all the lives that comprise it', that the poet finds in contact with the earth. Again, as in 'Anything Is Beautiful if You Say It Is', windows are both the poet's desire to see and his sense of being separated from the object of his desire. The open windows of the quiet room through which the sun enters are an indication of the contact that has taken place. The stasis of the moment is broken by the movement of the curtains. This small motion, a slight drifting, is none the less terrible; the poet feels that he is torn self from self as the tearing suggested by the moving curtains is assigned to the peaches.[11] The poet in his incompleteness becomes Angevine, lover, Spaniard and Russian in order to savour the fullness of the peaches, and yet another person when the peaches are fully realised, and this moment of integration is disturbed by the drifting curtains with their intimations of change and messages of interrupted vision. They stir like 'the never-resting mind' and the poet understands how much the peaches have moved him. 'Yellow Afternoon' is another description of a moment 'that answers when I ask' in which the poet 'was at the bottom of things / And of himself' – it, too, ends in a nightmare-like experience:

But he came back as one comes back from the sun
To lie on one's bed in the dark, close to a face
Without eyes or mouth, that looks at one and speaks.

The featureless face is like the poet's worst fears of losing identity
come true. Again the question is: who speaks?

'Woman Looking at a Vase of Flowers' shows how the object
reconciles these discordant elements. Thunder represents the
turbulent power of the imagination, associated with brooding blue-
black thunderheads, storms of rain at night, the lashing wind, and
the sound of the concert grand piano with its rumbling bass-notes,
black case and black keys (Liadoff in 'Two Tales of Liadoff' plays on a
black piano in a cloud). Here the thunder feelings become the
flowers; the object contains – in all senses of that verb – the
emotions:

It was as if thunder took form upon
The piano, that time: the time when the crude
And jealous grandeurs of sun and sky
Scattered themselves in the garden, like
The wind dissolving into birds,
The clouds becoming braided girls.
It was like the sea poured out again
In east wind beating the shutters at night.

The world is in pieces like innumerable droplets or spray, as if the
sea has been poured into the wind. The red sun and blue sky of
which it is composed scatter themselves in the garden, yet this is a
process in which the intangible dissolves into the tangible: wind
turns to birds, clouds to braided girls, thunder to a vase of flowers
upon the piano.

Hoot, little owl within her, how
High blue became particular
In the leaf and bud and how the red,
Flicked into pieces, points of air,
Became – how the central, essential red
Escaped its large abstraction, became,
First, summer, then a lesser time,
Then the sides of peaches, of dusky pears.

The process of definition continues. The high blue of the sky comes down to earth and the throbbing essential red that is the heart of reality changes into bright particles of air, summer, autumn, peaches and pears. As they combine, each becomes less abstract, and the flowers as the woman looks at them participate in both colours. The owl, the bird of night, wisdom and death, in this case an inner voice ('within her') whose cry sounds like 'who' is asked to tell how this happens:

> Hoot how the inhuman colors fell
> Into place beside her, where she was,
> Like human conciliations, more like
> A profounder reconciling, an act,
> An affirmation free from doubt.
> The crude and jealous formlessness
> Became the form and the fragrance of things
> Without clairvoyance, close to her.

The perception of a single object pieces the world together. Order is expressed as the closeness of two persons ('besides her,' 'where she was', 'close to her'). Reality is humanised, the inhuman and the human become 'like' and 'more like', but neither equivalent nor totally commensurate. Things remain 'Without clairvoyance'. The 'profounder reconciling' is one of those 'True reconcilings' described in 'Academic Discourse at Havana' that 'reconcile us to our selves'.

The object enables us to make contact with our feelings, 'as if in seeing we saw our feeling / In the object seen', and, thus, to know our selves. 'Prelude to Objects' describes such 'A profounder reconciling':

> If he will be heaven after death,
> If, while he lives, he hears himself
> Sounded in music, if the sun,
> Stormer, is the color of a self
> As certainly as night is the color
> Of a self, if without sentiment,
> He is what he hears and sees and if,
> Without pathos, he feels what he hears
> And sees, being nothing otherwise,
> Having nothing otherwise, he has not
> To go to the Louvre to behold himself.

Self-knowledge is a matter of seeing, of beholding – other things. We are the sum of our perceptions of the world and real, as long as we behold it without 'sentiment' and without 'pathos' – that is, without extraneous, intrusive, melodramatic false feelings. This makes the self an equation and of the same structure as metaphor, so that the metaphor-making for Stevens becomes part of a deliberate process of self-realisation. Of the Louvre he says, in 'Prelude to Objects', 'Granted each picture is a glass, / That the walls are mirrors multiplied . . .', and continues,

> granted
> One is always seeing and feeling oneself,
> That's not by chance. It comes to this:
> That the guerilla I should be booked
> And bound.

The self is a freedom-fighter that resists all efforts of capture; always on the move, hiding out in the wildest places, it makes war upon perception. This mode of seeing, of course, tends to personify Stevens' world, creating the sense that there is something lurking behind every object, and devaluing as it exalts the thing-its-self. This is why there are so many images of fixity – statues, museums, academies – and why the man in the Louvre is only a step from 'The Man on the Dump' (and Eliot's waste land with its 'heap of broken images'[12]). The Louvre is full of man-made images that are unnecessary if we have the world. The dump is another Louvre. 'The Dump is full / Of images. Days pass like papers from a press'. These images are the mind's print-out, its unending excogitations of things as they are. Each perception is a succession of similitudes, a copy that attempts to reproduce the vivid freshness of reality:

> The freshness of night has been fresh a long time.
> The freshness of morning, the blowing of day, one says
> That it puffs as Cornelius Nepos reads, it puffs
> More than, less than or it puffs like this or that.
> The green smacks in the eye, the dew in the green
> Smacks like fresh water in a can, like the sea
> On a cocoanut – how many men have copied dew
> For buttons, how many women have covered themselves
> With dew, dew dresses, stones and chains of dew, heads
> Of the floweriest flowers dewed with the dewiest dew.
> One grows to hate these things except on the dump.

Dew is one of poetry's oldest metaphors for the evanescence of the world, so that the copying of dew for buttons or any mundane purpose is doomed from the start. Of the men in 'Sunday Morning' who shall chant on a summer morn, 'whence they came and whither they shall go/ The dew upon their feet shall manifest'. Dew garments and dew ornaments, because they are no more than images, are a pathetic rhetoric – trash that arouses the poet's anger and that he consigns to the dump in an attempt to escape from thinking in images. The dump is a cemetery of dead metaphors.

> Now, in the time of spring (azaleas, trilliums,
> Myrtle, viburnums, daffodils, blue phlox),
> Between that disgust and this, between the things
> That are on the dump (azaleas and so on)
> And those that will be (azaleas and so on),
> One feels the purifying change. One rejects
> The trash.
>
>   That's the moment when the moon creeps up
> To the bubbling of bassoons. That's the time
> One looks at the elephant-colorings of tires.
> Everything is shed; and the moon comes up as the moon
> (All its images are in the dump) and you see
> As a man (not like an image of a man),
> You see the moon rise in the empty sky.

The dump is all the things of the world ('azaleas and so on') submitted to the judgement of time. The spring that confronts the poet with the idea of new growth, made precisely particular by the naming of the flowers, causes him to feel the dump, and his disgust, as a process. (This reciprocity between perceiver and the thing perceived is maintained throughout the poem.) At that moment when he understands that he is 'between the things / That are on the dump' and 'those that will be', the poet feels purified. Thus he abstracts his self from the continuous copying and, truly and completely himself (and not as an image of himself), sees the moon itself (divested of all its images) rise in the empty sky of the moment's purity. The parentheses separate the poet's second thoughts, and the whole poem is made studiously impersonal by the use of the indefinite pronoun *one*, except at the moment of vision. Then the shift is to the personal pronoun: *One looks*, but *you see* 'the moon come up as the moon' – this is the division that the poem seeks to resolve.

One sits and beats an old tin can, lard pail.
One beats and beats for that which one believes.
That's what one wants to get near. Could it after all
Be merely oneself, as superior as the ear
To a crow's voice? Did the nightingale torture the ear,
Pack the heart and scratch the mind? And does the ear
Solace itself in peevish birds? Is it peace,
Is it a philosopher's honeymoon, one finds
On the dump? Is it to sit among mattresses of the dead,
Bottles, pots, shoes and grass and murmur *aptest eve*:
Is it to hear the blatter of grackles and say
Invisible priest; is it to eject, to pull
The day to pieces and *cry stanza my stone*?
Where was it one first heard of the truth? The the.

The poet (like all of us) beats the drum – and it is a makeshift drum, shabby in its reality, devoid of any vestige of the ideal – for that which he believes. The struggle, as in 'Woman Looking at a Vase of Flowers', is for faith in perception, 'An affirmation free from doubt', and is expressed, as it is in that poem, as a matter of proximity – 'What one wants to get near'. Attempting to identify this 'what', the poet tries to sum up the experience of the dump and the poem dissolves into a series of unanswered questions, affirmations of doubt. For Stevens, 'Questions Are Remarks'. Like the child's question in the poem of that title, they are complete because they contain our utmost statement. The answer to all these questions, except the last, is – almost – a hesitant 'yes'. What we can believe is song or speech – is it oneself or some other, an internal or external voice? The raucous, painful and disagreeable nature of what he hears half persuades the poet that these songs are real.

'A romantic poet now-a-days', says Stevens in his Preface to William Carlos Williams' *Collected Poems 1921–1931* (after stating that 'All poets are to some extent romantic poets'), is 'one who still dwells in an ivory tower, but who insists that life would be intolerable except for the fact that one has, from the top, such an exceptional view of the public dump . . . . ' The poet, because he is a romantic, because he can look on mattresses, bottles, pots, shoes and grass and murmur *'aptest eve'*, needs the anti-poetic, needs the dump – the dump is the whole world seen as an unending source of the anti-poetic. Stevens' comments on Williams explain Stevens: 'The anti-poetic is his spirit's cure. He needs it as a naked man needs shelter or as an animal needs salt. To a man with a sentimental side the anti-poetic is that truth, that reality to which all of us are forever fleeing.'[13] This is why he can consider the dump as an image of peace or as a 'philosopher's honeymoon', when the solipsistic metaphysician feels totally married to reality (and the moon reappears in the poem in *honeymoon*), and this is how he comes to feel a disparity between his language and its objects (the italics functioning as the parentheses earlier). He deconstructs the day in order to reassemble it. The cry *'stanza my stone'* suggests that poetry is the rock upon which the poet builds his belief. The final question after all assumes that there is a truth. This question, which cannot be answered 'yes' or 'no', is not answered. Instead it is used to propose a definition of reality: 'The the.' Simpler even than Shakespeare's wonderfully simple metaphor in *Antony and Cleopatra* of images in the clouds losing their shape and becoming 'indistinct / As water is in water',[14] this definition has the simplicity of genius. 'The the' is utterly abstract, denoting all the nouns in the world – every definite object in all the particularity of its definiteness – without naming any of them. Stevens uses the power of grammar to make the world a single unity. It is the idea of the dump in the purest possible form.

The much later 'Study of Images. I' is more comfortable with the image as an idea:

> It does no good to speak of the big, blue bush
> Of day. If the study of his images
> Is the study of man, this image of Saturday,
>
> This Italian symbol, this Southern landscape, is like
> A waking, as in images we awake,
> Within the very object that we seek,
>
> Participants of its being. It is, we are.
> He is, we are. Ah, bella! He is, we are,
> Within the big blue bush and its vast shade
>
> At evening and at night. It does no good.

The perception of an object is an appropriation of its reality that enables us to conjugate the verb 'to be'. We live through it not vicariously, but truly. We begin in blue and end in red, or green – or 'Hartford in a Purple Light'. The object creates the world from which

it comes, as the big blue bush is Saturday, Italy and the South; it is
the fixed point, the centre, necessary to change chaos to order and to
communicate purpose – the jar in 'Anecdote of the Jar', the candle in
'Valley Candle' or the glass in 'The Glass of Water'. That we wake in
images reminds us, as all of Stevens' poetry seeks to do, that our
conscious life is composed of sleeping and waking. There is no poet
more fully aware of how we dream in the presence of an object or
that our daydreams can be nightmares – of which the most terrible is
that life is only a dream. This alternation between imagination and
reality is why Stevens can write, 'There is no such thing as life; what
there is is a style of life from time to time.' This now-and-then life
enables us to survive our disillusionments, even when we are
poetry-weary – as the concluding lines of 'Study of Images I' affirm:

> Stop at the terraces of mandolins,
> False, faded and yet inextricably there,
>
> The pulse of the object, the heat of the body grown cold
> Or cooling in late leaves, not false except
> When the image itself is false, a mere desire,
>
> Not faded, if images are all we have.
> They can be no more faded than ourselves.
> The blood refreshes with its stale demands.

6

Faithful Speech

Stevens' confidence and optimism as he worked on the final poems of *Parts of the World* is shown by his letter to William Carlos Williams dated 22 January 1942. He was sixty-two; Williams, fifty-eight.

Dear Bill,

Thanks for your postcard. I am just getting under way. Twenty or thirty years from now I expect to be really well oiled. Don't worry about my grey hair. Whenever I ring for a stenographer she comes in with a pistol strapped around her belt.

Best regards young feller and best wishes,

Wallace Stevens

His notion of his own development is accurate. He was in a sense 'just getting under way', and on the brink of starting his greatest long poem, 'Notes Toward a Supreme Fiction', the fullest and most comprehensive statement of his views on poetry. The poem was composed in four months. Dedicated to Henry Church, it developed out of their discussions (begun in 1940) about the chair of poetry that Church hoped to establish, and out of the preparation of a lecture, 'The Noble Rider and the Sound of Words', that Stevens gave in Princeton (May 1941) under Church's auspices (*L*, pp. 356, 392). 'No one', he writes to Simons, 'would be likely to suppose from that paper what a lot of serious reading it required preceding it, and how much time it took' (8 July 1941). The poem may be considered as what Stevens would have said as the incumbent of the chair. The idea is not a new one in his work: 'Poetry is the supreme fiction, madame', the poet asserts in 'A High-Toned Old Christian Woman' (1922); and in 'Asides on the Oboe' (1940) he writes, 'So, say that final belief / Must be in a fiction. It is time to choose.'

Katherine Frazier of the Cummington Press wrote to him in December 1941 asking whether he would allow them to publish a small book of his poems. He asked to see some samples of their work and, admiring what she sent, he replied, 'you can count on me for something, but not earlier than the end of June, unless I should have luck' (*L*, p. 397). A week after his letter to Williams he had still not started. On 28 January 1942 he tells Henry Church that, when the typing of *Parts of a World* is finished, 'which ought to be within about a week',

> Then I am going to write a very small book for a private press, which will certainly not be published until late in the summer or early autumn. As yet I have not written a word of it. I don't expect to have any difficulty. This is the best time of the year for me: this and spring and early summer.

By 14 May two of the three sections were complete and on 19 May he had only one more poem and the epilogue to do, and on 1 June, ahead of his schedule, he posted the manuscript to Miss Frazier (*L*, pp. 406–8). He had certainly had luck.

'By supreme fiction, of course, I mean poetry', Stevens states firmly to the Cummington Press (14 May 1942), but other comments show that it is not as simple as this. Above all, the poem is neither a system nor a theory, nor is it philosophy. To Henry Church, an avid reader of philosophy, he feels it necessary to insist upon this:

> It is only when you try to systematize the poems in the NOTES that you conclude it is not a statement of a philosophic theory. . . . But these are Notes; the nucleus of the matter is contained in the title. . . . But the NOTES are a miscellany in which it would be difficult to collect the theory latent in them. . . . It is true that the articulations between the poems are not the articulations that one would expect to find between paragraphs and chapters of a work of philosophy.   (8 Dec 1942)

And eight months before his death his conviction is unshaken. 'Say what you will', he writes to Robert Pack on 28 December 1954, 'But we are dealing with poetry, not with philosophy. The last thing in the world that I should want to do would be to formulate a system.'

Although, he tells Henry Church, 'It is implicit in the title that there can be such a thing as a supreme fiction . . .',

> I have no idea of the form that a supreme fiction would take. The NOTES start out with the idea that it would not take any form: that it would be abstract. Of course, in the long run, poetry would be

the supreme fiction; the essence of poetry is change and the essence of change is that it gives pleasure.   (8 Dec 1942)

After glossing many of the poem's difficulties for Hi Simons, Stevens concludes by emphasising the indeterminacy of the idea:

> I ought to say that I have not defined a supreme fiction. A man as familiar with my things as you are will be justified in thinking that I mean poetry. I don't want to say that I don't mean poetry; I don't know what I mean. The next thing for me to do will be to try to be a little more precise about this enigma. I hold off from even attempting that because, as soon as I start to rationalize, I lose the poetry of the idea.   (12 Jan 1943)

Some two weeks later he has second thoughts; he was concerned that he has said too much: 'I think I said in my last letter to you that the Supreme Fiction is not poetry, but I also said that I don't know what it is going to be. Let us think about it and not say that our abstraction is this, that or the other' (28 Jan 1943). The supreme fiction is poetry and it is not, and it will be poetry 'in the long run'. The supreme fiction is something that 'is going to be'; the poem goes *toward* it; it is a formless abstraction, which may or may not be formless in the future, that we can think about without saying what it is. Stevens does not know what he means; he does not want to say that he does not mean poetry – he does not want to say anything too particular.

When he thinks of trying 'to be *a little more* precise about this enigma', he holds off 'from even attempting that'. The indefiniteness, the elusiveness, of the idea – that it can be neither rationalised nor systematised – is precious to him. The supreme fiction appears to be of the sacred 'incommunicado element' that Winnicott identifies as for ever unfound at the centre of each person. Certainly Stevens' remarks to Robert Pack on this subject resemble those to Richard Eberhardt on the poet's need to protect 'his vital self': 'That a man's work should remain indefinite is often intentional. For instance, in projecting a supreme fiction, I cannot imagine anything more fatal than to state it definitely and incautiously' (28 Dec 1944).

Stevens tells Henry Church,

> At first I attempted to follow a scheme . . . . But I very soon found that, if I stuck closely to a development, I should lose all of the

qualities that I really wanted to get into the thing, and that I was less likely to produce something that did not come off in any sense, not even as poetry.   (8 Dec 1942)

For Stevens poetry is a mode of thought that is very different from philosophy. Although he plays with the concepts of ontology and epistemology as he plays with the idea of religion and the idea of system, the play is more important to him than the system, and he prefers those systems with the most play in them, the most slack, the most freedom, the most opportunities for improvisation and for changing his point of view, because only thus can they be made to bear on the nature of identity. Poetry is more satisfying than philosophy because it allows full scope to so-called irrational, or, more precisely, unconscious articulations, because (like the unconscious) it admits the coexistence of contradictions. This is why he commits himself to a supreme fiction rather to a supreme truth, and why the supreme fiction appears to him as an inexhaustible subject. To Church he writes,

> The truth is that this ought to be one of only a number of books and that, if I had nothing else in the world to do except to sit on a fence and think about things, it would in fact be only one of a number of books. You have only to think about this a moment to see how extensible the idea is. I could very well do a THEORY OF SUPREME FICTION, and I could try a BOOK OF SPECIMENS, etc. etc.
>
> (8 Dec 1942)

He tells Simons, 'As I see the subject, it would occupy a school of rabbis for the next few generations' (12 Jan 1943).

The 'school of rabbis' is only one of several religious comparisons that Stevens uses to try to make clear the function of a supreme fiction. He has the greatest ambitions: he is, he informs Simons, 'trying to create something as valid as the idea of God has been, and for that matter remains' (12 Jan 1943). He seeks to establish as a permanent possibility – rather than as the chance result of a random encounter with an object – that 'affirmation free from doubt' of 'Women Looking at a Vase of Flowers'. Underlying the poem, he states to his Harvard classmate Gilbert Montague,

> is the idea that, in the various predicaments of belief, it might be possible to yield or try to yield, ourselves to a declared fiction.

This is the same thing as saying that it might be possible for us to believe in something that we know to be untrue. Of course, we do that every day, but we don't make the most of the fact that we do it out of the need to believe, what in your day, and mine, in Cambridge was called the will to believe.   (22 Mar 1943)

This is a surrender or exchange of self in the interests of self-belief, a yielding to that which the poet knows exists because he has created it. The poet is so often compared to an actor in Stevens because he, too, is expected to sustain an illusion, to tell us (and himself) a story that will hold us so enthralled that we shall forget our scepticism. Stevens desires to trust or know the world if only for a moment, even if that knowledge is an illusion. The impossibility of belief rests on the impossibility of knowledge; if we know nothing for certain, then the world has no meaning; it is not a totality, system or language. To mean nothing is to be without purpose and not to be whole. His growing conviction that everything is without meaning or purpose strengthens his will to believe, causing him to invent meaning so as to feel purposeful (and whole) and to attempt to have total faith in his creations. He explains the matter at length to Henry Church:

One evening, a week or so ago, a student at Trinity College came to the office and walked home with me. We talked about this book. I said that I thought that we had reached a point at which we could no longer really believe in anything unless we recognised that it was a fiction. The student said that that was an impossibility, that there was no such thing as believing in something that one knew was not true. It is obvious, however, that we are doing that all the time. There are things with respect to which we willingly suspend disbelief; if there is instinctive in us a will to believe, or if there is a will to believe, whether or not it is instinctive, it seems to me that we can suspend disbelief with reference to a fiction as easily as we can suspend it with reference to anything else. There are fictions that are extensions of reality. There are plenty of people who believe in Heaven as definitely as your New England ancestors and my Dutch ancestors believed in it. But Heaven is an extension of reality.   (8 Dec 1942)

The supreme fiction integrates his certainty and uncertainty; it is derived from reality and is something that we experience deeply, real as the imagination is real – it exists not as a paradox, but as a feeling, as Stevens writes to Simons: 'Nothing mystical is even for a moment intended' (29 Mar 1943).

'Notes Toward a Supreme Fiction' is divided into three sections – 'It Must Be Abstract', 'It Must Change', 'It Must Give Pleasure' – with an eight-line introduction and a separate concluding poem that balance each other as prologue and epilogue. Each of the three major sections is composed of ten poems, each of seven three-line stanzas. As the concluding poem is also of this form, there are thirty-one of these poems altogether. 'My line', Stevens tells Katherine Frazier, 'is a pentameter line, but it runs over and under now and then' (19 May 1942). Thus, he gave himself in every way more space than in 'The Man with the Blue Guitar', and, with the division into three sections and a regular number of poems and stanzas, set himself carefully fixed limits, which he had not done in the earlier work. He left himself some leeway in the line length and completely free in the relation of sentences to stanzas (he rhymes only occasionally and randomly) and in the articulation of both stanzas and poems. Each poem is self-contained, complete in itself with its own definite conclusions. The sentences are relatively short, and uncomplicated, averaging two to three lines in the first two sections and three to four in the last section – which also has the longest sentences (one of sixteen-plus lines and one of fourteen, compared to ten in the first and ten-plus in the second). Similarly, most of the individual poems are composed either of many short sentences or of several longer ones.

There are slight differences in the organisation of the different sections. The first presents the most fully developed argument; the first four poems discuss the notion of the 'first idea' and the last four 'major man', the thinker of the first idea. The poet addresses the 'ephebe' – according to the *OED*, a Greek citizen of between eighteen and twenty who 'was occupied chiefly with garrison duty' but who in the poem is a young student, apprentice poet and *alter ego* of the poet, who is rejuvenated in the search for truth. The addresses to the ephebe in poems I, V and X, and the constant *we* and *us* establish a conversational tone, making the monologue feel like dialogue, and holding the section together. The ephebe is not mentioned in any of the other sections; nevertheless, the whole work can be considered as addressed to him. There is a shift or break in the fourth stanza of most poems in the first section: a full stop in line 10 or 12, or both, and the introduction of a new image or the sustained elaboration of an idea or image in the final three stanzas. This change does not occur in the poems in the other two sections. They are more fully integrated wholes (as if Stevens had become more comfortable in his form) and cannot be easily divided into parts.

The subject of change produces the most questions: the second section has nearly twice as many as either of the other two, and they occur in series (the ten questions in section 2 are distributed between poems II and IX, with four and six respectively. Most of the poems in the second section centre around a single protagonist: the seraph (I), the President (II), the statue of General Du Puy (III), the planter (V), the sparrow (VI), Nanzia Nunzio (VIII) and the unnamed man in the park (X). In this section more than any other the stanzas are the unit of thought, with full stops occurring regularly at the end of each triad. As if for contrast, this happens less in the third section than in either of the two, and notably in its first three poems. As in the second section, a number of poems are scenes with a single protagonist or central metaphor – the blue woman (II), the red stone face (III), the marriage of the captain and Bawda (IV), the fat girl (X); and, unlike in either of the first two sections, four poems (V, VI, VII, VIII) are devoted to a narrative: the story of Canon Aspirin, his sister and her children, and his vision of the Angel, with a shift in poems VIII – X to the first person.

'Notes Toward a Supreme Fiction' begins with a moment of completion. The poet addresses an unidentified 'you':

> And for what, except for you, do I feel love?
> Do I press the extremest book of the wisest man
> Close to me, hidden in me day and night?
> In the uncertain light of single, certain truth,
> Equal in living changingness to the light
> In which I meet you, in which we sit at rest,
> For a moment in the central of our being,
> The vivid transparence that you bring is peace.

The person addressed is the old woman in a wig, the regina of the clouds, 'the one of fictive music', the woman singer on the shore at Key West, the interior paramour and muse – one of the innumerable, maternal and queenly figures that appear throughout Stevens' poetry, necessarily abstract for presiding over the most intangible feelings, the ghostliest demarcations, so abstract that there is no indication of gender. Her presence turns perception, and poetry, into dialogue.

The poet has no being without her: it is *our being*. The initial question implies that she is the exclusive focus of the poet's love. He meets her in a light equal 'in living changingness' to the light of truth – that is, the light of fiction. The moment is very similar to 'the intensest rendezvous' of 'Final Soliloquy of the Interior Paramour', where:

> Out of this same light, out of the central mind,
> We make a dwelling in the evening air,
> In which being there together is enough.

The language is somewhat different in that poem because it is the paramour who speaks – and because of the living changingness of all ideas in Stevens. He uses the most ordinary words for his very complex purposes, modifying a few of them very slightly and combining them with rarer words such as *transparence*. He makes the more active *Changingness* out of the present participle, rejecting *changeableness* as only denoting potential. He converts an adjective, *central*, to a noun, again to make it more active and less obviously spatial than *centre*, to endow this newly created location with controlling power. This makes it a place that we have not visited before: '*the central* of our being'. These alterations are grammatical, matters of structure. The poet and his beloved sit together at rest; he experiences an extraordinary clarity, in which the act of vision, becoming total, becomes a state of mind without an object. for a moment the poet possesses what he desires: he is. He sees through everything, transparent to himself. Everything becomes clear. This is 'an emotion of two people . . . becoming one'.

'The real world seen by an imaginative man may very well seem like an imaginative construction', Stevens writes to Latimer (31 Oct 1935). This idea is the point of departure for the exposition of the supreme fiction. The world originates in an act of the imagination. To begin at the beginning, Stevens starts with *Begin* and invites a beginner, the ephebe, to conceive of an idea coming into existence without a mind to think it:

> Begin, ephebe, by perceiving the idea
> Of this invention, this invented world,
> The inconceivable idea of the sun.

> You must become an ignorant man again
> And see the sun again with an ignorant eye
> And see it clearly in the idea of it.
>
> Never suppose an inventing mind as source
> Of this idea nor for that mind compose
> A voluminous master folded in his fire.
>
> (1. i. 1–9)

The origin of the idea of the world is to be discovered in the idea of the sun and neither in the world nor sun itself. The essence or nature of things is to be grasped in the idea of them. Stevens is a Copernican, his world depends upon the sun. Because we see by its light, without it we would have no knowledge of reality; therefore, to see the sun in its idea is to understand how we see. The 'voluminous master folded in his fire' (reminiscent of Ulysses wrapped in a horn of flame in *Inferno*, xxxvi) is so powerful a metaphor as to negate the poet's command never to suppose an inventing mind. Seeing the first idea, as Stevens comes to call the supreme fiction, means seeing the world and sun as if for the first time, without preconceptions – without any other ideas. This act of regression that is rewarded by the recovery of the first self involves divesting oneself of all other acts of vision, of every myth and memory:

> How clean the sun when seen in its idea,
> Washed in the remotest cleanliness of a heaven
> That has expelled us and our images . . .
>
> The death of one god is the death of all.
> Let purple Phoebus lie in umber harvest,
> Let Phoebus slumber and die in autumn umber,
>
> Phoebus is dead, ephebe. But Phoebus was
> A name for something that never could be named.
> There was a project for the sun and is.
>
> There is a project for the sun. The sun
> Must bear no name, gold flourisher, but be
> In the difficulty of what it is to be.
>
> (1. i. 10–21)

The poem changes, with a characteristic modulation, from a succession of terse, sinewy abstract statements to a murmurous hymn on the death of the gods, repeating the same sounds over and over as if to conjure more meaning from them. *Ephebe* is, of course, virtually an anagram of *Phoebus* (another youth), a demonstration that our gods are ourselves transformed. By calling the supreme fiction a *project*, Stevens both affirms the existence of an encompassing design and puts its execution in the future. The plan is simple, if paradoxical: the sun must bear no name, because it is unnamable, because every name is the imposition of another idea – the enmeshing of the object in the imaginative system of language. If it exists, it must exist as all other things exist, in the difficulty of what it is to be.

The remotest cleanliness of a dehumanised, anti-anthropomorphic heaven, however, makes us dissatisfied and uneasy:

> It is the celestial ennui of apartments
> That sends us back to the first idea, the quick
> Of this invention; and yet so poisonous
>
> Are the ravishments of truth, so fatal to
> The truth itself, the first idea becomes
> The hermit in a poet's metaphors,
> Who comes and goes and comes and goes all day.
>
>   (1. II. 1–7)

'The celestial ennui of apartments' is an example of Stevens' ability to construct phrases that are grammatical, without lexical difficulties, yet strange, and almost without antecedents. He reduces the number of definite, explicit connections between the phrase and its context while increasing the connotative ones. 'The celestial ennui' is delicately comic; none the less, *ennui* carries the accumulated power of 'Les Fleurs du Mal'. An empty heaven is boring. Boredom is a form of loneliness, and it is this compelling need, profound longing and restless anguish, that sends us back to the first idea. Phoebus is dead. Long live Phoebus! Our need sends us back as if in time to the central vital substance of our imagined world, the idea made flesh in the word *quick*. This truth so removes us from the earth, so separates the spirit from the body, that it is self-destructive, so abstract that thinking about it necessarily changes it, giving it a form like Phoebus or Gold Flourisher, and causing it to lose its identity. It disappears, vestigially incarnate, momentarily present, only in a poet's metaphors. Again Stevens embodies an idea in a person. The first idea is the hermit that dwells apart in solitude, only intermittently present in some poet's metaphors – and by making the first idea a person he establishes a continuity that survives the hermit's coming and going. This is a statement which leads to the second major characteristic of the supreme fiction, that it must change, that there is an element in the second term of every metaphor that is discontinuous, a series of presences and absences. Every detail contributes to demonstrating the elusiveness of the first idea. The definite article of *hermit* indicates that the hermit is unique, while the indefinite article of *poet* produces a vague particularity: this is not a generic statement; the first idea cannot come and go generally.

These incessant appearances and disappearances cause their own anguish –

> May there be an ennui of the first idea?
> What else, prodigious scholar, should there be?
>
> (1. II. 8–9)

– and, in the midst of this loneliness, the forget-me-not (*Myosotis arvensis*) blooms, as blue as the sky at the end of winter.

> And not to have is the beginning of desire.
> To have what is not is its ancient cycle.
> It is desire at the end of winter, when
>
> It observes the effortless weather turning blue
> And sees the myosotis on its bush.
> Being virile, it hears the calendar hymn.
>
> It knows that what it has is what is not
> And throws it away like a thing of another time,
> As morning throws off stale moonlight and shabby sleep.
>
> (1. II. 13–21)

Desire is the hallucination of its object. To be filled with desire is to be possessed by the imagination. 'Not to have' is the precondition of desire that from time immemorial has turned itself, with the inevitability of the seasons, into 'To have what is not'. Desire, as long as it remains desire, is nothing, and cannot, for all its longing, truly change itself into its object; when it is confronted with the effortless changes of the weather, when it sees the myosotis being virile instead of merely wishing for virility, it becomes self-conscious and discards its imagined object as we awake from dreams. The calendar hymn is change conceived as music, a harmonious and orderly process in which the existence of each thing in the world is like a sound or note. The whole poem is pervaded by the feeling of temporality (*beginning, ancient, cycle, end, winter, weather, calendar, time, morning*), the idea of the coming and going of all things.

> The poem refreshes life so that we share,
> For a moment, the first idea ... It satisfies
> Belief in an immaculate beginning
>
> And sends us, winged by an unconscious will,
> To an immaculate end. We move between these points:
> From that ever-early candor to its late plural
>
> And the candor of them is the strong exhilaration
> Of what we feel from what we think, of thought
> Beating in the heart, as if blood newly came,
>
> An elixir, an excitation, a pure power.
> The poem, through candor, brings back a power again
> That gives a candid kind to everything.

(1. III. 1–12)

The poem (not poetry, as it is only a particular poem that can offer a dwelling-place to the first idea) is an emotion shared, a communal act, and, as long as it lasts, we are not alone. Because it is the tangible expression of intangibles, an incarnation of the imagination, it offers us for a moment a glimpse of the idea of a supreme fiction, thereby satisfying our desire for a pure and wholly known beginning. The power of the poem causes us to suspend our disbelief. We are winged (like Pegasus or the necessary angel), caught up, transported. *Candor* means brilliant whiteness, as in 'From the Packet of Anacharsis':

> In the punctual centre of all circles white
> Stands truly. The circles nearest to it share
>
> Its color, but less as they recede, impinged
> By difference and then by definition
> As a tone defines itself and separates
>
> And the circles quicken and crystal colors come
> And flare . . . .

Thus we move from the singular 'ever-early candor to its late plural', from the supreme fiction as the first idea to its intermittent incarnation in successive poems, and each time the idea is made real by speech we are exhilarated. 'Thought / Beating in the heart' is continuous incarnation and the successive appositions mimic the heart-beat. The pulsing heart is an image of change and of alternation; the blue blood becoming red as it takes in the world's oxygen. *Candor* and *immaculate* both denote purity. The candid is an approximation of transparence.

> We say: At night an Arabian in my room,
> With his damned hoobla-hoobla-hoobla-how,
> Inscribes a primitive astronomy
>
> Across the unscrawled fores the future casts
> And throws his stars around the floor. By day
> The wood-dove used to chant his hoobla-hoo
>
> And still the grossest iridescence of ocean
> Howls hoo and rises and howls hoo and falls.
> Life's nonsense pierces us with strange relation.

> (1. III. 13–21)

Stevens explains his metaphor to Simons as follows: 'The Arabian is the moon; the undecipherable vagueness of the moonlight is the unscrawled fores: the unformed handwriting' (12 Jan 1943). Like Wordsworth, Stevens associates poetry with an Arab, with the esoteric knowledge of the Orient. His 'hoobla-hoobla', suggesting the gutturals of Arabic (and the sound and name of the hubble-bubble?), is the imagination's gobbledegook, half-formed, half-chaotic thought. *Fores* are goings, traces, proceedings; Stevens employs an archaic and obsolete word to indicate the possibilities inherent in the future. The moonlight foreshadows and forelights things to come, creating forms that seem to have meaning, but are indecipherable. The wood-dove is moon-coloured and the ocean shines with the iridescence of the dove's feathers, and the 'hoobla-how' that seems to ask the question of origins (how things happen) strangely resembles the 'hoobla-hoo' and 'hoo . . . hoo' that ask the question of identity (who?). All resemblances, all relations, pierce us, strike us to the heart, at the central of our being. This piercing is like a moment of transparence.

> The first idea was not our own. Adam
> In Eden was the father of Descartes
> And Eve made air the mirror of herself,
>
> Of her sons and of her daughters. They found themselves
> In heaven as in a glass; a second earth;
> And in the earth itself they found a green –
>
> The inhabitants of a very varnished green.
>
> (1. iv. 1–7)

When Adam opened his eyes in Eden for the first time, the world was already there. The idea of its invention was not his. He had, like Descartes, to take his own consciousness as his point of departure in order to interpret his surroundings. He imposed his idea of order upon the world, naming all the animals: 'and whatsoever Adam called every living creature, that *was* the name thereof' (Genesis 2:19). As Stevens explains to Simons, 'Descartes is used as a symbol of the reason. But we live in a place that is not our own; we do not live in a land of Descartes; we have imposed the reason; Adam imposed it even in Eden' (12 Jan 1943). The same idea is stated very simply in the final section of the poem:

> We reason of these things with later reason
> And we make of what we see, what we see clearly
> And have seen, a place dependent on ourselves.
>
> (3. iv. 1–3)

Reason comes later. What we see when we first open our eyes is our point of departure; everything that we make of the world and of ourselves uses this original data, and it is, according to Stevens, poetry's task to recover a fresh vision of this primal ignorance; it is such seeing that enables us to behold the world in the pristine glory of the first idea. As Stevens writes to Simons,

> When a poet makes his imagination the imagination of other people, he does so by making them see the world through his eyes. Most modern activity is the undoing of that very job. The world has been painted; most modern activity is getting rid of the paint to get at the world itself. Powerful integrations of the imagination are difficult to get away from.   (18 Feb 1942)

Writing to Henry Church, he is even more specific and succinct: 'If you take the varnish and dirt of generations off a picture, you see it in its first idea. If you think about the world without its varnish and dirt, you are a thinker of the first idea' (28 Oct 1942). If Adam is the father of reason, Eve is the mother of imagination. She sees herself reflected in nothingness and produces heaven out of thin air. She and her children dwell in heaven as in a mirror, a habit of mind that causes them to find the earth a 'very varnished green', the idea of its invention overlaid by these successive projections of themselves. Stevens sums up in the fifth stanza, 'From this the poem springs: that we live in a place / That is not our own and, much more, not ourselves' (1. IV. 13–14). To understand what we see is difficult, but it is even more difficult to understand our selves, to be in 'the difficulty of what it is to be'. Implicit in this is that the self can only be understood in terms of some other. If the world was our selves, then, in apprehending the world, we should apprehend our selves and be complete; as it is, wholeness is only an idea, and we must interpret what we are in terms of what we are not. The poem consoles us for the alien nature of our surroundings.

This alienation is dramatised in the next poem:

> The lion roars at the enraging desert,
> Reddens the sand with his red-colored noise,
> Defies red emptiness to evolve his match,
>
> Master by foot and jaws and by the mane,
> Most supple challenger. The elephant
> Breaches the darkness of Ceylon with blares,

The glitter-goes on surfaces of tanks,
Shattering velvetest far-away. The bear,
The ponderous cinnamon, snarls in his mountain

At summer thunder and sleeps through winter snow.

(1. v. 1–10)

'Most of the things we know,' says William James, 'the tigers now in India, for example, ... are known only ... symbolically' or 'conceptually'.[1] For Stevens, all our knowledge is of this kind. His lion, elephant and cinnamon-bear who roar, blare and snarl in the present tense are like 'the tigers now in India'. The lion appears in 'The Man with the Blue Guitar' (xix), where, locked inscrutably in the stone that is the world, he stands for everything that the poet faces outside himself, nature in its monstrous aspect – which he hopes to match 'speaking (as a poet) with a voice matching its own'. 'One thing about life is that the mind of one man, if strong enough, can become the master of all life in the world. To some extent his is an everyday phenomenon. Any real great poet, musician, etc. does this' (Stevens to Simons, 8 Aug 1940). The lion, elephant and cinnamon bear are each poets in their own way, as Stevens explains to Simons apropos another poem, 'On an Old Horn' (1939): 'Animals challenge with their voices; birds comfort themselves with their voices, rely on their voices as chief encourager, etc. It follows that a lion roaring in a desert and a boy whistling in the dark, are alike, playing old horns ... ' (18 Feb 1942). The wild animals roaming the world are contrasted with the ephebe shut in his attic room 'with a rented piano', living a dimly suggested Bohemian life in an unnamed Paris, solitary and anguished.[2] He lies in silence upon his bed, clutches the corner of the pillow, writhes and presses a 'bitter utterance' from his writhing, a 'dumb/ Yet voluble dumb violence' (1. v. 15–16), that in the end makes him the master of the animals – and the world. He triumphs through the strength of his imagination. He is one of 'the heroic children whom time breeds/ Against the first idea – to lash the lion, / Caparison elephants, teach bears to juggle' (1. v. 19–21). The metaphor is exuberant. The animals are set not to work but to play. Poetry makes the world a circus.

The sixth poem offers us our first glimpse of the giant as Stevens moves from the first idea to its putative originator. Adam, Descartes and the ephebe all attempt to recover, dis-cover, the first idea, but who was the first thinker of the first idea? If the first idea is a fiction, then the thinker is also a fiction; if the first idea is the supreme fiction, then its thinker must be supremely powerful – a giant, a purely imaginary and utterly fictitious being. We see him first as 'the giant of the weather', because for Stevens the weather is the giant's counterpart: elemental brute reality. The weather in Stevens' poetry does not mean anything; it is itself, being in all its changingness, and 'ever-jubilant' like the weather in 'Waving Adieu, Adieu, Adieu'. 'The "ever-jubilant weather" is not a symbol', Stevens writes to Simons (9 Jan 1940). 'We are physical beings in a physical world; the weather is one of the things that we enjoy, one of the unphilosophical realities.' Thus, as he explains to Simons on 12 January 1943, the sixth poem moves back and forth between the extremes of imagination and reality:

> The abstract does not exist, but it is certainly as immanent: that is to say, the fictive abstract is as immanent in the mind of the poet, as the idea of God is immanent in the mind of the theologian. The poem is a struggle with the inaccessibility of the abstract. First I make the effort; then I turn to the weather because that is not inaccessible and is not abstract. The weather as described is the weather that was about me when I wrote this. There is a constant reference from the abstract to the real, to and fro.

'This', Stevens says, 'was difficult to do.' The poet, like the ephebe in the previous poem, struggles 'to master all the life in the world':

> Not to be realized because not to
> Be seen, not to be loved nor hated because
> Not to be realized. Weather by Franz Hals,
>
> Brushed up by brushy winds in brushy clouds,
> Wetted by blue, colder for white. Not to
> Be spoken to, without a roof, without
>
> First fruits, without the virginal of birds,
> The dark-blown ceinture loosened, not relinquished.
> Gay is, gay was, the gay forsythia

And yellow, yellow thins the Northern blue.
Without a name and nothing to be desired,
If only imagined but imagined well.

My house has changed a little in the sun.
The fragrance of the magnolias comes close,
False flick, false form, but falseness close to kin.

It must be visible or invisible,
Invisible or visible or both:
A seeing and unseeing in the eye.

The weather and the giant of the weather,
Say the weather, the mere weather, the mere air:
An abstraction blooded, as a man by thought.

(I. VI. 1–21)

The first four stanzas consist of three statements on the subject of
the supreme fiction alternating with two on the weather. The
abstractness of the supreme fiction makes itself felt in that none of
the statements about it is a complete sentence, and that each is a
series of negations, with neither subject nor object. The imaginative
power that the poet derives from contact with the earth (and its
weather) is demonstrated by the fact that these statements become
slightly less abstract, slightly less negative, as they interact with the
weather: the idea of realisation produces brush-strokes and the
brushy weather produces the fruits, birds and 'dark-blown
ceinture'. The alternation is a progress until in the final three stanzas
the poet is able to unite his imagination and his reality in a vision of
his house that is fictitious yet akin to what it is, a good
approximation of its reality.

At the start of the sixth poem perception is analysed into three
stages: vision, realisation, emotion (in which love and hate appear
as equally valuable). The poems of 'The Man with the Blue Guitar',
Stevens tells Latimer, 'are not abstractions . . . what they really deal
with is the painter's problem of realisation' (17 Mar 1937).
'*Realisation*, in all its meanings – understanding what is seen, feeling
and becoming real, converting property into money (obtaining
value) and the painter's (and poet's) problem of technique – is the
subject of 'Notes Toward a Supreme Fiction'. Stevens, who was very
conscious of being the descendent of Dutchmen, chooses a Dutch

painter, Franz Hals, whose brush-strokes are freer than those of most of his contemporaries and whose people are often painted enjoying the physical world with gusto. As the poet takes possession of the weather we see *his* realising brush-strokes, are aware of his composing of the scene, demonstrating to us that all seeing and unseeing is 'in the eye', a manifestation of the eye's (and mind's) structure. There can be no communication, however, with anything that does not inhabit a particular place and that does not disclose itself, *at least once*, in a palpable form: first fruits or virginal sounds, the belt of its concealing garment loosened if not relinquished. The sun-yellow forsythia (the previous flower, myosotis, was blue) brightens and warms the cold, dark-blown sky. This increase in reality in turn modifies the imagining of the supreme fiction in the poet's imagination. The prerequisites for its existence are now fulfilled: it is without a name and possessed; it is nothing to be desired, and therefore not part of the ancient cycle in which desire produces a hallucination of the absent object; and it is only imagined and imagined well. As a result the poet finds himself at home, under his own roof, in his imagined world, the visible and invisible merged in a feeling of familiar closeness, a metaphoric blood-tie, and we behold the weather and the giant of the weather. Stevens no sooner mentions the giant than he retreats from him, focusing insistently on the weather. However, he is engaged in a reciprocal process: the abstraction is realised as it is shaped, informed, by the world, as a man is realised, becomes what he is, through the continuous circulation of his thoughts. To be blooded is to be initiated: the face of the ephebe fox-hunter is smeared with the blood of his first kill, or a dog is given its first taste of the blood of the game it is to hunt. The ratio, *blood : abstraction :: thought : man*, while it fills the supreme fiction with the ever-changing world, fills the man with dreams. He exists as an abstraction – and, in the terms of the ratio, this is his health.

The seventh poem begins as the sixth ends, with a movement away from the giant, yet even negated he is present, and what follows appears as if it depends on this negative presence of the giant. He is virtually the condition of the three sentences beginning *Perhaps*. The final three poems of the first section develop the idea of major man out of that of the giant, and this poem with its celebration of the ordinary helps to establish things on a human scale. The supreme fiction is blooded by everyday life. There is another record of realisation. Again there is a see-sawing between faith and doubt. The truth is perhaps contingent (and the fiction?). The walk around the lake is perhaps imagined rather than actual (we cannot be certain), the problematic circumambulation of a blue object. We are invited to watch a definition growing certain and to wait within that certainty.

> It feels good as it is without the giant,
> A thinker of the first idea. Perhaps
> The truth depends on a walk around a lake,
>
> A composing as the body tires, a stop
> To see hepatica, a stop to watch
> A definition growing certain and
>
> A wait within that certainty, a rest
> In the swags of pine-trees bordering the lake.
> Perhaps there are times of inherent excellence,
>
> As when the cock crows on the left and all
> Is well, incalculable balances,
> At which a kind of Swiss perfection comes
>
> And a familiar music of the machine
> Sets up its Schwärmerei, not balances
> That we achieve but balances that happen,
>
> As a man and woman meet and love forthwith.
> Perhaps there are moments of awakening,
> Extreme, fortuitous, personal, in which
>
> We more than awaken, sit on the edge of sleep,
> As on an elevation, and behold
> The academies like structures in a mist.

                                                (I. VII. 1–21)

Certainty is a process, the arrestation of movement; definition, fixity. The walk is a stop, stop, wait and a rest. *Schwärmerei*, its ecstasy that happens, is a word for fanaticism that makes extreme faith synonymous with continuous, multitudinous movement. It refers to the swarming of bees, which must have appeared to its inventor like a delirious mob of true believers. (The bees return in section 2, representing the inextricably related concepts of change and being.) Hepatica is a very small flower that appears in the woods in early spring and is difficult to see, as it nestles in the shelter of a log or root or last autumn's leaves. There is considerable variation in the colour of the flowers. They are sometimes red, sometimes blue, sometimes purple, brighter, darker than the magnolia blossoms mentioned in the previous poem, which have only a purple blush or tinge – 'purple for victory', as Stevens says in 'Life on a Battleship', the imagination's victory in apprehending the world. *Swag* means to hang loosely or heavily, a swaying movement and stolen riches. The pines appear to be that green that 'smacks' the man on the dump in the eye, an unvarnished evergreen, and, as the idea that there was an order in the sea-surface full of clouds made the ocean a machine, the world in this case is a kind of Swiss music-box that runs of itself. The thought of 'balances that happen' is a holiday for the poet', it means that we do not have to do anything, but can allow the never-resting mind to stop and simply be. Peace as a balance suggests the wavering up and down of the scales that any Swiss clock-maker might possess, or the swaying of pine-boughs in the wind, emphasising that commonly a balance is a temporary counterpoising of elements or forces. 'Man and woman meet and love forthwith' – the second *and* withholds the *forthwith*, love is not quite at first sight; there is the slight separation as between vision, realisation and love or hate in vi. These separations are the poet's loneliness, and completion is again compared to love and being close to another person. We more than awaken and sit, resting as on an elevation, like the ephebe looking across the roofs. Here, looking closely at the real world (the lake, hepatica and pines) wakes us up to the dream world. Academies are buildings that stand for public order, the official homes of systematic thought and corporations or bodies of thinkers. The plurality of academies is a sign of our lack of any final certainty, like the impalpable, ghostly mist. We behold all our ideas as a system growing certain, balancing, changing, dissolving.

The next poem begins by asking whether it is possible to create a more substantial structure: 'Can we compose a castle-fortress-home ... And set MacCullough there as major man?' (1. viii. 1, 3). A castle is where giants live, the fortress is a never-failing bulwark against doubt and home is where we belong, our ordinary, everyday dwelling-place. The 'MacCullough' is Stevens' attempt to bring the giant down to earth. There can be very little doubt that Stevens' idea of major man owes something to Nietzsche's *Übermensch*.[3] At the beginning of *Also sprach Zarathustra*, Zarathustra, who has spent ten years as a hermit in the mountains meditating, decides to descend into the world to teach what he has learned. The *Übermensch* is Zarathustra's answer to the death of God. He tells the people in the village at the edge of the forest, '*I teach you the overman*. Man is something that shall be overcome. What have you done to overcome him?' The *Übermensch* is a goal for humanity in a world of bad faith. He stands for new human values: 'The overman is the meaning of earth. Let your will say: the overman *shall be* the meaning of the earth! I beseech you, my brothers, *remain faithful to the earth*, and do not believe those who speak to you of otherworldly hopes!'[4] The *Übermensch* resembles major man in that both are ways of personalising metaphysics, denoting human potential, affirming a secular ideal and establishing a man-centred cosmos. The two ideas are not the same: the *Übermensch* is a goal to be achieved in the future, a stage in human development yet to come; major man is a point of origin, an imaginative act to be performed in the present in order that present and past should be continuous. The *Übermensch* is the beginning of an ethics, major man, the beginning of an epistemology. Stevens writes to Church that Nietzsche is 'a perfect example' of 'how a strong mind distorts the world' (18 Dec 1942). 'The incessant job is to get into focus, not out of focus. Nietzsche is as perfect a means of getting out of focus as a little bit too much to drink.' The function of major man is to get the world into focus. He is a 'crystal hypothesis'. He is for Stevens a logical (and psychological) necessity. The first thinker of the first idea is the poetic expression of Stevens' genealogical researches (pursued with particular vigour at this time), the final and original imaginary ancestor who saves us from infinite regression into the unknown past. Imagination and reality are united as they are separated: in a man.

> The first idea is an imagined thing.
> The pensive giant prone in violet space
> May be the MacCullough, an expedient,
>
> Logos and logic, crystal hypothesis,
> Incipit and a form to speak the word
> And every latent double in the word,

Beau linguist. But the MacCullough is MacCullough.
It does not follow that major man is man.
If MacCullough himself lay lounging by the sea,

Drowned in its washes, reading in the sound,
About the thinker of the first idea,
He might take habit, whether from wave or phrase,

Or power of the wave, or deepened speech,
Or a leaner being, moving in on him,
Of greater aptitude and apprehension,

As if the waves at last were never broken,
As if the language suddenly, with ease,
Said things it had laboriously spoken.

(1. VIII. 4–21)

Major man is 'logos' (the creative word that was at the beginning: 'Εν ἀρχῇ ἦν ὁ λόγος[5] – 'The thesis of the plentifullest John' as Stevens calls it in 'Description without Place') and 'Incipit' (Latin for *begins*), a term used in the description of manuscripts for the opening words of a text). He is word and phrase, speech and writing, Greek and Latin – the two primary shaping languages of European culture. The several doubles testify to his synergic power. He forms the idea of the world as it is. He is an autonomous Adam speaking as if for the first time the name of reality. The doubleness latent in this naming is the difficulty that each person has in any act of perception of distinguishing what is imaginary from what is real. This is the difficulty of what it is to be. *If* he lay lounging by the sea – every statement in the poem is problematic in keeping with the abstractness and fictitiousness of the subject – MacCullough *might*, 'whether from wave or phrase', from without or within (again the latent doubleness) form a habit of mind that would ensure the continuity of being. The unbroken waves are an end to the intermittences of perception, the unbroken speech, 'the declaimed clairvoyance' (1. IX. 1) that makes all things transparent. 'The gist of this poem', Stevens replies to Simons (12 Jan 1943), 'is that the MacCullough is MacCullough, MacCullough is any name, any man' – that is, major man might be anybody, but must be a particular person. However, since the thinker of the first idea is a fiction, it 'does not follow that major man is man'. Major man is imaginary and particular (like a character in a novel), the ultimate fiction, a hypothesis with a definite logical function in Stevens' theory, while man is real, a generality, and an abstraction – without any special function. *MacCullough* is a name chosen for its prosaicness, to be the opposite of *Phoebus*, and Stevens makes his major man a Scot in order to make him as practical as possible, stubborn, industrious, hard-headed and tight-fisted, knowing the value of money and the world, someone without any vestige of the imagination's moon-light. 'How simply the fictive hero becomes the real', Stevens observes in the final poem. The particularity of the McCullough is in order to promote this merger.

'The MacCullough is McCullough' so as to be totally human, because he is to take the place of Phoebus and of God. Stevens sometimes thought that this humanism was insufficiently clear in 'Notes Toward a Supreme Fiction'. He tells Robert Pack, 'For a long time, I have thought of adding other sections to the NOTES and one in particular: *It Must Be Human*. But I think it would be wrong not to leave well enough alone' (28 Dec 1954). In the letter to Simons quoted above Stevens goes on to say, 'The trouble with humanism is that man as God remains man, but there is an extension of man, the leaner being, in fiction, a possibly more than human human, a composite human. The act of recognizing him is the act of this leaner being moving in on us.' Major man stands for our human potential and is an enhancement of self. He is 'a leaner being' – lean because he exists on the imagination's poverty – 'Of greater aptitude and apprehension', at once our imagined origin and final form, the limit of what is possible. Here (and in 1. IX and x) Stevens distinguishes between major man and MacCullough. *The* MacCullough is *the* major man, the thinker of the first idea; MacCullough is any man capable of projecting and reabsorbing the idea of major man, the leaner being who is a possibility, 'composite' of the imagination and reality. That he is in some sense beyond us is shown by his moving *in* on us.

'Apotheosis is not', Stevens states in the ninth poem, 'The origin of the major man' (1. IX. 5–6). His creation is not a deification; the ephebe is to produce major man through a process of self-realisation. He comes

from reason,
Lighted at midnight by the studious eye,
Swaddled in revery, the object of

The hum of thoughts evaded in the mind,
Hidden from other thoughts, he that reposes
On a breast forever precious for that touch . . . .

(1. IX. 7–12)

He is the product of the mind alone, of conscious reason and revery, and the unconscious: the hum, the almost-language, of what the mind does not want to think and hides from itself – and yet that which connects the mind, everlastingly and continuously, to reality. The child's first contact with the world is with its mother's breast, and, as Stevens says later in the poem,

The child that touches takes character from the thing,
The body, it touches.

(2. IV. 17–18)

The major man is the embodiment of this touching. He lives in order to maintain this contact: he *reposes* indefinitely and this ever-present *repose* (the word describes the state of mind that results from the action) endows the world with its value. Appropriately the poet then turns to the muse–mother: 'My dame, sing for this person accurate songs' (1. IX. 15). Even at this union of the palpable and the impalpable, his affirmation is interrupted by a doubt: 'He is and may be but oh! he is, he is' (1. IX. 16) – the repetition, his wish fulfilling itself. This poem closes with a reprise of major man's abstractness:

Give him
No names. Dismiss him from your images.
The hot of him is purest in the heart.

(1. IX. 19–21)

He exists unimaginably at the centre of our feelings.

'The major abstraction is the idea of man', Stevens states in the concluding poem of the first section:

And major man is its exponent, abler
In the abstract than in his singular,

More fecund as principle than particle.

(1. X. 2–4)

Major man is the *exponent* of the idea of man, the central figure in
Stevens' new humanism, in the three senses of the word: he brings
the idea outside (*ex-ponere*, to place without) the realm of pure
imagination, giving it a form, even if an abstract one; he expounds,
sets forth or interprets the idea of man *and* raises it to a higher
power, magnifying and enriching it with the power of our
aspirations, with all our imagined becomings. He is not a hero,
rather 'an heroic part, of the commonal'. This, however, is still too
abstract and the poet asks, 'Who is it?' The MacCullough is Stevens'
first attempt to *realise* major man so as to make him one of us; his
second is the somewhat ludicrous, backward-looking figure in old
clothes who now emerges. What rabbi or chieftain, the poet asks,

> Does not see these separate figures one by one,
> And yet see only one, in his old coat,
> His slouching pantaloons, beyond the town,
>
> Looking for what was, where it used to be?
> Cloudless the morning. It is he. The man
> In that old coat, those sagging pantaloons,
>
> It is of him, ephebe, to make, to confect
> The final elegance, not to console
> Nor sanctify, but plainly to propound.
>
> (1. x. 13–21)

This man is 'the old fantoche' of 'The Man with the Blue Guitar' and
reminiscent of the *persona* of Charlie Chaplin. With his clown-like
'sagging pantaloons' (Pantaloon is a stock figure of the *commedia
del'arte*), he is comedian and poet, shabby with the wear and tear of
reality. He lives 'beyond the town', possibly near the dump, like a
hobo, a nomad in a nomadic world, 'Looking for what was, where it
used to be', because all our knowledge is of the past. Our every
perception is of the moment that has just disappeared. His is comic
and emphatically ordinary, so that his appearance is the opposite of
an apotheosis. He is the way things are; and it is the ephebe's task to
propound rather than expound, simply to propose, to put forward,
things as they are.

In section 2, 'It Must Change', the idea of change calls forth from
Stevens a series of unusually self-contained poems, each (with the

exception of vii) tightly organised around a definite centre: a single perceiver–protagonist or object or idea–of which the most revealing is that of change as a constant. (His residual doubts about what he is saying are expressed in the number of questions.) The feeling of amorphousness demands strong forms, and perhaps none is as powerful and thoroughgoing as Stevens' idea of the immutability of change. Endlessness becomes 'A single text, *granite* monotony' (2. vi. 12; emphasis added). The section begins with the world as seen by an old seraph – the necessary angel, an abstract figure concealed in actual appearance. This shift from the highest man to the highest angel is a change in the direction of the imagination, motivated perhaps by change being so overwhelmingly a matter of reality that the poet needs to detach himself from it in order to see it and to create the possibility of any metaphysical meaning. (Meaning is always to some extent a meta-object.) The seraph's relation to reality is marked by his being parcel- (or partially) gilded. The expression is used especially of silver bowls and cups whose inner surface is gilt; thus, the seraph is the colour of both sun and moon, half-real, half-imaginary. Similarly, all the objects that he beholds partake of the ghostliness of past events:

> The old seraph, parcel-gilded, among violets
> Inhaled the appointed odor, while the doves
> Rose up like phantoms from chronologies.
>
> The Italian girls wore jonquils in their hair
> And these the seraph saw, had seen long since,
> In the bandeaux of the mothers, would see again.
>
> The bees came booming as if they had never gone,
> As if hyacinths had never gone. We say
> This changes and that changes. Thus the constant
>
> Violets, doves, girls, bees and hyacinths
> Are inconstant objects of inconstant cause
> In a universe of inconstancy.
>
> (2. i. 1–12)

The violets, doves, girls, bees and hyacinths recur like the seasons. Their continuous inconstancy is the 'permanence composed of impermanence' of 'An Ordinary Evening in New Haven' (x. 11), and produces, according to Stevens, a feeling of *déja vu* that causes us to turn away: 'It means the distaste we feel for this withered scene/ Is that it is has not changed enough.' (2. i. 15–16).

Everlasting change, however, is not immortality, and not even the most powerful man in the nation can make it so:

> The President ordains the bee to be
> Immortal. The President ordains. But does
> The body lift its heavy wing, take up,
>
> Again, an inexhaustible being, rise
> Over the loftiest antagonist
> To drone the green phrases of its juvenal?
>
> (2. ii. 1–6)

Life without death is beyond anyone's wish. Stevens avoids a simple negation in order to savour for a moment the possibility of 'inexhaustible being', and to ponder why we should have such longings. Immortality is unnecessary:

> Why should the bee recapture a lost blague,
> Find a deep echo in a horn and buzz
> The bottomless trophy, new hornsman after old?
>
> (2. ii. 7–9)

Again he finds being pervaded by dreams, the present object obscured in imagined pasts and futures. Why cannot spring be spring?

> Why, then, when in golden fury
>
> Spring vanishes the scraps of winter, why
> Should there be a question of returning or
> Of death in memory's dream? Is spring a sleep?
>
> This warmth is for lovers at last accomplishing
> Their love, this beginning, not resuming, this
> Booming and booming of the new-come bee.
>
> (2. ii. 15–21)

The statue of General Du Puy stands in the Place Du Puy in the next poem as if the President's command has been obeyed. It is the bronze fulfilment of his wish. Although the learned men who inspect the statue are described with a trace of the mockery Molière reserves for lawyers and doctors, their judgement is accurate; they decide that such permanence is a lie: the General cannot have existed because he does not change. 'The very Place Du Puy', the doctors conclude, where the other residents die and the General remains, 'belonged [the tense commits it to the past] / Among our more vestigial states of mind' – it is our lingering, enduring wish for immortality. Stevens then negates the Place Du Puy and the next moment brings it back with a *yet* in order to consign the General to the dump with laconic humour:

> Nothing had happened because nothing had changed.
> Yet the General was rubbish in the end.
>
> (2. iii. 20–1)

The poems of 'Notes Toward a Supreme Fiction' show us thought (life) as a succession of more or less discrete moods. This structure is created to allow for tonal shifts, changes in perspective, so that Stevens can continually oppose one mood to another. The poems are a third longer than a sonnet, short enough to have the lyric power of concentrated statement and long enough for a certain amount of analysis and improvisation. The division into seven unrhymed stanzas permits more development and repetition than the single unified statement of the sonnet. Each poem is long enough for an anecdote and to have its own distinctive bravura. While this structure makes for summing up in instalments, for many *dénouements* rather than a single conclusion, periodically (but irregularly with respect to the form) Stevens feels the need for a more comprehensive summation. Because these summaries occur irregularly and because there are a number of them, they are deprived of finality. They are not definitive. The desire for wholeness and integration is exhibited as a compulsion, everlastingly repeating itself. The form sets these summary poems equal to the other poems, showing us that theory is one more mood. The fourth poem is one of these summaries, more abstract, more serious, than any of the previous three:

Two things of opposite natures seem to depend
On one another, as a man depends
On a woman, day on night, the imagined

On the real. This is the origin of change.
Winter and spring, cold copulars, embrace
And forth the particulars of rapture come.

Music falls on the silence like a sense,
A passion that we feel, not understand.
Morning and afternoon are clasped together

And North and South are an intrinsic couple
And sun and rain a plural, like two lovers
That walk away as one in the greenest body.

In solitude the trumpets of solitude
Are not of another solitude resounding;
A little string speaks for a crowd or voices.

The partaker partakes of that which changes him.
The child that touches takes character from the thing,
The body, it touches. The captain and his men

Are one and the sailor and the sea are one.
Follow after, O my companion, my fellow, my self,
Sister and solace, brother and delight.

                                                    (2. IV. 1–21)

The whole poem is derived from the first sentence, a single, algebraic statement whose comprehensiveness is vitiated by its tentativeness: two things of opposite nature *seem* to depend on one another, and the nature of both the opposition and the dependence is unspecified. The ratios set up by the examples appear to contradict the conventions established by the poem as a whole. The order of the six terms surprises our expectations. A man may depend upon a woman as day depends upon night, but not at the same time as the imagined depends upon the real. Reality is usually associated with day, not night, and, more often than not, if both are present, man rather than woman is associated with reality. The terms have been arranged so as to suggest that a man depends on a woman as he depends on the night (presumably that of the imagination) *and* on the real. Such carefully nuanced choices and subtle arrangements are a characteristic of Stevens' later poetry. He uses language in order to overcome the paradox of his relation to the world, to effect the marriage that is his subject here. Each of his poetic paradoxes is the restatement of an original unity as seen from the point of view of the subsequent separation. The words in the interaction of their meanings (including their grammatical bonds) achieve an intricate and intimate harmony, detailed, local – a kind of invisible mending. This dependence of opposite natures curiously is not static but dynamic: it is the starting-point of change. As frequently happens, Stevens, when investigating a phenomenon, seeks its origin and finds it in a stated or implied sexual act. Change starts from unity, from the one body of two lovers, and change is rapture. To live in the world is to be gripped by a passion that one does not understand. It is like listening to music, if music is not a thing perceived but a mode of perception, trumpets that we hear even in solitude. We absorb the notes not knowing what they mean. Pure sounds are put into relation to each other without being translated. We are the music while the music lasts. We participate in it and are changed – apprehending the world is an active process, a partaking that results in incorporation. The man who depends on a woman is not simply a husband who depends on his wife, or one of the two adult lovers that the earlier metaphors suggest; he is also the son who depends on his mother. The child that takes character from the body that it touches is the child at its mother's breast. This is the primary partaking, the more obvious dependence. The 'trumpets of solitude' do not express, 'another solitude', because even in solitude we hear the 'crowd of voices' that is ourselves, the companion, fellow, self, sister, solace, brother and delight that the poet names within himself. It is in this sense that the captain is at one with the men who follow him and the sailor with the maternal sea that keeps him afloat, and we note that all the pairs – winter and spring, morning and afternoon, North and South, sun and rain – are things that the poet takes in from the world. There is no *other* person here, except the body that the child touches, and the final relations are not sexual. The poet knows himself to be both feminine and masculine, but the relation between this sister and brother is like that between the captain and his men, one of fellowship.

The essential loneliness of 'Notes Toward a Supreme Fiction' also manifests itself in the episode of the planter that follows. His story is told in his absence and set in the isolation of an island – and demonstrates how bright, exotic and lush loneliness can be in Stevens. The poem is the planter's immortality in that it occurs after his death. This is the point of view from which the old seraph sees the world and from which the equestrian statue of General Du Puy is seen. Change means death, and in choosing change as a subject the poet chooses to work through his feelings about his own death. The planter (the name affirms his deeply rooted connection to the earth and his commitment to growth) was a partaker of the world in which he dwelt, deriving from it all his values, although Stevens is careful to mark the discrepancy between what the planter perceives ('turquoise', 'orange blotches', 'zero green') and the reality ('blue', 'orange', 'garbled green'). This is another measure of the planter's solitude, especially evident in that the meagre, irregular, confused and multilated green of the limes is his standard, his 'zero green':

> On a blue island in a sky-wide water
> The wild orange trees continued to bloom and to bear,
> Long after the planter's death. A few limes remained,
>
> Where his house had fallen, three scraggy trees weighted
> With garbled green. These were the planter's turquoise
> And his orange blotches, these were his zero green,
>
> A green baked greener in the greenest sun.
> These were his beaches, his sea-myrtles in
> White sand, his patter of the long sea-slushes.
>
> There was an island beyond him on which rested,
> And island to the South, on which rested like
> A mountain, a pineapple pungent as Cuban summer.
>
> And là-bas, là-bas, the cool bananas grew,
> Hung heavily on the great banana tree,
> Which pierces clouds and bends on half the world.
>
> He thought often of the land from which he came,
> How that whole country was a melon, pink
> If seen rightly and yet a possible red.

An unaffected man in a negative light
Could not have borne his labor nor have died
Sighing that he should leave the banjo's twang.

(2. v. 1–21)

The poem was one of Stevens' favourites. He comments on it to Simons,

> Had I been attempting to imitate Zeno or Plotinus, this poem would probably not be in the book. As it happens, it is one of the things in the book that I like most. What it means is that, for all the changes, for all the increases, accessions, magnifyings, what often means most to us, and what, in a great extreme, might mean most to us is just as likely as not to be some little thing like a banjo's twang. This explanation should make it clear that the planter is not a symbol. But one often symbolizes unconsciously, and I suppose that it is possible to say that the planter is a symbol of change. He is, however, the laborious human who lives in illusions and who, after all the great illusions have left him, still clings to the one that pierces him.   (12 Jan 1943)

Zeno and Plotinus are mentioned, one supposes, to emphasise his rejection of any obvious paradoxes and any unworldly, alternative reality in favour of the sensuous specificity of the poem. No philosopher, he implies, would find, as he does, most of life's meaning in the mundane minutiae of everyday life, in 'some little thing', some random discord, like a banjo's twang. The poem is an imitation of Baudelaire's 'L'Invitation au voyage'; 'là-bas' is the mysterious, voluptuous, imaginary Holland where he wishes his beloved to go with him. Stevens transposes Baudelaire's luxurious, beautiful and ordered country into a tropical island 'to the South' of the planter's island, a real location with a plausible mountain and an unreal giant banana-tree that 'pierces clouds and bends on half the world'. This tree, introduced so casually into the poem and calling into doubt the existence of everything else, shows us how our fantasies are continuous with the world. The banana-palm at the end of the mind is different only in degree from the orange blotches approximating oranges and the planter's native land pink with the red of reality *if seen rightly*. This qualification allows for its distortion by fantasy, as the fact that it can be red allows for the possibility that it is real, although this possibility is made more problematic by the indefinite article: *a* possible red is not *the* supreme red. Similarly, the negatives deprive the final sentence of any decisiveness. The sentence as it stands is not about the planter. He is a man deeply affected by both his melon homeland (of which he 'thought often') and his island solitude, and it was this capacity for feeling deeply that enabled him to survive, be pierced by the banjo's twang and die with a sigh of regret for the little things of his world. That he dies with no more than a sigh shows both satisfaction and profound disillusionment, and suggests that they are related. A negative light is a kind of darkness; presumably this is the light of all our seeing, a light by which we cannot be positive that what we see is as we see it. Stevens' remarks on the planter as a symbol indicate that he is concerned with change as an inner condition. The labour of which he speaks is the labour of perception, interpretation, the difficulty that we have in cultivating our own gardens.

In the next poem Stevens turns from the tropics to the birds singing in a coppice, borrowing the imperative 'Be thou me' from Shelley's 'Ode to the West Wind' to describe their assertive, repetitive songs. This is what they sing because they cannot conceive of anything different from what they are, and their song seems like an attempt to impose their mode of being on the world, so insistent as to be almost insane ('idiot minstrelsy'). Although it appears as rigid and enduring as stone, nevertheless 'It is / A sound like any other. It will end' (2. VI. 20–1). Thus, the stone sparrow is disposed of with the same laconic terseness as the bronze General Du Puy. After the finality of this judgement, Stevens speaks in the seventh poem of our 'ever-ready love' and the 'accessible bliss' that it offers, the moment when we breathe the perfume of lilacs, and the order is absolute in that it evokes nothing and we know nothing as a result of the experience – except happiness. 'Our earthy birth' makes us lovers, and, although the text does not specify of what or whom, it intimates that it is this bliss that we love, the state of pure feeling – knowing that if it recurs it will not be the same. 'Accessible bliss' is that of

> The fluctuations of certainty, the change
> Of degrees of perception in the scholar's dark.
>
> (2. VII. 20–1)

The idea of the lover is developed in the eighth poem in the story of Nanzia Nunzio and Ozymandias. Shelley's 'Ozymandias' is a traveller's report of finding a broken statue in a desert. Only two enormous legs are still standing on the pedestal, and nearby, half-buried in the sand, is 'a shattered visage', the remains of a cold, frowning face. The inscription can still be read:

> 'My name is Ozymandias, king of kings:
> Look on my works, ye Mighty and despair.'[6]

The message is still valid, but time has reinterpreted it by changing the context. The bare, empty desert expanding in every direction shows that nothing of Ozymandias' works has survived except the 'colossal wreck' of the statue: the mighty may well despair, not at Ozymandias' achievements, but rather that not even the power of the 'king of kings' could create anything lasting. The works of Ozymandias, like the statue of General Du Puy, were 'rubbish in the end'. Nanzia Nunzio on her trip around the world confronts Ozymandias. She removes her necklace and stone-studded belt, stands before him as the spouse, 'the woman stripped more nakedly / Than nakedness' (2. viii. 10–11), and asks him to invest her with 'the spirit's diamond coronal' and clothe her 'in the final filament'. He is inflexible order, a metaphoric if bodiless figure from the same matrix as the President and the great red stone face (3. iii), and speaks for the irreducible imaginary element in all perception. The poem closes with his declaration of the impossibility of her request:

> Then Ozymandias said the spouse, the bride
> Is never naked. A fictive covering
> Weaves always glistening from the heart and mind.
>
> (2. viii. 19–21)

The imagination prevents any final or perfect marriage of reality and order. There is nothing more definite than gold, emerald, amethyst – or desire. The imagination's shining fictions are the supreme changes, endlessly combining, systematising, enveloping. The metaphor (again with a necklace and belt as symbols of union) is developed in 'The World as Meditation', where Penelope interweaves the sunrise and the approach of her husband, who keeps 'coming constantly so near'. The sun and Ulysses are two and they are one: 'The thought kept beating in her like her heart. / The two kept beating together'. While 'The World as Meditation' is located in Penlope's consciousness, the meeting of Nanzia Nunzio and

Ozymandias is a confrontation of two distinct powers, a dialogue in which nothing is marked as speech. Ozymandias' metaphor of an ever-weaving fictive covering unifies perception, imagination and poetry – a text is something woven – and implies the hiding of some nakedness, some absence and presence.

The poem in this changing world becomes for Stevens an inconstant thing, a glistening, flittering fiction. He sees it as in a continuous state of tension, always moving like a weaver's shuttle – and, thinking about it, his very thought changes form:

> The poem goes from the poet's gibberish to
> The gibberish of the vulgate and back again.
> Does it move to and fro or is it of both
>
> At once? Is it a luminous flittering
> Or the concentration of a cloudy day?
> Is there a poem that never reaches words
>
> And one that chaffers the time away?
> Is the poem both peculiar and general?
>
> (2. IX. 1–8)

The poem oscillates between private and public gibberish, as if it gains strength from meaninglessness, as if all language were ultimately unintelligible, incommensurable and out of phase with consciousness. The poem's exact nature is problematic (as it must be in a universe of continuous change) and defined by a series of questions. The poem may be one of two things or both at once, insubstantially real or densely and obscurely imaginary: a weak, erratic, intermittent illumination or an opacity of nuances. This is restated as a choice between the two extremes of a wholly private and wholly public poem, the possibility of a poem inaccessible to language and one that is only banter or haggling to pass the time:

> There's a meditation there, in which there seems
>
> To be an evasion, a thing not apprehended or
> Not apprehended well. Does the poet
> Evade us, as in a senseless element?

Evade, this hot, dependent orator,
The spokesman at our bluntest barriers,
Exponent by a form of speech, the speaker

Of a speech only a little of the tongue?
It is the gibberish of the vulgate that he seeks.
He tries by a peculiar speech to speak

The peculiar potency of the general,
To compound the imagination's Latin with
The lingua franca et jocundissima.

(2. ix. 9–21)

As so often in Stevens, a decision about the nature of things, which
almost always involves a choice between interpretations, becomes a
process in which both choices are made alternately and simultaneously. Meditation occurs instead of a decision (although, of
course, it is a decision not to decide) and a conscious response is
substituted for an unconscious one. Belief becomes a succession of
tentative affirmations *and* negations, a process of approximation in
an effort to maintain an intense conscious contact with some
primary object – the intermittence of belief reflecting the earliest
intermittence of the object. Nothing else seems adequately to
explain Stevens' continuous no–yes. Here the inability to decide
about poetry is seen as the result of an evasion, a deliberate
rejection, an inability to face some item of reality. The question
('Does the poet / Evade us, as in a senseless element?') occurs
because one thing is 'not apprehended or / Not apprehended well'.
Stevens is concerned that the poet may evade what we are – perhaps
because language is 'a senseless element' and we need to be
apprehended in the vividness of our sensations. The *us* is
ambiguous in that it can refer to the plurality of each self as well as to
the plurality of persons. The final question states the kind of
spokesman we require: a 'hot, dependent orator' who by the
formality of his speech expresses our dullness, our limitations, and
raises the non-sense of our inarticulate feelings to the power of
meaning. Speech that is only of the tongue is rhetoric in the
pejorative sense, mere words, mere forms. There is an element of
this in all poetry which is why Stevens calls the poet an orator. Both
orator and *spokesman* emphasise the public function of the poet. The

speech of the poet who does not evade us is of the tongue and of the whole person. He attempts with the language of his own uniqueness to make statements that have the nomothetic power of generalities. this is an affair of diction, of a compounding of languages, in this case not English and French, but a literary Latin and a spoken vernacular, or, judging from the actual words of the text, English and Latin. As an enormous number of the abstrct words in English are derived from Latin, the phrase *the imagination's Latin* emphasises the abstractness of every act of the imagination and the imaginary character of all general statements. A lingua franca is in itself a mixed language, compounded by people speaking different languages. This is the case, Stevens implies, with every language – each speaker contributes his own peculiar gibberish. The concluding sentence is constructed so as make 'the imagination's Latin' the equivalent of 'peculiar speech', and the 'lingua franca et jocundissima' the equivalent of 'the peculiar potency of the general' – a demonstration of how language offers us possibilities of integration and communion that cannot be achieved any other way.

The second section closes with an unnamed man sitting on a bench in the park, so absorbed in a meditation on change that he is as if in a cataleptic state, his body rigid in response to the continuous movement of his mind:

> A bench was his catalepsy, Theatre
> Of Trope. He sat in the park. The water of
> The lake was full of artificial things,
>
> Like a page of music, like an upper air,
> Like a momentary color, in which swans
> Were seraphs, were saints, were changing essences.

(2. x. 1–6)

The man is as in a trance and a spectator of his own thoughts. The lake full of artificial things is an image of the inner world merging with the outer world that emphasises the fluidity of his perceptions. What he apprehends are symbols that fade, becoming like an upper air or momentary colour. A trope is a rhetorical figure, a form. Perception is a notation in which events of the body stand for other events as a page of music represents a group of sounds. The seraphs remind us of the seraph of the first poem, and this vision of the upper air foreshadows Canon Aspirin's dream in the final section. The most powerful statement is that essence changes. Swans become seraphs become saints become changing essences – the alteration marking their vestigial similarity. This is an assertion of the necessity of change. 'The casual, is not/ Enough'. Random variation or disorder is not a substitute for the completeness of changes in form. Only transformation, changing essences, offers the necessary refreshment of rebirth:

> The casual is not
> Enough. The freshness of transformation is
>
> The freshness of a world. It is our own,
> It is ourselves, the freshness of ourselves,
> And that necessity and that presentation
>
> Are rubbings of a glass in which we peer.
> Of these beginnings, gay and green, propose
> The suitable amours. Time will write them down.
>
>   (2. x. 14–21)

The will to change is 'that necessity and that presentation'. The rubbings are the polishing of a lens or attempts to remove the condensation (of our breath?) from a mirror or window so that we can see more clearly the origins of things and invent their histories, which will be of amours – as change is an affair of copulars. Every event in a world of transformations is a beginning; hence its freshness and the difficulty of knowing where it is going. Only time makes history come true. Rubbings are also copies (easily made from brass, impossible from a smooth pane of glass); time is presented as an author and what is real is written down. Reality is writing, notation like a page of music.

The title of the poem's final section, 'It Must Give Pleasure', specifies the third characteristic of the supreme fiction. Writing to Henry Church, Stevens says that, of all the comments that the French philosopher, Jean Wahl, had made on the poem, the 'one thing that I like more than anything else … is that it gave him pleasure to read the NOTES', and, considering the reviews of *Parts of a World*, issued a few months earlier, he observed, not without a certain irony,

> I think I am right in saying that in not a single review . . . was there even so much as a suggestion that the book gave the man who read it any pleasure. Now, to give pleasure to an intelligent man, by this sort of thing, is as much as one can expect . . . .
>   (8 Dec 1942)

He tells Simons, apropos the reviews of 'Notes Toward a Supreme Fiction',

> People never read poetry well until they have accepted it; they read it timidly or they are on edge about it. . . . All this is proved by the fact that I have yet to see any review in which the reviewer let himself go and said that he really enjoyed the book.   (12 Jan 1943)

One might say that the purpose of the supreme fiction is to overcome our timidity with regard to the world, to enable us to accept it so that we can let ourselves go.

Stevens begins this final section distinguishing between pleasures. 'To sing jubilas at exact, accustomed times', to exalt as part of a multitude, this 'is a facile exercise' compared to Jerome's translation of the Bible:

>   Jerome
> Begat the tubas and the fire-wind strings,
> The golden fingers picking dark-blue air:
>
> For companies of voices moving there,
> To find of sound the bleakest ancestor,
> To find of light a music issuing
>
> Whereon it falls in more than sensual mode.
>
>   (3. I. 7–13)

Jerome is seen as concerned, like Stevens, to find the primary principle of all utterance, the creative word of every beginning (note also *Begat*) and to go beyond the senses. The idea of this 'more than sensual' choral illumination prepares us for Canon Aspirin's vision of 'the amassing harmony' at the conclusion. The text of Jerome discovers a music of light such that our mode of apprehension is changed and we see things differently. We are translated by

Jerome's 'lingua franca et jocundissima', and Stevens' poem
becomes in this tacit comparison a poetic Vulgate. Yet the creation of
a secular text that performs the functions of sacred scripture is more
difficult than Jerome's task and depends upon something different:

> But the difficultest rigor is forthwith,
> On the image of what we see, to catch from that
>
> Irrational moment its unreasoning,
> As when the sun comes rising, when the sea
> Clears deeply, when the moon hangs on the wall
>
> Of heaven-haven. These are not things transformed.
> Yet we are shaken by them as if they were.
> We reason about them with a later reason.

                                                    (3. 1. 14–21)

The moment of perception is fraught with irrationality. That which
is most difficult is apprehending the images of the senses in all their
irrationality – as they are – to get at the unreason of the irrational. To
do this we work on images in order to lay hold of the changing
essences of fugitive moments. This is such a hardship and a
discipline because our modes of apprehension are rational,
transforming everything with which they come in contact. We
reason and reality is unreasonable. The world happens, we respond
and reason comes later. The sun rises, the sea clears deeply, the
moon hangs at home in the sky (all of these examples are of effects of
light occurring in the present) and we are moved, shaken, as if they
had been the objects of meditation. 'A later reason' suggests the
existence of an earlier reason, which would be the process of
perception itself. That the untransformed things shake us as if they
were transformed can be understood as an assertion of the
imagination's power; however, there is a paradox in their being
apprehended without being transformed, unless we say that this is
how Stevens allows for unconscious perception. According to
Stevens, it is the immediacy of the untransformed things, when we
reason by the light of unreason, that offers us the profoundest
satisfaction, as deep as the clearing of the sea. This still makes the
catching of the unreasoning of the irrational moment as impossible
by definition, and indeed this is the view of the poem, and the

supreme fiction is a transformation of that impossibility. This ambiguity emphasises the problematic nature of perception – and ambiguity is Stevens' *solution* to the problem.

The next three poems introduce in turn the blue woman at her window (II), the great red masculine stone face (III) and the celebration of 'a mystic marriage' (IV). Then there are three poems on the dream vision of Canon Aspirin (V–VII), then three more poems in which the poet speaks in his own person (VIII–X), taking Canon Aspirin's 'angel in his cloud' as his point of departure, and the final coda on the soldier and the poet. For the blue woman who is pure imagination, what she remembers suffices. She does not desire any change in the world, because everything, having happened, is in its proper place, corresponding to, and validating, her memory. This congruence makes possible a more accurate seeing:

> The blue woman looked and from her window named
>
> The corals of the dogwood, cold and clear,
> Cold, coldly delineating, being real,
> Clear and, except for the eye, without intrusion.
>
> (3. II. 18–21)

This is one of a series of acts of improved vision that occur in this section of the poem. The series concludes when, seeing the world revolving in the cold, fully delineated clarity of crystal, the poet calls the green, fluent world by name. Similarly, the blue woman's seeing is a warning. What we are offered is the virtual identity of the imagination and the world, of reason and unreason. This correspondence is a function of the blue woman's memory and the world's becoming static and of her consciousness becoming zero, so that she sees only with the eye – all impossibilities. For Stevens her vision is the equivalent of Canon Aspirin's; they are two approaches to the same fiction. He writes to Simons,

> One of the approaches to fiction is by way of its opposite: reality, the truth of the thing observed, the purity of the eye. The more exquisite the thing seen, the more exquisite the thing unseen. Eventually there is a state at which any approach becomes the actual observation of the thing approached. Nothing mystical is even for a moment intended.   (19 Mar 1943)

Where the supreme fiction emerges by implication in the blue woman's concentration on the 'corals of the dogwood', it is incarnate in the stone face. The perceiver–subject is the protagonist in the former case, the object perceived in the latter. The face metaphor is derived, in part, from the third chapter of Exodus, in which God speaks to Moses out of a burning bush – 'a lasting visage in a lasting bush', as Stevens puts it. 'The first thing one sees of any deity is the face, so that the elementary idea of God is a face ...', Stevens tells Simons (28 Jan 1943). 'Adoration is a form of face to face.' Again concentration changes what is perceived: 'We struggle with the face, see it everywhere & try to express the changes. In the depths of concentration, the whole thing disappears.' The Old Testament visage is abruptly replaced in the poem by the New Testament image of a shepherd. The idea of 'face to face', it will be noted, also refers to the situation of mother and baby. The stone face is the colour of reality, 'an unending red' that changes as we look at it, becoming 'Red-emerald, red-slitted blue, a face of slate' (3. III. 2–3), permeated and infused with the imagination's power as perception becomes memory, as if of a blue woman.

> We reason of these things with later reason
> And we make of what we see, what we see clearly
> And have seen, a place dependent on ourselves.
>
> (3. IV. 1–3)

Thus, the start of the fourth poem returns us to the beginning of the section, bringing the blue woman's remembering and our search for an idea of God into relation with the sun rising, sea clearing and moon hanging, except that we reason *about* or around, only approaching, the sun, sea and moon, and *of* memory and the idea of God – they are the substance of our thought. Stevens does not say that we create the world; rather, he says that we make out of our past and present perceptions a place that is contingent upon what we are, and that this dependence appears as an interpretation. Our constant need is to locate ourselves in our perceptions and to be independent of our surroundings, to be King of the Ghosts.

Stevens then describes the 'mystic marriage in Catawba' of the great captain and Bawda, 'mystic' because it is a marriage that cannot actually take place, the union of the perceiver with the world that can be no more than a legal or supreme fiction:

> They married well because the marriage-place
> Was what they loved. It was neither heaven nor hell.
> They were love's characters come face to face.
>
> (3. IV. 19–21)

Here 'face to face' is a metaphor of total, loving confrontation, recognition and reciprocity. This mutuality takes the place of the stone face that 'might have been'. The metaphor is one of seeing rather than touching; it is as if they *read* each other:

> Each must the other take as sign, short sign
> To stop the whirlwind, balk the elements.
>
> (3. IV. 14–15)

Personified, the world is more comfortable to live in because it is understandable. The whirlwind of change becomes a response, a communication; however, in order to be made meaningful the world is made double, incomplete and dependent: assigned a value, it becomes a sign, and this doubleness informs the whole of Stevens' mystic fable. The great captain and Bawda are separate from that for which they stand as they are separate from each other, 'face to face.' The anonymous captain is a version of the hero and major man. His presence transforms the anecdote into an account of origins, a version of the Eden story.

'Canon Aspirin is simply a figure, not a symbol', Stevens explains to Church (28 Oct 1942). 'This name is supposed to suggest the kind of person he is.' A canon is a member of an ecclesiastical chapter who lives according to the rules or canons of his church, and an aspirin is a cure for the headache (of conflicting thoughts?) as well as a word that contains almost all of *aspiring*. The canon is, therefore, associated with two edifices of belief, one of stone (a collegiate church or cathedral) and one of law, and, as a man living a life of disciplined faith, is, for Stevens, like the rabbi or Franciscan don. He is, Stevens says to Simons, the 'sophisticated man . . . (the man who has explored all the projections of the mind, his own particularly)' who 'comes back, without having acquired a sufficing fiction – to, say, his sister and her children' (29 Mar 1943). His sister, who 'has never explored anything at all', is in this his opposite. As she is a widow with two children, together they form a 'mystic' family (as the great captain and Bawda celebrate 'a mystic marriage'), and the episode can be seen as another myth of origins. The sister, who has no interest in the projections of the mind, is as close to reality as it is possible to be. 'The words [her children] spoke were voices that she heard' (not words), and, when she 'looked at them', she 'saw them as they were' (3. v. 13–14). She avoids so far as she can the distortions of language. Her children she 'hid ... under simple names' and 'what she felt fought off the barest phrase' (3. v. 11, 15). The canon declaims all these things to praise the 'sensible ecstasy' in which his sister 'lived in her house', but, where 'in the excitements of silence' the sister 'Demanded of sleep' for her children 'Only the unmuddled self of sleep', Canon Aspirin, as he reflects after having spoken, hums 'an outline of a fugue' to fill the silence.

The fifth poem begins with dinner: Meursault, lobster Bombay, mango chutney. (The vineyards of Meursault are not far from those of 'Montrachet-le-Jardin'.) The menus is an indication of the Canon's sophistication, and part of the sensuous texture of the whole poem: the 'glitter-goes' and 'velvetest far-away', the fragrance of magnolias, Italian girls with jonquils in their hair and the 'red-blue dazzle' of flags in the wind – all of which is a demonstration of the pleasure that poetry must give and of the need for 'imperishable bliss'. The Meursault and lobster Bombay are the counterpart of the late coffee and oranges in 'Sunday Morning'. The profundity of Canon Aspirin's dissatisfaction, his emptiness, is shown by his having dined so well and so agreeably. After declaiming his sister's virtues and humming a sketch of the harmony to which he aspires, he goes to bed. From the phrasing 'came to sleep', we cannot be certain whether what follows is day dream or night dream:

> When at long midnight the Canon came to sleep
> And normal things had yawned themselves away,
> The nothingness was a nakedness, a point,
>
> Beyond which fact could not progress as fact.
> Thereon the learning of the man conceived
> Once more night's pale illuminations, gold
>
> Beneath, far underneath, the surface of
> His eye and audible in the mountain of
> His ear, the very material of his mind.

So that he was the ascending wings he saw
And moved on them in orbit's outer stars
Descending to the children's bed, on which

They lay. Forth then with huge pathetic force
Straight to the utmost crown of night he flew.
The nothingness was a nakedness, a point

Beyond which thought could not progress as thought.
He had to choose. But it was not a choice
Between excluding things. It was not a choice

Between, but of. He chose to include the things
That in each other are included, the whole,
The complicate, the amassing harmony.

                                        (3. VI. 1–21)

The Canon thinks himself to 'the very material of his mind' and
beyond, to the whole, complicate, amassing harmony that is the
supreme fiction. His vision is a response to nothingness, the
conversion of absence into presence.

He fills his own emptiness with himself (his self?). He beholds an
inner light born of learning, his accumulated experience. (The man
of imagination in Stevens' poetry is always a scholar, forfeit or
otherwise, ephebe or master.) The gold light is a re-creation out of
knowledge of what has been; it is 'night's illumination' *once more*.
That 'learning' is the subject of the verb makes it appear that this is a
virtually automatic response, which is in keeping with Stevens'
comment to Simons that Canon Aspirin 'doesn't have much choice
about yielding to "the complicate the amassing harmony"' (29 Mar
1943). This is, none the less, a conscious act. Aspirin is both the
subject and object of his own vision. He sees himself moving within
himself, the Daedalus of his own mind: 'he was the ascending wings
he saw'. Stevens' epigram in *Adagia* that 'There is no wing like
meaning' (*OP*, p. 162) confirms that this imaginative flight is a
creation of meaning and suggests even that meaning is the
substance of the self.[7] Characteristically, one might say inevitably,
Canon Aspirin's journey is in two stages: he starts beyond reality
(the 'point / Beyond which fact could not progress as fact') and goes
beyond the imagination (the 'point / Beyond which thought could
not progress as thought'), exchanging one nothingness for another.

The pathos of human dependence that he feels when he contemplates the sleeping children – his pity and the sadness at his own humanity – forces him to face the limits of the imagination. Nothingness is not only filled, but conceived of as a point, as limited, contained by the poem. The end of the mind becomes a destination. Belief is not thought, it is a choice; but this choice is itself limited – and, like everything so far, man-made. Canon Aspirin cannot choose to exclude things. His choice is of all or nothing and he chooses wholeness, totality, relationship. The present participle *amassing* indicates that this is a dynamic, a changing harmony, with a hint, perhaps, that it grows as a result of having been chosen.

Thought, however, has not been surpassed. The seventh poem shows us Canon Aspirin imposing 'orders as he thinks of them':

> But to impose is not
> To discover. To discover an order as of
> A season, to discover summer and know it,
>
> To discover winter and know it well, to find,
> Not to impose, not to have reasoned at all,
> Out of nothing to have come on major weather,
>
> It is possible, possible, possible. It must
> Be possible. It must be that in time
> The real will from its crude compoundings come,
>
> Seeming, at first, a beast disgorged, unlike,
> Warmed by a desperate milk. To find the real,
> To be stripped of every fiction except one,
>
> The fiction of an absolute – Angel,
> Be silent in your luminous cloud and hear
> The luminous melody of proper sound.

> (3. VII. 7–21)

Again there is the effort to escape from reason, from the mind, that with each *possible* appears more unlikely. The increased activity of the will marks an increase in doubt, until the statement shifts from *is* to *must* and the poet's hopes emerge as double: the uncompounded beast and angel. The real is savage, *unlike*, without the analogues necessary to perception, and *disgorged*, as if vomited forth, uneaten, raw and at the nursing-stage. Here, however, the poet does not wish for an unmitigated, unmediated real, but desires the real enclothed in a solitary fiction. The world without the supreme fiction would be without an absolute, and thus without a single certainty. The angel is merely associated with this emergence, present yet syntactically apart, silent but shedding light. This final sentence demonstrates the vestigial, ineffable effectiveness of the supreme fiction in Stevens' thought. The angel, so human in form, presides over the possibility of the apprehension of the real *together* with 'The fiction of an absolute', although no casual connection is stated. The dash separates the absolute from the angel in such a way that the possibility is preserved of the two being in apposition. Moreover, the presence of the angel enables dialogue (the commands 'Be silent' and 'hear') to take place at this crucial moment. These many nuances suggest that wholeness, integration and harmony may depend not on any particular form of statement, but rather upon all the troubling items being included in the poem. Antithesis and all other figures of exclusion are forms of connection. Naming prevails over syntax. This is the deeper structure of the poem.

Everything is thrown into doubt by the question that begins the eighth poem: 'What am I to believe?' The poet speaks suddenly in his own person as if he were an incredulous witness to Canon Aspirin's narrative; nevertheless, he concentrates on the angel, re-experiencing his flight and, like the Canon, trying to find himself in the experience:

> Is it he or is it I that experience this?
> Is it I then that keep saying there is an hour
> Filled with expressible bliss, in which I have
>
> No need, am happy, forget need's golden hand,
> Am satisfied without solacing majesty,
> And if there is an hour there is a day,
>
> There is a month, a year, there is a time
> In which majesty is a mirror of the self:
> I have not but I am and as I am, I am.

These external regions, what do we fill them with
Except reflections, the escapades of death,
Cinderella fulfilling herself beneath the roof?

(3. VIII. 10–1)

The poet like the angel 'Forgets the gold centre, the golden destiny' (3. VIII. 6) of reality that it has been belief's function to establish, so that no connection is made between belief and the possibility of an hour of 'expressible bliss' – a possibility maintained by the unidentifiable voice that keeps saying that it exists. The experience is that of merely being, oblivious of making, taking, of all the hand's activities; a finite time of unspecified duration of the self; the feeling that 'I am and as I am, I am.' This is defined in contradistinction to the feeling of possession ('I have') and is a declaration of self-unity in two parts: the poet asserts that he exists and that his existence is identical with itself; no change intervenes to affect the continuity of his identity ('as I am, I am'). This is a more primary statement than Descartes's *cogito ergo sum*, which makes consciousness the basis of knowledge of the world. Stevens proclaims a subject without an object, utterly intransitive; none the less, this too is a notion of the self requiring confirmation or validation, and the introduction of the mirror, which makes everything double, shows that the completeness of this experience is virtual rather than absolute. The 'as I am, I am' refers back to the eroded, unending red stone face, 'a lasting visage in a lasting bush'. This face, 'the idea of God', does not speak in Stevens. In Exodus 3, however, God (whom Moses is afraid to look at) speaks at length, and, in answer to Moses' question as to his name, replies from the burning bush, 'I AM THAT I AM' (v. 14) – a more positive and unambiguous statement of identity than any that the poet is able to make. The poet is momentarily a falling or hovering angel speaking in the absence of God, or, like Jacob at Peniel, wrestling with the angel in order to know his own name – or myth. The poem closes with a question that emphasises the poet's uncertainty and creates a new inner space by consigning everything that has gone before to 'external regions'. What has appeared as a radically introspective exploration of the centre of inwardness becomes exterior to a new interior dwelling-place, which is, for all this, the same old home. This happens because all thought is *reflections*, self-alienating, decentralising by its very nature, a mirror that we make for ourselves. We are Cinderellas in a fairy or angel story, fulfilled without going to the ball – the wish, the fiction, is self-sufficient. The final metaphor restores us to a reassuringly structured inwardness in that these external regions, including 'the violent abyss', are 'beneath the roof'.

Stevens closes the poem with an address to the earth as his beloved. His tone is formal and intimate, appropriate for a beloved who despite long familiarity is still a stranger, always different from what she was, incomplete and aberrant, for ever straying from the straight path of any formulation. At her most mundane, she is evasive, remaining 'more than natural', becoming *the* phantom in his thoughts:

> Fat girl, terrestrial, my summer, my night,
> How is it I find you in difference, see you there
> In a moving contour, a change not quite completed?
>
> You are familiar yet an aberration.
> Civil, madam, I am, but underneath
> A tree, this unprovoked sensation requires
>
> That I should name you flatly, waste no words,
> Check your evasions, hold you to yourself.
> Even so when I think of you as strong or tired,
>
> Bent over work, anxious, content, alone,
> You remain the more than natural figure. You
> Become the soft-footed phantom, the irrational
>
> Distortion, however fragrant, however dear.
> That's it: the more than rational distortion,
> The fiction that results from feeling. Yes, that.
>
> They will get it straight one day at the Sorbonne.
> We shall return at twilight from the lecture
> Pleased that the irrational is rational,
>
> Until flicked by feeling, in a gildered street,
> I call you by name, my green, my fluent mundo.
> You will have stopped revolving except in crystal.

>   (3. x. 1–21)

The world is named (as it is personified) so that communication can take place, in order to create the conditions for dialogue, the fiction that someone is listening. Everything comes down to this. Each time the poet names her, he uses a different name. Such is her elusive changingness that even his *final* formulation changes with each repetition: she is 'the irrational / Distortion', 'the more than rational distortion', 'The fiction that results from feeling', each phrase emphasising her unapprehensible ghostliness, until, at last, it is as if the world has become the supreme fiction. The poet does not escape from his reality–imagination complex, but he does make his peace with it – by an imagined reconciliation in the foreign country of the future. The task of definition is transferred to the teachers at the Sorbonne, while he and his beloved as a single *we* return together in the half-light, sharing the same pleasure at the same thoughts *until* he calls her by name. She will have stopped revolving except in the enduring transparency of his language. Stevens in an earlier draft had, 'You will have stopped revolving, will rest in crystal.'[8]

This stasis, however, was unacceptable. There is no rest. Even *within* the crystal act of naming, the world changes. Stevens was not satisfied with ending the poem at this point; like Shakespeare in *The Tempest* he chose to add an epilogue in order to effect the transition from the text back to the world. Stevens now addresses the soldier, as if the preceding speech to the woman made necessary speech with a man, and love calls forth thoughts of war. Stevens asserts an affinity between the poet and the soldier:

> Soldier, there is a war between the mind
> And sky, between thought and day and night. It is
> For that the poet is always in the sun,
>
> Patches the moon together in his room
> To his Virgilian cadences, up down,
> Up down. It is a war that never ends.
>
> Yet it depends on yours. The two are one.
> They are a plural, a right and left, a pair,
> Two parallels that meet if only in
>
> The meeting of their shadows or that meet
> In a book in a barrack, a letter from Malay.
> But your war ends. And after it you return

With six meats and twelve wines or else without
To walk another room . . . Monsieur and comrade,
The soldier is poor without the poet's lines,

His petty syllabi, the sounds that stick,
Inevitably modulating, in the blood.
And war for war, each has its gallant kind.

How simply the fictive hero becomes the real;
How gladly with proper words the soldier dies,
If he must, or lives on the bread of faithful speech.

They are both warriors, only the poet's war, 'a war between the mind / And sky, between thought and day and night', is 'a war that never ends'. The poet's war depends upon the soldier's and is the same war: 'The two are one.' Similarly their tasks are interchangeable:

How simply the fictive hero becomes the real;
How gladly with proper words the soldier dies,
If he must, or lives on the bread of faithful speech.

It is on this elegiac, almost Homeric, note that Stevens ends the poem, with the world as a battleground where the bread of poetry sustains us.

'Notes Toward a Supreme Fiction' was published in two limited editions (1942 and 1943) and in *Transport to Summer* (1947). *Transport* is a means of conveyance and a state of ecstasy. 'Summer', Stevens says in 'Credences of Summer', is when 'the mind lays by its trouble'. The title *Transport to Summer* suggests that the book is a vehicle for removing the poet to the warmth of the changing, growing, physical world and the record of a single rapture, as if all the poems were concerned with the same powerful emotion – in both senses it presents poetry as a way of taking the poet out of himself. Within the poems themselves, this is achieved by an effort to set limits to thought by a general theory of thinking. To use Stevens' words, the credences of summer are founded on the pure good of theory.

The majority of the poems are a further thinking through of the material of 'Notes Toward a Supreme Fiction', which Stevens rightly regarded as 'the most important thing in the book' (letter to Herbert Weinstock, 12 Nov 1946). They are more abstract than those of any previous collection. Their subtleties are more nuanced, and they are more generally allusive, but with stronger arguments and an unyielding intentness of purpose. There is not in *Transport to Summer* the same focus on particular objects as in *Parts of a World*. There is less detailed observation as poetry's function is understood as to 'make the visible a little hard / To see' ('The Creations of Sound') and it becomes more difficult 'to accept the structure / Of things as the structure of ideas' ('The Bed of Old John Zeller'). The specifics of carnations, pears and peaches give way to the 'Debris of Life and Mind', 'Pieces' and the possibility of 'A Completely New Set of Objects'. As the object becomes an abstraction, any object will do and then the idea of an object, as in 'Man Carrying Thing'. For Stevens, the success of 'Notes Toward a Supreme Fiction' was the creation of an object and mode of belief, the establishment of a new rigour and, consequently, the development of a new language: the poem's hypothetical, conditional form of statement, a heuristic reasoning in which the tentative is energetic and antitheses are employed to make a texture of connections. The composition of the poem was like the creation of an algebra for the solution of the problem of reality and imagination.

The desire for new language causes Stevens to explore the limits of intelligible speech. *Transport to Summer* is alive with sounds of all kinds. There are a zither, shouts, shuffling and bugles, the hard sound of the hammer of red and blue, and sounds negated: the stillness of the 'cricket in the telephone', angry machines with wheels 'too large for any noise', inaudible tapping on skeleton drums and, on an old shore, even 'the vulgar ocean rolls / Noiselessly, noiselessly'. The groan of Vesuvius is heard as well as the ting-tang of Old John Zeller's bed, wood-doves singing rou-coo along the Perkiomen and a 'Late Hymn from the Myrrh-Mountain'. These sounds are the chaos and order of the world – 'The buzzing world and lisping firmament' – its meaning and its nonsense. Poetry is so important because:

> It is a world of words to the end of it,
> In which nothing solid is its solid self.

('Description without Place', vii. 5–6)

We are 'Men Made out of Words' who live in a 'Description without Place':

> We say ourselves in syllables that rise
> From the floor, rising in speech we do not speak.
> ('The Creations of Sound')

7

The World is What You Make of It

'Late Hymn from the Myrrh-Mountain' concludes,

> The deer-grass is thin. The timothy is brown.
> The shadow of an external world comes near.

This shadow in Stevens' sixth book of poetry, *The Auroras of Autumn* (1950), and in *The Rock*, the section of new poems in *The Collected Poems* (1954), is also the shadow of death. The poet was seventy-one when *The Auroras of Autumn* appeared. Seventy was the mandatory age of retirement at the Hartford Accident and Indemnity Company, and, although Stevens had been granted permission to continue working, he was concerned that the sustaining routine of his life should not be disturbed. The death of Henry Church, who was a year younger than he, in 1947, focused his attention on the approaching end of his own connection with the external world. 'The Owl in the Sarcophagus', is one of five long poems in *The Auroras of Autumn*. 'This', Stevens writes to Barbara Church, 'was written in the frame of mind that followed Mr Church's death. While it is not personal, I had thought of inscribing it somehow, below the title, as for example, Goodbye H. C. . . . ' (5 Nov 1947). This does not mean that most of the poems of *The Auroras of Autumn* are about death, rather that death is assimilated in terms of Stevens' other major concerns. The confrontation of death in 'The Owl in the Sarcophagus' is literally that – a face-to-face meeting – and produces a group of figures: two brothers and a mother. He invents 'the mythology of modern death' (vi. 1) as in 'Notes Toward a Supreme Fiction' he invents a mythology of modern poetry.

Death is seen as a change in time and/or place:

> That of itself stood still, perennial,

271

> Less time than place, less place than thought of place
> And, if of substance, a likeness of the earth,
> That by resemblance twanged him through and through,
>
> Releasing an abysmal melody,
> A meeting, an emerging in the light,
> A dazzle of remembrance and of sight.
>
> (II. 6–12)

Existence is of the earth; it is to be a body; and, as death exists, it is attributed a hypothetical earth-like substance. Death is a special case of 'the way what was has ceased to be what is' (v. 9). The two brother forms 'move among the dead'. The mother is the figure of transition, the midwife, the mistress of the rites of passage:

> she that says
> Good-by in darkness, speaking quietly there,
> To those that cannot say good-by themselves.
>
> (I. 4–6)

She assumes the poet's function. As our mother teaches us our first words – in the mother tongue – it is fitting that she speak the last words, and here it is as if there is no action without speech and existence ceases when one stops speaking. This notion has such force in Stevens that in the earlier 'Burghers of Petty Death' (1946) he distinguishes between petty death and total death so as to obtain an antithetical music – poetry without end. The petty death of individuals is only 'a slight part' of the all-encompassing 'total death:

> an imperium of quiet,
> In which a wasted figure, with an instrument,
> Propounds blank final music.

Even nothingness must exist as an 'abysmal music'.

The goodbye of 'The Owl in the Sarcophagus' echoes in the successive farewells of 'The Auroras of Autumn'. The idea of death in subsequent poems, however, is increasingly transformed, becoming an absolute state of the imagination, a condition of metaphor and negative being. It generates images of impending winter, ghosts, bells, angels, black violets and black rivers, and translates itself into a concern for the ultimate poem. These poems of life's sunset are filled with a sense of what Stevens calls, in 'Our Stars Come from Ireland', 'The Westwardness of Everything'. As he states in 'Metaphor as Degeneration',

> these images, these reverberations,
> And others, make certain how being
> Includes death and the imagination.

This inclusiveness is his determined desire for wholeness and continuity (the two are interchangeable in Stevens). This desire is satisfied by death as another time; 'blank, final music'; the black river, Swatara, that becomes 'the flecked river' of being (three images of endlessness), and by the appearance of the parents, the agents of wholeness in the child and proofs of its continuity with the human past.

The father and, more especially, the mother, appear again and again in the poems of *The Auroras of Autumn* and *The Rock*, as if presiding over rebirth, the guarantors of another childhood. The mythologic figures of 'The Owl in the Sarcophagus' are 'The pure perfections of parental space' (VI. 6) – as if the parents' corporeality, transformed through the power of the child's emotions, persists as the sense of three dimensions, as if the objects of our first love are always synonymous with the world and the measure of all other feeling. (These are 'milky matters'.) The idea recurs in 'The Auroras of Autumn' when Stevens postulates a beginning to our knowledge of reality, a time in which we are innocent of the earth:

> That we partake thereof,
> Lie down like children in this holiness,
> As if, awake, we lay in the quiet of sleep,
>
> As if the innocent mother sang in the dark
> Of the room and on an accordion, half-heard,
> Created the time and place in which we breathed ....

(VIII. 19–24)

The music of the accordion, which like the harmonium is a wind instrument, is produced by an in-and-out movement that resembles breathing. The accordion also resembles the harmonium in the significance of its name, which indicates its function here: the creation of an accord. Half-heard, it is both conscious and unconscious. The mother's singing and playing is the origin of the child's being and gives depth to everything, creating the interrelated perspectives of time and space, the co-ordinates of identity. From her we learn who we are – that is, a specific location in the world – knowledge that, even if imaginary, is a blessing and a sanctification. At the close of 'The Owl in the Sarcophagus' Stevens asserts the primacy of the imagination in this process:

> It is a child that sings itself to sleep,
> The mind, among the creatures that it makes,
> The people, those by which it lives and dies.
>
> (VI. 9–12)

The mind is a child, always beginning, for ever dependent, never itself the master or originator of anything except its songs. The child creates the parents. At the same time the mind is the father of a whole people, surrounding us with a ghost population who are everything to us. The poet's purpose – and everybody's purpose – is to keep himself company. The poem is another being. The sound of the human voice, even if it is the sound of us humming to ourselves, becomes infinitely sustaining if no one else is really there.

If the mind is a child, the decisive persons in its life are the parents, even if imaginary presences. They are in every sense the giants of the first idea, and, along with the poet himself, they are the major figures in 'The Auroras of Autumn'. As a way of coming to terms with death, the poet finds that he needs to say an explicit farewell to the ideas of a mother and a father. They are, he discovers, the sources of the meaning of living in the world, its most fundamental forms. His farewell is a theoretical encompassing of existence, a myth of parenthood, and in the process he introduces as an aside the equation: 'The mother's face, / The purpose of the poem' (III. 1–2). The two are interchangeable, synonymous, closer than the two terms of a metaphor and to be stated without the verb 'to be'. Nothing could be simpler or make the poetic processes more intimate, more intensely unique and private, or more backward-looking. Wordsworth makes this same equation when he sees the relation between the child and the 'one dear Presence' of the mother as 'the first / Poetic spirit of our human life.'[1] This is for Wordsworth the starting-point of every poet's life, and his autobiographical poem can be understood as an expansion of this moment. For Stevens the mother's face is the end-point, the destination, of the poem. Unlike Wordsworth, when he elaborates this thought, Stevens does not engage in psychological analysis. He avoids any specifically historical account of his own development. He glosses over the personal and abstracts the poem from the poet. Instead he offers an evocation of the mother's presence growing old in the house of the mind. This mood is created with the full sense of its, and the poet's, impending destruction; it is evoked only to be overwhelmed by the Heraclitean fire. Stevens' achievement is his ability to combine great passion and moral neutrality so that our sense of the profundity and vividness of the peace is undisturbed by the dissolving, crumbling and burning:

> Farewell to an idea ... The mother's face,
> The purpose of the poem, fills the room.
> They are together, here, and it is warm,
>
> With none of the prescience of oncoming dreams.
> It is evening. The house is evening, half dissolved.
> Only the half they can never possess remains,
>
> Still-starred. It is the mother they possess,
> Who gives transparence to their present peace.
> She makes that gentler that can gentle be.
>
> And yet she too is dissolved, she is destroyed.
> She gives transparence. But she has grown old.
> The necklace is a carving not a kiss.
>
> The soft hands are a motion not a touch.
> The house will crumble and the books will burn.
> They are at ease in a shelter of the mind
>
> And the house is of the mind and they and time,
> Together, all together.
>
> (III. 1–17)

The mother's presence is palpable, composed of kisses and touches, verifications of the solidity of the world. To possess her is to be certain. 'She gives transparence': knowledge of reality without a shadow of a doubt. Thus it is that 'the innocent mother' in the passage cited above created 'the time and place in which we breathed'. This thought is elaborated in the ninth poem, where the coming of the mother is definitive:

> This sense of the activity of fate –
>
> The rendezvous, when she came alone,
> By her coming became a freedom of the two,
> An isolation which only the two could share.

(IX. 12–15)

This rendezvous is the moment of meeting of the dedicatory poem of 'Notes Toward a Supreme Fiction' and the moment in 'Of Modern Poetry' when an invisible audience listens 'to itself, expressed / In an emotion as of two people, as of two / Emotions becoming one'. Stevens' interest in how we apprehend the world had always been a concern for the way in which the perception of external reality helps to define the internal reality, and, while being had always involved a meeting with a half-mythical woman, in these later poems he is concerned with the agency of the parents, and especially with the originating and informing power of the mother in the establishment of being. This means looking beyond the everlasting interaction of imagination and reality to the individual whole that is the result of this interaction; and, as he sees the end of this process, he sees its beginning.

'An Ordinary Evening in New Haven' (also colleced in *The Auroras of Autumn*) is the last of Stevens' three great theoretic poems. They are the working out of the most comprehensive statement of the nature of poetry ever made by a poet, the creation of a method rather than a set of conclusions, poems of self-examination where the poetic process is the most satisfying response to the uncertainties of an ever-changing world because it is the only mode in which knowing and being are virtually synonymous.

> Poetry is the subject of the poem,
> From this the poem issues and
>
> To this returns.

This discovery of 'The Man with the Blue Guitar' (xxii. 1–3) is expanded and reaffirmed in a more tentative, abstract and nuanced form in 'An Ordinary Evening in New Haven':

> This endlessly elaborating poem
> Displays the theory of poetry,
> As the life of poetry. A more severe,
>
> More harassing master would extemporize
> Subtler, more urgent proof that the theory
> Of poetry is the theory of life,
>
> As it is, in the intricate evasions of as . . . .

(xxviii. 10–16)

The vitality of poetry is in the elaboration of the theory, in going beyond the single object or act to making statements of relation. The thing itself matters as the gate to an encompassing system; the interest is not so much in perceiving as in accounting for, interpreting perception. The repetition of 'theory' stresses the uncertain and personal nature of this enterprise, that it is the activity of a single mind making what it can out of its own resources. The phrase 'the theory of life, / As it is' where the qualifying 'As it is' can apply either to 'theory', with which it seems at odds, or 'life', is a good example of 'the intricate evasions of as' and of how much more complicated the world – and poetry as the subject of the poem – has become for Stevens.

'An Ordinary Evening in New Haven' is in many ways a reworking of 'Notes Toward a Supreme Fiction', but with the opposite emphasis: on truth not fiction, on everyday mundanity instead of all-mastering invention, and it obtains some of its form from this countervailing of 'Notes Toward a Supreme Fiction'. Both poems consist of thirty-one sections composed of blank-verse triads, seven in 'Notes Toward a Supreme Fiction', six in 'An Ordinary Evening in New Haven' (where the blank verse is so free as almost to disappear). There are innumerable echoes of the former poem in the latter. 'The vulgate of experience' (i) recalls 'the imagination's Latin' (2. ix) and the celebration of Jerome (3. i); the statue of Jove that is blown up (xxiv) reminds us of the statue of General Du Puy that 'was rubbish in the end' (2. iii); the land of the lemon-trees (xxix) seems another version of the planter's island with its orange- and lime-trees (2. v) and of Catawba (3. iv). The last leaf that has fallen in the penultimate poem (xxx) is the spinning leaf of the penultimate poem (3. ix) of 'Notes Toward a Supreme Fiction' – and the robin is in both poems; and 'the late president, Mr Blank' (xxxi) might be the President who ordains (2. ii). The ephebe is present in 'An Ordinary Evening in New Haven' (xiii) as well as a mature scholar, Professor Eucalyptus, presumably of Yale (xiv–xv, xxii). Professor Eucalyptus, who appears in the second half of the poem and who 'does not look / Beyond the object' (xiv. 3–4), is the counterpart of Canon Aspirin in 'Notes Toward a Supreme Fiction' who sees himself as the angel of the absolute beyond whom 'thought cannot progress as thought'(3. vi–vii). Eucalyptus listens to the ramshackle sound of the rain in the ramshackle spout of his house, while Aspirin listens to 'the whole, / The complicate, the amassing harmony'. Their equivalence is confirmed by the Professor's statement that 'The search / For reality is as momentous as / The search for god' (xxii. 1–3).

Reality or god, what Stevens is looking for is certainty, whether 'Beneath, far underneath . . . the very material of his mind' or in the streets of New Haven. As certainty is unobtainable, he moves back and forth between the idea of a supreme fiction and the idea of total disillusionment, creating out of the antithesis a substitute for certainty and out of the tension of opposites a substitute for possession. This, as Stevens was aware, is the fundamental movement of his thought: a continuous alternation from belief in the possibility of a totally successful act of the imagination to belief in the possibility of an act of pure perception, from the mind's night visions to the 'plainness of plain things', and back again. 'What underlies this sort of thing', he writes to Heringman, 'is the drift of one's ideas. From the imaginative period of Notes I turned to the ideas of Credences of Summer' (3 May 1949). 'At the time when that poem was written my feeling for the necessity of a final accord with reality was at its strongest . . . ', he tells Charles Tomlinson (19 June 1951). 'Later I followed this up . . . in a long poem called "An Ordinary Evening in New Haven" ' (with, of course, 'The Owl in the Sarcophagus' and 'The Auroras of Autumn', imaginative excursions on death, the ultimate unreality, intervening). His purpose in 'An Ordinary Evening in New Haven', as he confides to Heringman, is 'to get as close to the ordinary, the commonplace and the ugly it is possible for a poet to get. It is not a question of grim reality but of plain reality. The object is of course to purge oneself of anything false.'

Stevens begins with the data of perception and sets it aside with a single gesture:

> The eye's plain version is a thing apart,
> The vulgate of experience. Of this,
> A few words, an and yet, and yet, and yet –
>
> As part of the never-ending meditation ....
>
> (I. 1–4)

What we see is separate from what is; it is a 'vulgate', a 'version' of reality even if a plain one: the act of apprehension is an act of interpretation. Here what engages the poet is not that perception is endless, one *an* or item after another (although that is implied), but that every *an*, being untranslatable, gives rise to innumerable *and yets*. The 'never-ending meditation', the mind's unending effort to understand its experience, is produced by the impossibility of any final knowledge. The 'and yet, and yet, and yet - ' also indicates the order of the poem. Each poem follows clearly enough from the previous poem and some are very closely connected, but there is neither an argument nor a division into parts and no plot except that of the ruminating mind. As Stevens says to Tomlinson (19 July 1951), 'This ... poem may seen diffuse and casual' – it is only an 'endlessly elaborating poem' that can represent 'the drift of one's ideas'. Diffuseness is its form.

The poet considers the town of New Haven, which for the purposes of the poem constitutes the external world. Suppose, he says, that 'these houses are composed of ourselves', that everything we apprehend as exterior is a projection of the interior, that the houses are 'transparent dwellings of the self', then New Haven is 'an impalpable town, full of / Impalpable bells', moving with 'the movement of the colors of the mind':

> The far-fire flowing and the dim-coned bells
> Coming together in a sense in which we are poised,
> Without regard to time or where we are,

> In the perpetual reference, object
> Of the perpetual meditation, point
> Of the enduring, visionary love,
>
> Obscure, in colors whether of the sun
> Or mind, uncertain in the clearest bells,
> The spirit's speeches, the indefinite,
>
> Confused illuminations and sonorities,
> So much ourselves, we cannot tell apart
> The idea and the bearer-being of the idea.

(II. 7–18)

Sense data are obscure, uncertain and indefinite, because they are at once the data of self and the data of the world – both us and New Haven. As thinkers we are always in the act of referring, but without knowing to what. We cannot tell where we end and our idea of the world begins. We are asked to distinguish the thought from its thinker. This is an analysis that begins and ends in the mind. That there are two entities indicates that something other than ourselves exists, that a world is there somewhere beyond our sense data, however indefinite and confused its 'illuminations and sonorities', The fire is the sun's fire which illuminates the mind's intrinsic darkness. The fire flowing, no matter how far away, is an intimation of reality. The houses represent Stevens' desire to be at home in the world, and the bells show us both how the world calls to him and how intolerable it is that any home should be mute. The image of the container-like bells, I think, further suggests that communication is an enveloping structure like a house.

This is one of the many places in 'An Ordinary Evening in New Haven' in which Stevens sounds as if he is echoing *Four Quartets* (especially 'Burnt Norton'). Stevens' 'sense in which we are poised' resembles Eliot's 'still point of the turning world' in 'Burnt Norton', and the technique is very similar:

> The inner freedom from the practical desire,
> The release from action and suffering, release from the inner
> And the outer compulsion, yet surrounded
> By a grace of sense, a white light still and moving,
> *Erhebung* without motion, concentration

> Without elimination, both a new world
> And the old made explicit, understood
> In the completion of its partial ecstasy,
> The resolution of its partial horror.[2]

The two passages have a similar rhythm. Eliot's repetition of words, negative definitions, successive restatements, radical enjambments, his use of *without* and meditative tone all have their counterpart in Stevens. Both passages contain many phrases composed of two or more abstractions, such as 'concentration / Without elimination', 'object / Of the perpetual meditation', 'understood / In the completion of its partial ecstasy', 'poised, . . . In the perpetual reference', and enjambed so as to disturb the balance of the phrase. In both the syntax is such that the words so emphasised at the end of a line are set off against words at the beginning or in the middle of the next line (for example, *inner, surrounded, concentration* and *understood* against *compulsion, elimination* and *completion* in Eliot and *poised, object, point* and *indefinite* against *time, reference, meditation, obscure* and *uncertain* in Stevens). *Perpetual*, repeated twice by Stevens, occurs at the start of 'Burnt Norton':

> What might have been is an abstraction
> Remaining a perpetual possibility
> Only in a world of speculation.

There are enough similarities to suggest that the increasing abstraction of Stevens' verse from 1942 on was in part a response to the abstraction of Eliot ('Ash Wednesday' was first published in 1930, 'Burnt Norton' in 1936, 'East Coker' in 1940, 'The Dry Salvages' in 1941, 'Little Gidding' in 1942).

That 'we cannot tell apart / The idea and the bearer-being of the idea' means that we cannot fully know who we are. This is 'the difficulty of what it is to be' and Stevens attempts to solve the problem with a myth:

> Inescapable romance, inescapable choice
> Of dreams, disillusion as the last illusion,
> Reality as a thing seen by the mind,

Not that which is but that which is apprehended,
A mirror, a lake of reflections in a room,
A glassy ocean lying at the door,

A great town hanging pendent in a shade,
An enormous nation happy in a style,
Everything as unreal as real can be,

In the inexquisite eye. Why, then, inquire
Who has divided the world, what entrepreneur?
No man. The self, the chrysalis of all men

Became divided in the leisure of blue day
And more, in branchings after day. One part
Held fast tenaciously in common earth

And one from central earth to central sky
And in moonlit extensions of them in the mind
Searched out such majesty as it could find.

(v. 1–18)

We continuously offer ourselves a choice of two dreams: illusion or disillusion, appearance or reality – not because the world is double, but because we are. This division is not explained; it is something given: 'The self ... Became divided in the leisure of blue day' – something that happened without any apparent cause, in a leisurely, unforced way and at a very early stage, the chrysalis stage, of our development. The mythic note implies that this happened once and for all, that this divided self is our common human nature and not a matter of individual development.

This primary uncertainty about who we are produces a hunger for everything definite. When we feel 'that which was incredible' become, in 'misted contours, credible day again' (vii. 17–18),

We fling ourselves, constantly longing, on this form.
We descend to the street and inhale a health of air
To our sepulchral hollows. Love of the real

Is soft in three-four cornered fragrances
From five-six cornered leaves, and green, the signal
To the lover, and blue, as of a secret place

In the anonymous color of the universe.
Our breath is like a desperate element
That we must calm, the origin of a mother tongue

With which to speak to her, the capable
In the midst of foreignness, the syllable
Of recognition, avowal, impassioned cry,

The cry that contains its converse in itself,
In which looks and feelings mingle and are part
As a quick answer modifies a question,

Not wholly spoken in a conversation between
Two bodies disembodied in their talk,
Too fragile, too immediate for any speech.

(VIII. 1–18)

We are hollow, full of longing for reality. To us the air of any
particular place is substantial and inhaling it fills the inside with the
outside – the poet's search for an 'exterior made / Interior' (XII. 5–6).
The flinging suggests desperation. It is an act of abandonment and
self-forgetfulness; nevertheless, Stevens is careful to specify that it is
'this form' and not reality itself on which we fling ourselves. The
fragrances and leaves have corners, and a specified number of
corners, in order to emphasise their definiteness as things of the
world. They are 'three-four' and 'five-six cornered', because all that
we know of reality is a form and all form is approximation. Stevens
makes *her* a pronoun without a clear antecedent; it refers
inconclusively and tenuously to *mother, the real* and *this form*,
but most clearly to what follows: she is 'the capable / In the midst of
foreignness' to whom we speak 'the syllable / Of recognition'. The
structure of the sentence (that *her* refers to *mother tongue* and *mother*
only by implication, that the clearest referent is a
postcedent rather than an antecedent, that *mother tongue, the capable*
and *the syllable* appear to be in apposition) reinforces the
identification of the mother with the act of communication, of the

recipient with the message, as if she inheres in the poet's language. 'These are', as Stevens says in the concluding poem, 'the edgings and inchings of final form' (XXXI. 10) and can be said to have been developed to enable Stevens to get as close as possible to the reality of his feelings, in which the vestigial, elusive and disembodied memory of his mother is the forming presence. Existence is a conversation with her. The world is an answer to a question not wholly spoken, a relation between two bodies, too fragile, too immediate for any speech. Reality hovers on the edge of language. The poem shows us our breath on the verge of becoming our mother tongue. We have a syllable and a cry but neither words nor sentences. The question is only partially spoken and the state of the two bodies apparently makes any speech impossible. This is as contradictory as the cry 'that contains its converse in itself' and is composed of non-verbal 'looks and feelings'. This cry – reminiscent of Tennyson's crying infant 'with no language but a cry'[3] – with its overtones of sorrow and desperation at its own inarticulateness is heard throughout Stevens' later poetry. Stevens' language is an attempt to incarnate the original, ineffable intimacy of the two bodies. This is why the sentences are lengthened, the elements repeatedly restated and the syntax loosened so as to maximise the amount of grammatical modification. The final phrase, 'Too fragile, too immediate for any speech', like the pronoun *her*, has several possible antecedents: it can modify *their talk* (or *conversation*) or *two bodies* or, more probably, *question or cry*. The ambiguity is increased in that the final four lines are part of a simile: 'looks and feelings mingle and are part' (the intransitive *are part* further adding to the ambiguity). '*As* a quick answer' (suggesting that there are other answers) modifies the question – this is another of 'the intricate evasions of as'. This ambiguity, this condition of divided and 'perpetual reference', is the ambiguity that the poet feels when he beholds the world. The mingling of looks and feelings, of outside and inside, reality and imagination, is, of course, the central concern of Stevens' poetry, and the cry is so important because it enables them to mingle. As Stevens says later, 'The poem is the cry of its occasion' (XII. 1).

> We keep coming back and coming back
> To the real: to the hotel instead of the hymns
> That fall upon it out of the wind. We seek

The poem of pure reality, untouched
By trope or deviation, straight to the word,
Straight to the transfixing object, to the object

At the exactest point at which it is itself,
Transfixing by being purely what it is,
A view of New Haven, say, through the certain eye,

The eye made clear of uncertainty, with the sight
Of simple seeing, without reflection. We seek
Nothing beyond reality. Within it,

Everything, the spirit's alchemicana
Included, the spirit that goes roundabout
And through included, not merely the visible,

The solid, but the movable, the moment,
The coming on of feasts and the habits of saints,
The pattern of the heavens and high, night air.

(IX. 1–18)

'We keep coming back and coming back / To the real . . . .' This is the movement of the whole poem. New Haven in its complete and total ordinariness is both the setting and the goal, 'the transfixing object'; it is the standard by which everything is judged. The scholar in his Segmenta writes: 'The Ruler of Reality, / If more unreal than New Haven, is not / A real ruler, but rules what is unreal' (XXVII. 2–4). 'If it should be true that reality exists / In the mind . . . it follows that / Real and unreal are two in one: New Haven / Before and after one arrives . . . .' (XXVIII. 1–2, 4–6).

This continuous effort to return to the real is a roundabout indication of what an exile our existence is and of our alienation from reality. We exist in a state of seeking, of hunger and restlessness, a state of between meanings, returning for ever from that unspecified location that is our selves. Even our ultimate goals are approximations: we return to a hotel, a home away from home, seek 'The poem of pure reality' (whose very conception appears unreal) and end with no more than a view of New Haven even when we look through 'the certain eye'. 'We seek / Nothing beyond reality. Within it / Everything . . . .' Everything of the spirit, all our moments and all our absolutes are to be found within reality. Stevens, thus, establishes a limit to our fantasies. They become part of the spectrum of the real: our spirit resides in 'a permanence composed of impermanence' (x. 11) and so we inhabit 'the metaphysical streets of the physical town' (xi. 1).

When Professor Eucalyptus seeks for god in New Haven he does so with 'an eye that does not look / Beyond the object'. He seeks him 'in the object itself, without much choice'. This is analogous to the search for the 'poem of pure reality ... Straight to the transfixing object' that is 'At the exactest point at which it is itself'. Both searches are a matter of finding the right language:

> It is a choice of the commodious adjective
> For what he sees, it comes in the end to that:
>
> The description that makes it divinity, still speech
> As it touches the point of reverberation – not grim
> Reality but reality grimly seen
>
> And spoken in paradisal parlance new
> And in any case never grim, the human grim
> That is part of the indifference of the eye
>
> Indifferent to what it sees. The tink-tonk
> Of the rain in the spout is not a substitute.
> It is of the essence not yet well perceived.
>
> (xiv. 8–18)

The choice is of adjective; the noun is given by perception. The adjective needs to be commodious so as to include all the qualities of the thing. Description is the assignment of value, the encompassing of the reverberating by the 'still'. Speech must make contact with the centre of origin of the world's echoing, copying changes ('the point of reverberation'). This speech must be in a new language or system of discourse as fresh as paradise in order to denote the pristine 'essence' of what the speaker sees. To do this he cannot be indifferent. The speaker–perceiver must care for the object. A fierce and relentless concentration on the thing itself is necessary for victory in the struggle against illusion. 'The plainness of plain things is savagery' (iv. 1), and *grim* is a synonym for *savage*. Merely by introducing Professor Eucalyptus, Stevens reserves his own position. That Professor Eucalyptus seeks 'without *much* choice' suggests that there is a chance that god might be found without the object. The final statement in making everything a matter of perception, with all that that implies in the poem (along with the object being the *sound* of the rain in the spout), seems to negate any possibility of certainty. Or perhaps it can be said that the poet achieves certainty of a kind in affirming the world's uncertainty, and wholeness, in an accurate statement of his doubts.

For the poet every object is as problematic as the houses of New Haven:

> These houses, these difficult objects, dilapidate
> Appearances of what appearances,
> Words, lines, not meanings, not communications,
>
> Dark things without a double, after all . . . .

(I. 7–10)

His every thought 'contains its converse in itself': the houses are appearances of appearances, then 'Dark things without a double, after all'. There is a difficulty in apprehending objects without meaning, because thinking is the creation of meaning – the incorporation of an object in the system that is our character or memory or self – and this involves relating it to other objects: that is, expressing it in terms other than itself. Language is, among other things, a way of systematically doubling objects. Moreover, there is the difficulty denoted by *dilapidate*, that objects are always changing – and that we become tired of old imaginings. When, in the penultimate poem, the last leaf has fallen, the robins have migrated and the 'wind has blown the silence of summer away', what is present is neither residue nor static essence:

> The barrenness that appears is an exposing.
> It is not part of what is absent, a halt
> For farewells, a sad hanging on for remembrances.
>
> It is a coming on and a coming forth.

(xxx. 7–9)

Any feelings of nostalgia are rejected by the poet. He welcomes the change from summer to winter as the occasion for a new look at reality:

> It was something imagined that has been washed away.
> A clearness has returned. It stands restored.
>
> (xxx. 14–15)

This is 'a visibility of thought', a new imagining. As only that which was imagined 'has been washed away', we approach for a moment, at least, a little closer to reality – and to ourselves. The world does not disappear. That clearness is *returned* and *restored* indicates the enduring presence of reality. *Exposing, coming on* and *coming forth* show us the barrenness as emerging from the present. Their gerundive form converts the negativity of barrenness into an on-going process. *Clearness* is a quality of something not an entity in itself. How can we see 'transparency? We know our thoughts are invisible. The 'visibility of thought' is metaphoric, it owes its existence to the poem.

'An Ordinary Evening in New Haven' concludes with intimations of final form:

> The less legible meanings of sounds, the little reds
> Not often realized, the lighter words
> In the heavy drum of speech, the inner men
>
> Behind the outer shields, the sheets of music
> In the strokes of thunder, dead candles at the window
> When day comes, fire-foams in the motions of the sea,
>
> Flickings from finikin to fine finikin
> And the general fidget from busts of Constantine
> To photographs of the late president, Mr Blank,
>
> These are the edgings and inchings of final form,
> The swarming activities of the formulae
> Of statement, directly and indirectly getting at,
>
> Like an evening evoking the spectrum of violet,
> A philosopher practicing scales on his piano,
> A woman writing a note and tearing it up.

It is not in the premise that reality
Is a solid. It may be a shade that traverses
A dust, a force that traverses a shade.

(XXXI. 1–18)

Final form is the supreme fiction, of which only flickings, edgings and inchings are available. The three similes at the end indicate that form is temporary and approximative. The evening only evokes 'the spectrum of violet'. Playing scales is preparation for the final form of performance; it is an exercise rather than the real thing. Similarly, that it is a philosopher and not a musician at his piano indicates that this is a man at least slightly out of his element. The woman who writes a note and tears it up is also in a sense practising – and has just struck the wrong note. Her action is the image of a communication 'that contains its converse in itself'. The metaphors in the three similes are related in that scales are spectrums of sounds composed of notes, and that each event represents the evocation or imposition of an order and, with increasing definiteness, the conversion of sense data to communication.

The poem begins very tentatively with a Brownian movement of phrases. The opening sentence is ambiguous in that we cannot in most cases be certain whether these phrases are in apposition or a series. The 'less legible meanings of sounds', for example, appear to be different from the 'lighter words', but they may be among, or the same as, 'the little reds / Not often realized'; and are 'the inner men' behind their shields 'lighter words' inside the drum of speech? These phrases, in simultaneously including and excluding each other, create a problematic wholeness. Whatever their relation to each other, the meanings, reds, words, men, sheets, candles and fire-foams all appear to be 'Flickings from finikin to fine finikin'. To flick is to strike briefly and quickly, and in this context *flickings* suggests *flickerings*. *Finikin* has, according to the *OED*, only two meanings as a noun: a finicking person and a variety of pigeon – both obsolete. Having used the word three times previously as an adjective (and only in long poems), Stevens now makes a noun out of its adjectival meaning of fastidious, 'excessively precise in trifles' and over-delicately wrought. Final form is approached by a series of meticulous touches, sharp, light, rapid and highly finished, an accuracy of flashes and glimmerings. The thought is that of 'Like Decorations in a Nigger Cemetery':

> Poetry is a finikin thing of air
> That lives uncertainly and not for long
> Yet radiantly beyond much lustier blurs.

The finikin flickings are accompanied by a fidgeting with images of authority, and the change from sculpture to photography, a movement in the direction of greater, up-to-the-minute realism. Constantine and Mr Blank are rulers of reality (the subject of the scholar's meditations in xxvii), only vestigially present in their busts and photographs, which are yet more examples of approximate form. Their presence suggests that the search for reality is a search for a human face, and that every order has a human centre or origin.

The 'swarming activities of the formulae' are demonstrated in the syntax of the first three stanzas, the three-part simile in the fifth stanza and finally by the three-part statement of the last stanza. The swarming is all the more indefinite because we are not told what it is 'getting at', although presumably this is the final form – of reality. Stevens employs a transitive verb without an object so that we have activity with only an implied purpose. The uncertainty is increased by the use of *it* as an anticipatory subject in the second sentence and then immediately as a pronoun for *reality*, and also by the sudden introduction of *the premise*, when up to this point no premise has been stated. Is 'the premise' 'final form'? The two short declarative sentences of the concluding stanza are as tentative and elusive as the preceding long, complex accumulation of clauses – and to the same end: to show the insubstantiality of reality and to suggest its all-pervasive power. Stevens does not consider the possibility that reality does not exist. The *may be* refers not to whether it is, but to the difficulty or impossibility of knowing what it is. According to the final tercet, reality is insubstantial, moving and within an object: an intangible shade traversing tangible dust, then an imperceptible force, like electro-magnetism, traversing the intangible shade – the final restatement making it more inward, darker. Nothing could be more down-to-earth than the dust, and there are biblical overtones: the word reminds us of the clods from which Yahweh made Adam, the dust that we were, are, and to which we shall return. *Solid, shade, dust* and *force* are marked by the indefinite article. We do not know where they are. This locates them *au pays de la métaphore. Traverses* does not specify any particular relation between subject and object. The force acts, if at all, in incalculable ways. We are left with an impression of unknowable power.

After Henry Church's death, Stevens looked forward to his own end and then backward to his beginnings. He was disposed to sum up and see his life as a whole, and in this final period his old poems often echoed in his mind. His feelings of being separated from the world and from himself deepened as he confronted the impending separation of death. It was 'As if nothingness contained a métier'. This phrase from 'The Rock' is a definition of his vocation. That métier is poetry. Nothingness is the poet's *raison d'être*. He works to create an end to his primary loneliness: to make a communication that is like the presence of another person, a message sent that has the effect of a message received. As a poet, Stevens lived always in the hope of such a transformation and he was aware that in the poems of his final years he was engaged with the same old concerns, humming or hymning the prologues to the possibility of achieving 'the intensest rendezvous' with the interior paramour, some 'point of central arrival'.[4] As he says in 'Long and Sluggish Lines' (1952):

> It makes so little difference, at so much more
> Than seventy, where one looks, one has been there before.

'The Planet on the Table' (1953) is a reworking of the central metaphor of 'Someone Puts a Pineapple Together', the pineapple that is 'an object on a table' which stands for 'everybody's world'. Stevens' mood is elegiac, but his language is spare, plain and dispassionate, denuded of any sentimentality. The subject is a poet looking back over his poetic career:

> Ariel was glad he had written his poems.
> They were of a remembered time
> Or of something seen that he liked.
>
> Other makings of the sun
> Were waste and welter
> And the ripe shrub writhed.
>
> His self and the sun were one
> And his poems, although makings of his self,
> Were no less makings of the sun.

It was not important that they survive.
What mattered was that they should bear
Some lineament or character,

Some affluence, if only half-perceived,
In the poverty of their words,
Of the planet of which they were part.

As his poet Stevens has chosen Ariel, the ethereal singer whose words have the magic power of altering reality and who appears and disappears throughout Shakespeare's last great play (often said to be his farewell to the theatre). The planet on the table is the world reduced to a manageable, domestic totality. Stevens looks back on his work and is glad. Of all the 'makings of the sun' only his poems have any significance for Ariel, and as a result of writing them he is at one with reality. 'Makings' is ambiguous, showing us poetry as both the creator and creation of self and sun. What is important is neither the poet's nor the poems' immortality (or mortality), but that he has succeeded in making some contact, however tenuous, with reality.

'As You Leave the Room' (1954), published after Stevens' death, is another of these poems of last things. It resumes his early work in two ways, by being the reworking of an earlier poem, 'First Warmth' (1947), and by referring to four earlier poems:

You speak. You say: Today's character is not
A skeleton out of its cabinet. Nor am I.

That poem about the pineapple, the one
About the mind as never satisfied,

The one about the credible hero, the one
About summer, are not what skeletons think about.

I wonder, have I lived a skeleton's life,
As a disbeliever in reality,

A countryman of all the bones in the world?
Now, here, the snow I had forgotten becomes

Part of a major reality, part of
An appreciation of a reality

And thus an elevation, as if I left
With something I could touch, touch every way.

And yet nothing has been changed except what is
Unreal, as if nothing had been changed at all.

The 'poem about the pineapple' is 'Someone Puts a Pineapple Together'; 'the one / About the mind as never satisfied' is 'The Well Dressed Man with a Beard'; the 'one about the credible hero' is 'Examination of the Hero in a Time of War'; and 'the one / About summer' is 'Credences of Summer'. As the title suggests, 'As You Leave the Room' is about the fear of separation and the poet's feeling of incompleteness, his separation from, or disbelief in, reality. It is his poems (what he thinks about) that enable him to feel that he has a body rather than merely a skeleton, and the snow that he has forgotten (another mental event – an unconscious memory?) becomes part of a reality with which he is able to make contact. (*Appreciation* means the enjoyment of fine distinctions, a high estimation and an increase in value.) This coldness – and the imagination is always cold in Stevens' poetry – is an *elevation*: that which uplifts and transports. How this happens is unexplained, but it is, the poem makes clear, a change of imagination, in what is unreal, and therefore '*as if* nothing had been changed at all'. Faced with the impending separation, very tentatively, in the here and now of the poem, the poet decides, in spite of the fact that everything is very unreal to him, that he has not lived a skeleton's life.

'As You Leave the Room' is an expression of the apparent tenuousness of significant mental events – and all knowledge. It is deliberately located between being (in the room) and leaving, at the moment of change from one state to another. This process of exchange is also represented by the dialogue form. The difficulty of knowing who is speaking to whom is in keeping with the difficulty of determining what change has occurred. The poet appears to be talking to himself. He is divided: *you* suggests that part of him is always other; *Today's character* suggests that his character may be different every day; while the *I* that also seems to change is none the less distinguished from this less stable, more discontinuous 'character'. This inner inventory is continued in the enumeration of past poems and can be seen as a final effort of integration in response to the final separation of death. The skeleton is a *memento mori*. The metaphor is one of deprivation and spectral ghostliness, and, at the same time, of an articulated, fundamental order. The skeleton is as hard and certain as the rock in the poem of that name and connects the poet 'to all the bones in the world'. The snow that has passed out of memory ('Mais ou sont les neiges d'antan?'[5]) none the less has its effect in the present. 'A major reality' implies other possible realities, major and minor. It is *'a reality'* rather than *the* reality. *Appreciation* is neither the exact nor the full counterpart of being a *disbeliever*. *Could touch* is only a possibility and even so dependent on another *as if*. Scepticism and faith are of the same substance, a tissue of uncertainties and qualifications, and as temporary as the forgotten, evanescent snow.

According to the chronology established by his daughter, 'Of Mere Being' is the last poem that Stevens completed. His whole poetic career can be described as a search for the feeling of being, and this succession of clear, positive, unequivocal statements is the confident and joyful affirmation that that search has been successful. The poet in envisaging 'the end of the mind' is thinking about death. This limit is necessary in order to hold and define what he is (as in 'As You Leave the Room', the skeleton is conceived of in its cabinet and the poet within the limits of the room). His being is predicated on the existence of something beyond himself:

> The palm at the end of the mind,
> Beyond the last thought, rises
> In the bronze decor,
>
> A gold-feathered bird
> Sings in the palm, without human meaning,
> Without human feeling, a foreign song.
>
> You know then that it is not the reason
> That makes us happy or unhappy.
> The bird sings. Its feathers shine.
>
> The palm stands on the edge of space.
> The wind moves slowly in the branches.
> The bird's fire-fangled feathers dangle down.

This is Yeats' golden bird that sang in Byzantium 'To keep a drowsy Emperor awake. . . . Of what is past, or passing, or to come';[6] this is

Valéry's palm, the mobile arbiter between the shadow and the sun.[7] It is the 'cloudy palm remote on heaven's hill' of 'Sunday Morning' brought near at hand; it is the bantam of 'Bantams in Pinewood', the damned universal cock with its blazing tail, come home to roost. In 'A Mythology Reflects its Region', also composed in the year of his death, Stevens states,

> Here
> In Connecticut, we never lived in a time
> When mythology was possible

'Of Mere Being' is an attempt to provide a mythology for Connecticut. Palm and bird are the fulfilment of the poet's wish for the world and immortality. We are reassured by the idea of a limit (or form) to amorphousness, that if life has a conclusion it may also have a meaning (or form). Stevens writes to Elsie Moll (31 January 1909): 'How deeply one gets into one's mind! Poetry only lies in the remoter parts of it.' The self is secured by the poem at the end of the mind.

On 2 August 1955 Wallace Stevens died. A few days before his death he was baptised as a Catholic. According to Peter Brazeau, 'Holly Stevens vigorously denies that her father was converted to Catholicism during his last illness. While at St Francis Hospital, she recalls, Stevens complained of visits by clergy but he said he was too weak to protest' (*B*, p. 310). The Reverend Arthur Hanley, the priest who visited Stevens every day in the hospital and who baptised him, told Brazeau, 'He gave me the impression he knew quite a bit about the Church. The impression he gave me was there were just a few little things that kept him from being a Catholic.' The most important was the problem of evil in the world (the subject of his long meditative poem 'Esthétique du Mal', 1944):

> And he was always coming back to the goodness of God: how could a good God allow all this evil in the world? . . . So we talked along that line quite a bit, and he was thinking and thinking and thinking. One day he had a bit of a spell. He called for me, and he said, 'I'd better get in the fold now.' And then I baptised him, and the next day I brought him Communion.

This was only a few days before he died. According to Hanley, 'He seemed very much at peace, and he would say, "Now I'm in the fold." It was not a nervous reaction, it was a real steady reaction.' (*B*, pp. 294–5.)

We are unlikely to know much more about exactly what happened. However, considered as a poetic decision, his conversion is logical and psychologically consistent. At the start of his essay 'Imagination as Value' (1948), written after his poems of death 'The Owl in the Sarcophagus' and 'The Auroras of Autumn', Stevens focuses on Pascal's deathbed: 'As he lay dying, he experienced a violent convulsion ["a bit of a spell"].... He repeatedly asked that he might receive communion.' Stevens then quotes from Pascal's sister's account of the scene:

> *God, who wished to reward a desire so fervent and so just, suspended this convulsion as by a miracle and restored his judgement completely as in the perfection of his health ... and as the priest approached to give him communion, he made an effort, he raised himself half way without help to receive it with more respect; and the priest having interrogated him, following the custom, on the principal mysteries of the faith, he responded distinctly: 'Yes, monsieur, I believe all that with all my heart.' Then he received the sacred wafer and extreme unction with feelings so tender that he poured out tears. He replied to everything, thanked the priest and as the priest blessed him with the holy ciborium, he said, 'Let God never forsake me.'*

On this ceremony, in which he himself was later to participate, Stevens comments, 'Thus, in the very act of dying, he clung to what he himself had called the delusive faculty.' Belief is an act of the imagination and without any particular moral value, because value is created by the imagination: 'The imagination is the power of the mind over the possibilities of things; but if this constitutes a certain single characteristic, it is the source not of a certain single value but of as many values as reside in the possibilities of things.' (*NA*, pp. 134–6.)

There is also a sense in which he had been pondering this decision for much of his life. On Sunday, 10 August 1902, he writes in his journal,

Last night I spent an hour in the dark transept of St Patrick's Cathedral where I go now and then in my more lonely moods. An old argument with me is that the true religious force in the world is not the church but the world itself: the mysterious callings of Nature and our responses. What incessant murmurs fill that ever-laboring, tireless church! But today in my walk I thought that after all there is no conflict of forces but rather a contrast. In the cathedral I felt one presence; on the highway I felt another. Two different deities presented themselves; and though I have only cloudy visions of either, yet I now feel the distinction between them. The priest in me worshipped one God at one shrine; the poet another God at another shrine.   (*SP*, p. 104)

The argument was already 'old' when Stevens was twenty-three, and even at this early stage he feels a 'contrast' rather than a 'conflict'. The idea that the world can be a religion is fully stated in 'Sunday Morning' and the image of the poet meditating in a cathedral occurs in 'The Comedian as the Letter C' and 'The Man with the Blue Guitar'. 'The priest in me' is the rabbi, Franciscan don and Canon Aspirin. As a believer Stevens felt he needed to be the officiating agent, to be the maker of the song he sang, and he was prepared to believe in the world and the church as mutually inclusive alternatives.

His notions of the relation between the world and the church are very clearly expressed in his letter to Elsie Moll on 10 March 1907. He does not find religious practice incompatible with disbelief and accepts unhesitatingly the church as a mother:

I am not in the least religious. The sun clears my spirit, if I may say that, and an occasional sight of the sea, and thinking of blue valleys, and the odor of the earth, and many things. Such things make a god of a man; but a chapel makes a man of him. Churches are human. – I say my prayers every night – not that I need them now, or that they are anything more than a habit, half-conscious. But in Spain, in Salamanca, there is a pillar in a church (Santayana told me) worn by the kisses of generations of the devout. One of their kisses are [*sic*] worth all my prayers. Yet the church is a mother for them – and for us.

His two gods were imagination and reality and, when he could no longer devise his own supreme fiction, he accepted one ready-made.

Throughout his poetic career Stevens saw poetry as taking the place of religion. He saw the creation of new faith as the primary activity of the imagination, necessary in order for life to have any meaning, and a process tht can never be completed because its results are always approximate, partial and inconclusive. Perhaps nothing indicates more clearly the function of poetry in Stevens' life than that, when he knew that he would not be able to write any more poems, he converted to a religion. When he could no longer create an order out of himself, he looked for an order outside himself and independent of his efforts. Forced by circumstances to give up the sustaining-process of searching for a tentative order, he chose a fixed order, and, recognising that he could no longer continue as a poet, reached out for such permanence as was available to him. His poem 'To an Old Philosopher in Rome' (1952) shows that the example of Santayana in the convent of the Blue Nuns in Rome – his scepticism secure within the safety of an established church – was very much in his mind. The poem concludes with the city of Rome and the Catholic religion appearing as a single structure that the old philosopher has himself created, as if his words have come true:

> Total grandeur of a total edifice,
> Chosen by an inquisitor of structures
> For himself. He stops upon this threshold,
> As if the design of all his words takes form
> And frame from thinking and is realized.

Stevens in becoming a Catholic chose the oldest religion in his culture, almost as venerable and full of myths as poetry itself. The choice was of something slightly foreign, analogous to including French as part of English, like trying to choose reality and imagination simultaneously.

To Simons in explanation of the second section of 'Owl's Clover', Stevens comments:

> The idea of God is a thing of the imagination. We no longer think that God was, but was imagined. The idea of pure poetry, essential imagination, as the highest objective of the poet, appears to be, at least potentially, as great as the idea of God, and for that matter, greater, if the idea of God is only one of the things of the imagination.   (28 Aug 1940)

He had not abandoned this view when on 6 June 1955, some three weeks before he died, he inscribed a copy of *The Collected Poems* for Elias Mengel: 'When I speak of the poem, or often when I speak of the poem, in this book, I mean not merely literary form, but the brightest and most harmonious concept, or order, or life; and the references should be read with that in mind' (*B*, p. 288). There is no reason to suppose that he ever abandoned this belief in poetry. There is a possibility that both Father Hanley and Holly Stevens are right: that he did convert to Catholicism, and that at the same time he did not change his mind about religion, but 'clung to what he himself had called the delusive faculty'. Whatever his state of mind, the decision was the private act of a man who spent his whole life 'thinking and thinking and thinking' in poetry.

Epilogue: The Whole of Harmonium

What, precisely, is 'thinking'? When, at the reception of sense-impressions, memory-pictures emerge, this is not yet 'thinking'. And when such pictures form series, each member of which calls forth another, this too is not yet 'thinking'. When, however, a certain picture turns up in many such series, then – precisely through such return – it becomes an ordering element for such series, in that it connects series which in themselves are unconnected. Such an element becomes an instrument, a concept. I think that the transition from free association or 'dreaming' to thinking is characterised by the more or less dominating role which the 'concept' plays in it. It is by no means necessary that a concept must be connected with a sensorily cognizable and reproducible sign (word); but when this is the case thinking becomes by means of that fact communicable.

With what right – the reader will ask – does this man operate so carelessly and primitively with ideas in such a problematic realm without making even the least effort to prove anything? My defense: all our thinking is of this nature of a free play with concepts; the justification for this play lies in the measure of survey over the experience of the senses which we are able to achieve with its aid. The concept of 'truth' can not yet be applied to such a structure; to my thinking this concept can come in question only when a far-reaching agreement (*convention*) concerning the elements and rules of the game is already at hand.

For me it is not dubious that our thinking goes on for the most part without use of signs (words) and beyond that to a considerable degree unconsciously. For how, otherwise, should it happen that sometimes we 'wonder' quite spontaneously about some experience? This 'wondering' seems to occur when an experience comes into conflict with a world of concepts which is already sufficiently fixed in us. Whenever such a conflict is experienced hard and intensively it reacts back upon our thought world in a decisive way. The development of this thought world is in a certain sense a continuous flight from 'wonder'.[1]

This attempt by Stevens' exact contemporary, Albert Einstein (1879–1955), to describe what is distinctive about his thought-processes is also a description of the thinking in Stevens' poetry. The emphasis on pictures, especially as ordering- and connecting-elements, on the way certain pictures keep turning up, the ready transformation of pictures into concepts, the homogenity of dreaming and reasoning, the complexity of pre-verbal states, and thought as 'a problematic realm' are all to be found in Stevens. His thought, like Einstein's, is dominated by idea-pictures that he is constantly trying to connect with sets of signs.

The 'free play of concepts' became in both cases a triumphant reimagining of the world, making it strange in order to make it more real and in order to read 'the experience of the senses'. For each man this play was part of an intensely personal quest, a reorganisation of his own thought-world. Welcoming the freshness of the new, they were disturbed by the possibility of its incomprehensibility. The poetry of Stevens, notwithstanding, is a flight to wonder.

Einstein's early papers are remarkable for their non-mathematical character. 'There are relatively few equations – often not even numbered sequentially.'[2] The results are obtained from the analysis of what he called 'thought-experiments' (*Gedankenexperiments*). There is perhaps no better description of Stevens' poems than 'thought-experiments'. He creates a succession of new worlds in order to test the possibility of ideas. Each poem is a new order, a hypothetical mode of being. Each theory is the model of a moment of experience in a form easily assimilable to, if not interchangeable with, the moments of the theory-maker's life. Working from a specific situation is a way of establishing a relation between several complex variables, especially when there is a long series of values for some or all of the variables. The thought-experiment is a response to a dynamic problem, a way of analysing a set of forces (including emotions).

In his speech on Max Planck's sixtieth birthday (1918) Einstein remarked,

Nobody who has really gone deeply into the matter will deny that in practice the world of phenomena unambiguously determines the theoretical system, in spite of the fact that there is no logical bridge between phenomena and their theoretical principles; this is what Leibniz described so happily as a 'pre-established harmony'.

When he says that 'the longing to behold this pre-established harmony' is the source of Planck's 'inexhaustible patience and endurance', he is also speaking for himself – and for Stevens, except that Stevens, for all his longing, was never entirely certain that the harmony was pre-established.[3] 'The world of phenomena' was always ambiguous. For him, that there was 'no logical bridge between phenomena and their theoretical principles' was decisive, and he resorted to poetic bridges.

Einstein was never happy with the statistical character of quantum mechanics. He hated the idea that physics should be a matter of probabilities, and for over thirty years he attempted to combine quantum and relativity theory in a single comprehensive aesthetically satisfying formulation. The unified field theory was his supreme fiction. He did not wish 'to prove anything'. The purpose of his thought, says his friend and biographer, Abraham Pais, 'was neither to incorporate the unexplained nor to resolve any paradox. It was purely a quest for harmony.'[4] Wallace Stevens wanted to call his collected poems 'THE WHOLE OF HARMONIUM'.

Notes

CHAPTER 1: I WAS THE WORLD IN WHICH I WALKED

1. *L*, pp. 4–5; *SP*, pp. 4, 7.
2. *SP*, p. 9.
3. *SP*, pp. 6–7; *L*, pp. 3–4.
4. *SP*, p. 6.
5. *L*, pp. 4, 454; *B*, pp. 257, 262–4.
6. Jerald Hatfield, 'More About Legend', *The Trinity Review*, VIII (May 1954) 30, as cited in Michael Lafferty, 'Wallace Stevens, A Man of Two Worlds', *The Historical Review of Berks County*, XXIV (1959) 110.
7. Ibid., p. 110.
8. Hatfield, as cited ibid., p. 110.
9. *B*, p. 266.
10. *L*, p. 13.
11. *L*, pp. 14, 20.
12. *SP*, p. 71.
13. Garrett Stevens to Wallace (27 Sep 1897); *L*, p. 14.
14. *SP*, pp. 4–5.
15. *B*, p. 258.
16. *B*, p. 258.
17. *B*, pp. 256, 261–2, 263–4.
18. *B*, p. 259.
19. *B*, p. 258.
20. *SP*, pp. 208–9.
21. On Elsie Stevens, see *B*, pp. 234–5, 257, 259–60.
22. *B*, p. 264.
23. *SP*, pp. 9–12.
24. *SP*, p. 11; 'Gold Medals Awarded on "Alumni Night"', *The Reading Eagle*, 23 Dec 1896, p. 5.
25. 'Commencement of the Reading High Schools', *The Reading Eagle*, 24 June 1897, p. 3.
26. 'Gold Medals Awarded on "Alumni Night"', *The Reading Eagle*, 23 Dec 1896, p. 5.
27. *L*, pp. 17, 22, 33–4 (Holly Stevens has here transcribed the Harvard records).
28. *E*, p. 189.
29. *E*, pp. 189–94.
30. The entire journal (1898–1909 with two entries in 1912) is published in *SP*.
31. Up to the ellipsis, letter from Murray Seasongood to Holly Stevens (29 June 1964), after ellipsis, from Samuel Morse, *Wallace Stevens: Poetry as Life* (New York, 1970) p. 27, as cited in *SP*, p. 37.
32. *SP*, pp. 72, 74–5, 78, 87–9; *E*, p. 194.
33. *L*, p. 57; *SP*, pp. 137–8; *B*, pp. 255–6.

34. *L*, pp. 77–8, 318.
35. *B*, pp. xxi, 5; cf. *L*, p. 93.
36. *L*, p. 102.
    B, p. 261. Cf. Stevens' letter to Elsie Moll, 4 Jan 1907: 'I dream now of writing golden odes; at all events I'd like to read them.'
38. *SP*, pp. 186–7; *L*, p. 94.
39. *SP*, p. 189; *B*, p. 5.
40. *SP*, pp. 190–6.
41. *SP*, p. 203; *B*, pp. 256, xii.
42. *SP*, pp. 227–34.
43. *SP*, pp. 246–7.
44. *L*, p. 166.
45. *B*, pp. xii, 3–4, 300, 6.
46. C. T. Lewis and T. A. Ingram, 'Insurance', *The Encyclopaedia Britannica*, 11th edn (Cambridge, 1910) xiv, 656–73.
47. *B*, p. 7.
48. *B*, pp. 11–12, 61, 63, 172.
49. *B*, pp. 10–12, 17–18.
50. *B*, p. 12.
51. *B*, pp. 24–5.
52. *B*, p. 25.
53. *B*, p. 24.
54. *B*, p. 22.
55. *B*, pp. 63, 67.
56. *B*, p. 67. On his 'psychic intuitiveness' about bond cases, see *B*, p. 37.
57. *B*, p. 77.
58. *B*, p. 67.
59. Wallace Stevens, 'Surety and Fidelity Claims', *The Eastern Underwriter*, 25 Mar 1938, p. 45.
60. *B*, p. 20.
61. *B*, p. 39.
62. *B*, pp. 48, 77.
63. *B*, p. 192.
64. *B*, p. 197.
65. *B*, pp. 25, 34, 50, 57.
66. *B*, p. 23.
67. *B*, pp. 23, 38.
68. *B*, p. 68.
69. *B*, p. 25.
70. *B*, p. 40.
71. *B*, p. 38.
72. *B*, p. 192.
73. *B*, pp. 94–5, 109, 216.
74. *B*, p. 188.
75. *B*, pp. 27, 29, 30, 77, 15, 63.
76. *B*, pp. 41–2, 45, 66–7, 292–3.
77. *B*, p. 21, 51, 33.
78. *B*, p. 78.

79. Wilson Taylor, 'Of a Remembered Time', *WSC*, p. 95.
80. *B*, pp. 58–9.
81. *B*, p. 31.
82. *B*, pp. 11, 48.
83. *B*, p. 49.
84. *B*, pp. 80–1, 53–4.
85. *B*, pp. 51, 58, 80.
86. *B*, pp. 88, 37.
87. Wilson Taylor, 'Of a Remembered Time', *WSC*, pp. 93, 95.
88. *B*, pp. 41, 56
89. *B*, p. 62; cf. pp. 14, 73.
90. *B*, p. 44.
91. *B*, pp. 28, 40.
92. *B*, p. 33.
93. *B*, p. 37, 'But the greatest thing by far is to have a command of metaphor. This alone cannot be imparted by another; it is the mark of genius, for to make metaphors implies an eye for resemblances' – Aristotle, *The Poetics*, 1459a, in S. H. Butcher, *Aristotle's Theory of Poetry and Fine Art* (1951) pp. 86–7.
94. *B*, pp. 103, 15, 76. The photograph is on the seventh page of photographs in *B*, following p. 174.
95. *B*, pp. 11, 13, 50, 146, 173, 195.
96. *B*, pp. 21, 32, 55.
97. *B*, p. 243.
98. *B*, p. 236.
99. *B*, pp. 72, 199. Stevens started to have his suits made in East Orange in 1905 when he lived there. When the father, Axel Lofquist, retired, he patronised his son, Spencer (*L*, p. 682).
100. *B*, p. 211.
101. *B*, p. 140.
102. *B*, pp. 245; 102–3, 15, 50, 233.
103. *B*, p. 13.
104. Peter Brazeau, 'A Trip in a Ballon: A Sketch of Stevens' Later Years in New York', *WSC*, p. 122; *B*, pp. 92, 247.
105. *B*, p. 141.
106. *B*, pp. 49, 54, 68, 79, 97.
107. *B*, pp. 246, 193.
108. *B*, p. 139.
109. *B*, p. 50.
110. *B*, p. 72.
111. Wilson Taylor, 'Of a Remembered Time', *WSC*, pp. 83–4, 86.
112. *B*, p. 98.
113. *B*, p. 65.
114. The references to Ceylon in his poetry occur after his first letter to van Geyzel. See, for example, 'A Weak Mind in the Mountains' (1938), 'Connoisseur of Chaos', 'Extracts from Addresses to the Academy of Fine Ideas', VII, 'Notes Toward a Supreme Fiction', 1. v (and his letter to Simons, 12 Jan 1943), and 'Description without Place', III.

115. *B*, p. 115.
116. *B*, pp. 156–7, 27.
117. *B*, pp. 232–3, 247.
118. *B*, pp. 231, 245, 239.
119. Holly Stevens, 'Holidays in Reality', *WSC*, pp. 105–6, 113.
120. *B*, pp. 141–2. The sentence is from Henry James' notebook entry dated 23 October 1891 – *The Notebooks of Henry James*, ed. F. O. Matthiessen and Kenneth Murdock (1947) p. 112. Stevens found it in F. O. Matthiessen's *Henry James: The Major Phase* (1944) 10; see *L*, p. 506.
121. *L*, p. 77; *SP*, p. 115; *B*, p. 150.
122. *B*, p. 157.
123. *B*, pp. 260, 281.
124. *B*, p. 260. There are photographs of Elsie Stevens in *L* and *B*.
125. *SP*, pp. 81–2.
126. *SP*, pp. 128.
127. *SP*, p. 142.
128. *SP*, pp. 186, 190, 227.
129. Carl Van Vechten, 'Rogue Elephant in Porcelain', *The Yale University Library Gazette*, xxxviii (Oct 1963) 49. Stevens opens his letter to Elsie Moll of 6 January 1909: 'O Muse'.
130. *SP*, p. 227. cf. *B*, p. 235.
131. *B*, p. 175.
132. *L*, p. 155. Plate ix in *L* is a photograph of the Weinman head. See also *B*, pp. 250, 87, 91.
133. *SP*, p. 247.
134. Van Vechten, 'Rogue Elephant in Porcelain', pp. 47–50.
135. *B*, p. 243.
136. *B*, pp. 65, 43–4.
137. *SP*, p. 137.
138. *B*, p. 252.
139. *B*, pp. 234, 236, 238, 245, 279. See the photograph of her and Stevens in about 1938 in *L*, plate xiv.
140. *B*, pp. 250, 235, 279 (housekeeping); Van Vechten, 'Rogue Elephant in Porcelain', pp. 47–8, and *B*, pp. 79, 97 (disapproval of Stevens' drinking); *B*, p. 250 (objection to smoking).
141. *B*, p. 232.
142. *B*, pp. 234, 258.
143. *B*, pp. 49, 236, 247, 276, 279. For examples of Stevens not inviting people to his house or not introducing them to his wife, see *B*, pp. 80, 87, 137, 138–9, 145, 114, 246.
144. *B*, pp. 235, 250, 279, 238.
145. *B*, pp. 234, 255, 270; see also Milton Bates, 'To Realize the Past: Wallace Stevens' Genealogical Study', *American Literature*, lii (1981) 609.
146. *B*, pp. 237, 252, 43, 122–3, 72; see also Wilson Taylor, 'Of a Remembered Time', *WSC*, p. 86; and see Stevens' letter to Taylor (11 Aug 1954), ibid., pp. 88–9.
147. *B*, pp. 161–2; *L*, p. 397; *B*, p. 270.

148. Milton Bates, 'To Realize the Past', *American Literature*, LII, 610.
149. Ibid., 607.
150. *B*, p. 74.
151. *B*, p. 97.
152. Ernest Hemingway, *Selected Letters 1917–1961*, ed. Carlos Baker (London, 1981) pp. 438–46; *B*, pp. 97–8.
153. *B*, pp. 52–3.
154. *B*, p. 17.
155. *B*, p. 68.
156. *B*, p. 202.
157. *B*, p. 83.
158. *B*, pp. 292–3.
159. *B*, p. 291.
160. *B*, p. 292.
161. *SP*, pp. 29–36. The early poems (up to 1910) are reprinted and discussed in *SP*. For the whole period up to 1915, see Robert Buttell, *Wallace Stevens: The Making of Harmonium* (Princeton, NJ, 1967), which also includes most of the poems.
162. The following are some examples of early poems foreshadowing later ones. The first of the sonnets for English 22 has the poet walking in his world as on a seashore (*SP*, p. 29), the ninth contrasts the ceremonies inside a cathedral with the weather outside (*SP*, pp. 32–3) and the eleventh sets 'the scarlet rose' against blue forget-me-nots and the bluer ocean (*SP*, p. 33). There are circling pigeons in 'The Pigeons' (*SP*, p. 61), and an 'old-time wig' and 'pink parasol' in *Ballade of the Pink Parasol* (*SP*, pp. 66–7). Perhaps it can be said that the red roses 'Red with a reddish light' of *Outside the Hospital* (*SP*, p. 58) dimly suggest the 'rubies reddened by rubies reddening' of 'Description without Place', VII. 20.
163. *SP*, pp. 68, 269.
164. *SP*, p. 68.
165. *SP*, pp. 77, 98–9.
166. *SP*, p. 100.
167. *SP*, p. 101.
168. *B*, p. 7.
169. *B*, p. 57.
170. *L*, p. 291.
171. Stevens to Harriet Monroe, 29 May 1916; *L*, p. 195.
172. *L*, p. 201.
173. R. P. Blackmur, *Language as Gesture* (1952) pp. 221–2.
174. *OP*, p. 166.
175. *OP*, p. 161.
176. *OP*, p. 161.
177. This statement by Santayana was a favourite one of Richard Blackmur's and I have cited it in the form in which he used to repeat it. What Santayana wrote is: 'for everything in nature is lyrical in its ideal essence, tragic in its fate, and comic in its existence' – George Santayana, 'Carnival', *Soliloquies in England and Later Soliloquies* (Ann Arbor, Mich., 1967) p. 142.

178. His salary increased from $10,000 (1 May 1923) to $15,000 (1 Jan 1929). The Depression caused a reduction to $13,500 (1 July 1932), but it la.er increased to $17,500 (1 Feb 1934) and continued to increase for the rest of his working life. Stevens bought 118 Westerly Terrace in 1932 in the middle of the Depression and paid about $20,000 in cash for it (*B*, p. 232).
179. *L*, p. 242.
180. *B*, p. 244.
181. *L*, pp. 241–2.
182. *L*, p. 242.
183. *L*, p. 259; *B*, p. xiii.
184. *B*, p. 59.
185. Theodore Weiss, *The Man from Porlock* (Princeton, NJ, 1982) p. 67.

CHAPTER 2: THE GRAND POEM: PRELIMINARY MINUTIAE

1. William Blake, 'Auguries of Innocence', *The Complete Poems*, ed. Alicia Ostriker (Harmondsworth, Middx, 1977) p. 506.
2. See *WBMP*, esp. pp. 163, 215–16.
3. William Wordsworth, 'Lines Composed a Few Miles above Tintern Abbey', *The Poems*, ed. J. O. Hayden (Harmondsworth, Middx, 1977) I, 360.
4. Sigmund Freud, *The Interpretation of Dreams*, tr. James Strachey in *The Standard Edition of the Complete Psychological Works of Sigmund Freud*, ed. James Strachey, V (London, 1975) 577.
5. Martin Heidegger, *Poetry, Language, Thought*, tr. Albert Hofstadter (1971) p. 4.

CHAPTER 3: AMERICANS ARE NOT BRITISH IN SENSIBILITY

1. Paul Valéry, 'La Crise de l'esprit', *Oeuvres*, ed. Jean Hytier, I (1957) 992–3 (the ellipsis is Valéry's), 991–2. Valéry entitled the five volumes of his collected essays *Variété*.
2. On this whole subject see *WBMP*, esp. pp. 17–43, 74–9, 202–13.
3. Hart Crane, *The Complete Poems and Selected Letters and Prose of Hart Crane*, ed. Brom Weber (Garden City, NY, 1966) pp. 218–19.
4. Ezra Pound, 'The Approach to Paris, I', *The New Age*, n.s., XIII, no. 19 (4 Sep 1913) 551–2, as cited in Cyrena Pondrom, *The Road from Paris* (Cambridge, 1974) p. 172.
5. Ezra Pound, 'The Approach to Paris, II', *The New Age*, n.s., XIII, no. 20 (11 Sep 1913) 577–9 as rep. (in an edited version) in Pondrom, *The Road from Paris*, pp. 174–5.
6. W. B. Yeats, *Uncollected Prose*, ed. John Frayne and Colton Johnson, II (London, 1975) p. 413. The text is from 'An account of his speech' that appeared in *Poetry* (Apr 1914). The dinner was given by the Poetry Society of Chicago at Cliff Dwellers on 1 Mar 1914.
7. T. S. Eliot, 'A Commentary', *The Criterion*, XIII (Apr 1934) 451.

8.   T. S. Eliot, *'Baudelaire and the Symbolists. Five Essays*. By Peter Quennell', *The Criterion*, IX (Jan 1930) 359, 357.

9.   Ezra Pound, 'What I feel about Walt Whitman', *Selected Prose 1909–1965*, ed. William Cookson (1973) pp. 145–6.

10. W. C. Williams, *The Autobiography of William Carlos Williams* (1967) pp. 53–4.

11. Ibid., p. 107.

12. Ibid., p. 311.

13. Buttel, *Wallace Stevens: The Making of Hamonium*, pp. 195–8. Crispin is 'Like Candide, / Yeoman and grub', 'The Comedian as the Letter C' (v. 73–4).

14. *Focus Five: Modern American Poetry*, ed. B. Rajan (London, 1950) pp. 183–4, as cited in R. H. Pearce, *The Continuity of American Poetry* (Princeton, NJ, 1961) pp. 379–80.

15. Jane Harrison, *Prolegomena to the Study of Greek Religion* (1955) pp. 288–92; H. R. Patch, *The Goddess Fortuna in Medieval Literature* (London, 1967); E. R. Curtius, *European Literature and the Latin Middle Ages*, tr. W. R. Trask (1953) pp. 195–200.

16. Curtius, *European Literature and the Latin Middle Ages*, p. 195.

17. Stevens told Elder Olson 'that he had originally intended to put in something like Helen of Troy but decided the poor girl was overworked, especially in poetry, and so he thought of another beautiful woman. . . . I said, "That's fine, but what about the rouge?" "Oh," he said, "that's just to dress her up a bit" ' (*B*, p. 210). One can think of her as the counterpart of the blue woman in 'Notes Toward a Supreme Fiction', 3.II.

18. S. T. Coleridge, 'Kubla Khan', *Selected Poetry and Prose of Coleridge*, ed. D. A. Stauffer (1951) pp. 43–5. Stevens in a letter to his wife from Havana states, 'There are a good many Chinese here. . . . One came up to me on the street with a big box swung over his shoulder and said "Hot Peanuts!" That's the life' (4 Feb 1923). A. Walton Litz, in *Introspective Voyager* (1972) p. 143, nicely observes that this man is 'the comic prototype for the "mythy goober khan" '.

19. Andrew Marvell, 'Upon Appleton House', *The Complete Poems*, ed. Elizabeth Story Donno (Harmondsworth, Middx, 1972) p. 84. I am grateful to David Reid for bringing this passage to my attention. The poem also contains the idea of a house in a park and woods, the beating of drums (XXXVII. 4), a parade (XXXIX), a reference to manna and the Israelites (LI. 8) and a nightingale (LXV. 1).

20. The idea of the poem as a tomb is explicit in the *tombeaux* poems of Mallamé. Cf. also 'Toast funèbre' and 'Prose', where he uses the word 'sépulcre'. Stéphane Mallarmé, *Oeuvres complètes*, ed. Henri Mondor and G. Jean-Aubry (1945) pp. 69–71, 54–7.

21. Hi Simons, 'Wallace Stevens and Mallarmé, *Modern Philology*, XLIII (1946) 235–59.

22. William Shakespeare, *A Midsummer Night's Dream*, ed. H. F. Brooks (London, 1979) IV. i. 203–15.

23. 'Harmonium' is the name given to 'a free-reed keyboard instrument with compression bellows' manufactured in Paris after 1840 by

Alexandre Debain, then for all types of keyboard instruments with free vibrating metal tongues or 'free reeds' – 'free' because they pass through the openings in which they operate – 'set in periodic motion by a current of air produced by a compression or suction treadle bellows'; also known as 'orgue expressif'.

Pipes with free reeds were added to a piano in Copenhagen (1763–70). Abbé Vogler incorporated this idea in his 'orchestrion', the portable organ built to his specification in Holland in 1789. This is the instrument that Browning has him play in his 'Abt Vogler'. Stevens certainly might have known this poem (as well as 'A Toccata of Galuppi's', which has a similar theme).

From about 1800 to about 1950 the harmonium was 'an important and popular instrument, favoured for home music making alongside the piano', used in churches instead of an organ and in cinemas before sound films. It was mass-produced in the United States after 1860. 'As a substitute for the orchestra the harmonium has been indispensable for almost 100 years [approximately 1830–1930], especially in domestic music and in light music arrangements. It reached the height of its technical perfection between 1900 and 1925 and suffered a decline of interest beginning around 1930.' See Alfred Berner, 'Harmonium', *The New Grove Dictionary of Music and Musicians*, ed. Stanley Sadie (London, 1980) VIII, 169–75.

As a metaphor in Stevens, it is worth noting its name, which implies the creation of harmony; its range of sound; the several analogies between human sound production and its method – that it works, we might say, by *inspiration*; and that it was a domestic and popular instrument, in no sense archaic or esoteric.

24.   Letter to Alfred Knopf, 25 May 1954.
25.   Charles Baudelaire, 'Salon de 1846', *Oeuvres complètes*, ed. Y.-G. Le Dantec (1956) p. 615.
26.   Baudelaire, 'Exposition Universelle de 1855', ibid., pp. 689–90.
27.   René Taupin, *L'Influence du symbolisme français sur la poésie américaine (de 1910 á 1920)* (1929) p. 276.
28.   Joachim du Bellay, '*Les Antiquitez de Rome*' et '*Les Regrets*', ed E. Droz (1960) p. 56.
29.   Baudelaire, 'L' Invitation au voyage', *Oeuvres complètes*, pp. 127–8.

CHAPTER 4: 'MY REALITY – IMAGINATION COMPLEX'

1.   D. W. Winnicott, *The Child, the Family, and the Outside World* (Baltimore, 1964) p. 69.
2.   Ibid., 73–4.
3.   Ernst Cassirer, *Kant's Life and Thought*, tr. James Haden (New Haven, Conn., 1981) p. 15.
4.   W. C. Williams, 'Kora in Hell', *Imaginations* (1970) p. 15.
5.   Wallace Stevens to Ronald Latimer, 5 Nov 1935: 'It is difficult to make much of this in personal terms, because there is nothing that kills an idea like expressing it in personal terms . . . .' (L, 292).

6. John Keats, 'Ode to a Nightingale', *The Complete Poems*, ed. John Barnard (Harmondsworth, Middx, 1973) pp. 346–8.

7. Paul Valéry, *Cahiers*, ed. Judith Robinson, II (1974) 302.

8. Keats, 'Ode to a Nightingale' *The Complete Poems*, p. 348; Alfred Tennyson, 'Ulysses', *The Poems of Tennyson*, ed. Christopher Ricks (London, 1969) p. 563.

9. D. W. Winnicott, 'On Communication', *The Maturational Processes and the Facilitating Environment* (London, 1972) pp. 186–7.

10. The painting, now in the Bartlett Collection of the Art Institute of Chicago, has had three owners: Ambroise Vollard, John Quinn and Bartlett. See *The Complete Paintings of Pablo Picasso, Blue and Rose Periods*, intro. by Denys Sutton, notes and catalogue by Paola Lecaldano (London, 1968) p. 95 and plate xv. Stevens' friend Walter Arensberg, also an art-collector, knew Quinn (*L*, pp. 821, 850–1) and Stevens writes to Weldon Kees (10 November 1954) that Walter Pach knew Quinn 'quite as well as he knew Walter Arensberg, whereas I knew John Quinn only slightly', so there is a possibility that Stevens might have seen the painting while it was in Quinn's possession.

The picture, in haunting and melancholy shades of blue, shows an old man (whose gaunt, angular head and torso, slight beard and long thin hands are reminiscent of El Greco's figures) sitting cross-legged on a window seat, playing a six-stringed guitar. He is bent over his instrument, his head somewhat awkwardly, even painfully, perpendicular to his body, his left shoulder raised higher than his head. He is literally turned in upon himself. There is a large hole in his loose shirt showing the point of his bare left shoulder and part of his upper arm. His trousers are torn and reach only to his calves (owing to the way he is sitting, his right leg is bare from the knee) and his feet are bare. His head, painted in profile, shows his sunken left eye as a slit, the eyeball missing. He stares straight down unseeing, focused on his music, lost in himself, his mouth open as if in speech or song. The corner of the big open window behind his head emphasises his blindness and the sadness of the picture in that there is nothing to see: a dark, flat, featureless plain, reaching to an empty, streaky sky. This emptiness, together with the apparent barrenness of the room, the old man's ragged clothes and haggard look, suggests an inner poverty or asceticism. The body of the guitar is brown with grey sides, grey bridge and a grey fingerboard so long that it extends out of the picture.

Many years later Stevens rejected any particular connection with Picasso. Writing to Renato Poggioli, who was translating the poem, he states (1 July 1953): 'I had no particular painting of Picasso's in mind and even though it might help to sell the book to have one of his paintings on the cover, I don't think we ought to reproduce anything of Picasso's' – presumably in order to protect his 'vital self'. This is one of Stevens' characteristic attempts to evade any suggestion that his work is dependent on someone else's. The poem contradicts the letter: 'Is *this picture* of Picasso's this "hoard/ Of destructions"', a picture of ourselves . . . ?' (xv. 1–2) emphasis added. The phrase 'hoard of destructions' is an English version of a remark Picasso made to Christian Zervos: 'Chez moi, un tableau est une somme de destructions' – Christian Zervos, 'Conversation avec Picasso', *Cahiers d'Art*, VII, 10 (1935) 173. This is, moreover, the only Picasso painting of a guitarist; it is blue, the colour of the guitar and its creations in the poem; and there are several other specific correspondences. Stevens tells Poggioli that his description of the guitarist as 'A shearsman of sorts' (I. 2) 'refers to the posture of the speaker, squatting like a tailor (a shearsman) as he works on his cloth' (25 June 1953). The position of Picasso's old man bent over his work, sitting cross-legged on a raised seat by a window, is that of a tailor. The poem stresses 'the man bent over his guitar' (I. 1), his 'hunched' (IX. 4) aspect, as does Picasso, and the poem's many references to the poverty of the artist are in keeping with the appearance of the guitarist in the painting. The idea that the world seen from a particular point of view is seen in one colour is implicit in Picasso's blue and rose paintings, virtually the same two colours that Stevens chooses to represent the imagination and reality.

The Old Blind Guitar Player is no more than a point of departure, an idea, a form, that Stevens uses for his own purposes, very different from those of Picasso, and in taking possession of it he makes his own picture. 'The fruit and wine, / The book and bread' (XIV. 11–12) are his additions. There is no 'table on which the food is cold' (XV. 9) nor any 'spot upon the floor' (XV. 11) in the painting. The only object in the room is the guitar and the floor is not visible. Perhaps this is what Stevens meant when he said that he 'had no particular painting of Picasso in mind'. More important perhaps, Stevens himself played the guitar. On 17 August 1906 he writes in his journal, 'Tonight – after dinner a harp, a violin, a bad piano, Mrs Yeager and Louise singing hymns, my rusty guitar in vindictive opposition, bawling crickets . . .' (*SP*, p. 170); and in a letter to Elsie Moll he describes how he fell asleep after 'lying on my bed playing my guitar lazily' (10 Mar 1907). Almost two years later he tells her,

> Tonight, after dinner, for example, I thought I should like to play my guitar, so I dug it up from the bottom of my wardrobe, dusted it, strummed a half-dozen chords, and then felt bored by it. I have played those half a dozen chords so often. I wish I were gifted enough to learn a new half dozen. – Some day I may be like one of the old ladies with whom I lived in Cambridge, who played a hymn on *her* guitar. The hymn had thousands of verses, all alike. She played about two hundred every night – until the house-dog whined for mercy, and liberty.   (7 Dec 1908)

The guitar, in both instances, is associated with the idea of repetition, perhaps the principal formal characteristic of Stevens' hymn of many verses (*SP*, p. 202).

The acrobats in Stevens may owe something to Picasso's painting of acrobats (1905) of his so-called Rose Period.

11.   Marcel Raymond, *De Baudelaire au surréalisme* (1952) pp. 11–12.

12. Percy Shelley, 'To a Skylark', *The Selected Poetry and Prose of Percy Bysshe Shelley*, ed. Carlos Baker (1951) pp. 397–400. Cf. Stevens' 'A poem is a pheasant' in *Adagia*; *OP*, p. 168.
13. Leo Tolstoy, *War and Peace*, tr. Louise and Aylmer Maude (1942) p. 1076 (bk xii, ch. 3).

CHAPTER 5: PARTS OF A WORLD

1. T. S. Eliot, 'The Dry Salvages', *The Complete Poems and Plays* (1952) p. 136.
2. Curtius, *European Literature and the Latin Middle Ages*, pp. 138–40.
3. Richard Blackmur often used the phrase in conversation and it is the title of the third lecture that he gave at the Library of Congress (23 Jan 1956) under the auspices of the Gertrude Clarke Whittall Poetry and Literature Fund – R. P. Blackmur, *Anni Mirabiles 1921–1925* (Washington, DC, 1956). Raymond is cited on pp. 12 and 15.
4. *The Poetical Works of William Wordsworth*, ed. E. de Selincourt and Helen Darbishire, iv (Oxford, 1970) 464.
5. The phrase 'figure of capable imagination' occurs in 'Mrs Alfred Uruguay'.
6. Alain, 'Division et opposition à l'intérieur de l'esprit' (Sep 1928), *Propos*, ed. Maurice Savin (1956) pp. 789–9.
7. This phrase is used as a title by Holly Stevens when she reprints the text in *Palm*, p. 206.
8. *Palm*, see p. 402.
9. 'The Comedian as the Letter C', ii. 5; 'Lions in Sweden'; 'Saint John and the Back-ache', 'Connoisseur of Chaos'; 'The Sense of the Sleight-of-Hand Man'; 'Late Hymn from the Myrrh-Mountain'.
10. Du Bellay, *'Les Antiquitez de Rome' et 'Les Regrets'*, p. 56.
11. Compare Mallarmé's image of moving curtains in 'Une Dentelle s'abolit', *Oeuvres complètes*, p. 74. For a discussion of the poem, see my ' "Une dentelle s'abolit" de Mallarmé', *Nineteenth-Century French Studies*, i (1973) 162–73.
12. Eliot, *The Waste Land*, *The Complete Poems and Plays*, p. 38.
13. 'Williams', *OP*, pp. 256, 255. Stevens writes to James Powers (12 May 1933), 'You may remember that Westerly Terrace is situated on one of the slopes of Prospect Hill: the declivity runs towards a public dump . . .', and his daughter comments, 'During the depression in the thirties a man said to be a Russian refugee built a shack out of old boxes, tin cans, etc., on this dump and lived there, as a semi-hermit, for several years' (*L*, p. 266).
14. William Shakespeare, *Antony and Cleopatra*, ed. M. R. Ridley (London, 1964) iv. xiv. 10–11.

CHAPTER 6: FAITHFUL SPEECH

1. William James, 'The Tigers in India', *'Pragmatism' and Four Essays from 'The Meaning of Truth'* (1955) p. 225.

2.　The description of the ephebe in his 'mansard' looking 'Across the roofs' echoes Baudelaire's 'Paysage', the first of the 'Tableaux parisiens' in *Les Fleurs du mal*:

> Je veux, pour composer chastement mes églogues,
> Coucher auprès du ciel, comme les astrologues,
> Et, voisin des clochers, écouter en rêvant
> Leurs hymnes solennels emportés par le vent.
> Les deux mains au menton, du haut de ma mansarde,
> Je verrai l'atelier qui chante et qui bavarde;
> Les tuyaux, les clochers, ces mâts de la cité,
> Et les grands ciels qui font rêver d'éternité.
>
> (Oeuvres complètes, p. 154)

> I wish, in order chastely to compose my ecologues,
> To go to sleep near the sky, like the astrologers,
> And, the neighbour of steeples, to hear while dreaming
> Their solemn hymns carried off by the wind.
> My chin in my hands, from the top of my mansard,
> I will see the workshop which sings and gossips;
> The down pipes, the steeples, those city masts
> And the big skies which make us dream of eternity.

I am grateful to Michael Alsop for helping me to find this passage. Baudelaire's poem also contributes to our understanding of 'the celestial ennui of apartments' (1. ii. 1).

3.　See *L*, p. 409, which is at once a denial and an admission; and also *L*, pp. 431–2, 461–2, which shows that Stevens read Nietzsche in German and in English. Henry Church, whom Stevens met in November 1939 (*B*, p. 216), was very interested in Nietzsche (*L*, pp. 431, 570, 636) and presumably they talked about him before 1942. The 'bright *scienza*' and its 'gaiety that is being' of 'Of Bright & Blue Birds & the Gala Sun' (1940) suggest Nietzsche's *Die fröhliche Wissenschaft* (usually translated as *The Gay Science*) and the 'no' and 'yes' of 'The Well Dressed Man with a Beard' (1941) suggest the sacred 'no' and 'yes' of Zarathustra's speech 'On the Three Metamorphoses'. This speech, moreover, contains a lion that can be compared to Stevens' lion who 'roars at the enraging desert' (1. v. 1–5). Zarathustra says, 'In the loneliest desert, however, the second metamorphosis occurs: here the spirit becomes a lion who would conquer his freedom and be master in his own desert' – Friedrich Nietzsche, *Thus Spoke Zarathustra*, *The Portable Nietzsche*, tr. Walter Kaufmann (1954) p. 138. Stevens' 'Less and Less Human, O Savage Spirit' (1944) is vaguely reminiscent of Nietzsche's *Menschliches, Allzumenschliches* (*Human, All-Too-Human*) and Nietzsche himself appears in 'Description without Place' (1945).

4.　Nietzsche, *Thus Spoke Zarathustra*, *The Portable Nietzsche*, pp. 124, 125.

5.　'In the beginning was the word', the opening words of the Gospel of John; 'το κατα ΙΩΑΝΝΗΝ', i. 15. 1, *Novvm Testamentvm Graece*, ed.

Alexander Souter (Oxford, 1936).
6.   Shelley, 'Ozymandias', *Selected Poetry and Prose*, p. 375.
7.   'There must be some wing on which to fly' (*OP*, p. 176).
8.   Houghton Library MS. fms Am 1333. I owe this reference to the kindness of Walton Litz.

CHAPTER 7: THE WORLD IS WHAT YOU MAKE OF IT

1.   William Wordsworth, *The Prelude, 1799, 1805, 1850*, ed. Jonathan Wordsworth, M. H. Abrams and Stephen Gill (1979), 1850 text, II. 238, 260–1. See the whole passage in both versions: II. 237–303 (1805) and II. 232–84 (1850); and *WBMP*, pp. 102–4, 210–15.
2.   Eliot, 'Burnt Norton', *The Complete Poems and Plays*, p. 119.
3.   Tennyson, *In Memoriam A. H. H.*, LIV. 20, *Poems*, p. 909.
4.   'Final Soliloquy of the Interior Paramour'; 'Prologues to What is Possible'.
5.   François Villon, 'Ballade des dames du temps jadis', *Oeuvres*, ed. Auguste Longnon and Lucien Foulet (1932) pp. 22–3.
6.   W. B. Yeats, 'Sailing to Byzantium', *The Collected Poems of W. B. Yeats* (London, 1956) pp. 191–2.
7.   Valéry, 'Palme', *Oeuvres*, pp. 153–6.

EPILOGUE: THE WHOLE OF HARMONIUM

1.   Albert Einstein, 'Autobiographisches' ('Autobiographical Notes') tr. Paul Schilpp in *Albert Einstein: Philosopher–Scientist*, ed. Paul Schlipp, I (LaSalle, Ill., 1969) pp. 6–9.
2.   Jeremy Bernstein, *Einstein* (London, 1976) p. 139.
3.   Albert Einstein, 'Principles of Scientific Research', *The World as I See It*, tr. Alan Harris (London, 1935) p. 126. 'Planck', writes Stevens, 'was a much truer symbol of ourselves; and in that true role is a more significant figure for us than the remote and almost fictitious figure of Pascal.... It is unexpected to have to recognise even in Planck the presence of the poet' – 'A Collect of Philosophy' (1951), *OP*, 200–1; see also pp. 195–6.
4.   Abraham Pais, *'Subtle is the Lord ...'* (1982) p. 4.

Index

EP17